Shariʿa in the Secular State

Words in both law and religion can shape power relationships and are often highly disputed. *Shariʿa* lies within the overlap of these two spheres and provides a unique subject for the study of meaning in that liminal space. This book contributes important insights related to Islamic jurisprudence and secularism in the Turkish context and regarding the role of language in contested legal and religious contexts.

The study begins by providing a historical framework for the ideas and terms covered, including concepts of religion in general, *Shariʿa* in particular, and secularism in the Turkish state. It goes on to examine empirical research to describe and analyze contemporary Turkish understandings of religion and *Shariʿa*. The author's research indicates that there is often a disconnect between supporting the adoption of *Shariʿa* and supporting the regulation of everyday behavior through civil codes. Thus, "*Shariʿa*" seems to have taken on new meanings as groups have sought either to appropriate or criticize it. It is a quintessential example of fractured and contextual meaning at the center of both religious and legal traditions.

This book is essential reading for both academics and those interested in law, linguistics, history, political science, anthropology, sociology, religious studies, or Near Eastern studies.

Russell Powell is Professor of Law and Associate Provost for Global Engagement at Seattle University, USA. He has previously worked as a diplomat and holds degrees in Near Eastern Studies, Philosophy, and Law. He has published widely on law, religion and secularism, and Islamic jurisprudence.

Law, Language and Communication

Series Editors

Anne Wagner

Université du Littoral Côte d'Opale, France

and

Vijay Kumar Bhatia

formerly of *City University of Hong Kong*

This series encourages innovative and integrated perspectives within and across the boundaries of law, language and communication, with particular emphasis on issues of communication in specialized socio-legal and professional contexts. It seeks to bring together a range of diverse yet cumulative research traditions in order to identify and encourage interdisciplinary research.

The series welcomes proposals – both edited collections as well as single-authored monographs – emphasizing critical approaches to law, language and communication, identifying and discussing issues, proposing solutions to problems, offering analyses in areas such as legal construction, interpretation, translation and de-codification.

Other titles in the series:

Language and Culture in EU Law: Multidisciplinary Perspectives
Edited by Susan Šarčević
ISBN 978-1-4724-2897-4

Towards Recognition of Minority Groups: Legal and Communication Strategies
Edited by Marek Zirk-Sadowski, Bartosz Wojciechowski and Karolina M. Cern
ISBN 978-1-4724-4490-5

The Ashgate Handbook of Legal Translation
Edited by Le Cheng, King Kui Sin and Anne Wagner
ISBN 978-1-4094-6966-7

Legal Lexicography: A Comparative Perspective
Edited by Máirtín Mac Aodha
ISBN 978-1-4094-5441-0

Shariʿa in the Secular State

Evolving meanings of Islamic jurisprudence in Turkey

Russell Powell

Routledge
Taylor & Francis Group
LONDON AND NEW YORK

First published 2016 by Routledge

2 Park Square, Milton Park, Abingdon, Oxfordshire OX14 4RN
52 Vanderbilt Avenue, New York, NY 10017

Routledge is an imprint of the Taylor & Francis Group, an informa business

First issued in paperback 2020

British Library Cataloguing in Publication Data
A catalogue record for this book is available from the British Library

Library of Congress Cataloging-in-Publication Data
A catalog record for this book has been requested

ISBN: 978-1-4724-7954-9 (hbk)
ISBN: 978-0-367-59645-3 (pbk)

Typeset in Times New Roman
by Apex CoVantage, LLC

Contents

Figure and tables

Figure

Tables

Glossary

Bektashi A Sufi order from the early period of the Ottoman Empire. The *Bektashi tariqat* played a liminal role between Sunni and Shiʿi communities as the teachings included veneration of Ali and other practices normally associated with Shiʿism. The *Bektashi* order became the official order of the Janissary Corps, affording it a certain protected status that ordinary Shiʿism did not have.

Dershane Private teaching centers found throughout Turkey. Although a *dershane* may offer broad academic support throughout a student's time in school, it emphasizes preparation (*hazırlık*) for the intensive university entrance examination (*sınav*).

Diyanet In the government of the Republic of Turkey, the Directorate of Religious Affairs. *Diyanet* controls religious education, ordination/licensing, and appointment of imams, the construction of mosques, and (at times) even contents of Friday sermons throughout the country.

Fiqh Islamic jurisprudence. The human endeavor to ascertain and understand *Shariʿa*. It also refers to the bodies of jurisprudential literature which form the bases for legal norms within the traditional schools of Islamic jurisprudence.

Hadd/Hudud Criminal acts with specific religious implications as "claims of God." These crimes have specific punishments in the canonical texts of the Quran and the *Sunna*. These crimes include adultery, highway robbery, theft, fornication, false accusation of adultery or fornication, winedrinking, and apostasy. Traditions differ somewhat as to the exact offenses and their definitions.

Hadith *Hadith* are recorded stories and teachings regarding the Prophet. They consist of two parts: the text of the story or teaching, called the *matn*, and the chain of narrators reporting the text, called the *isnad*.

Hazırlık After school preparatory classes for the university entrance examination in Turkey. Generally, the term *hazırlık* refers to the near- or post-graduation intensive preparation courses provided by a *dershane*.

Hizmet *Hizmet*, also known as the *Gülen Cemaati* or just the *Cemaat*, is arguably the largest religious network in Turkey. The movement is inspired by the writing and preaching of *Fethullah Gülen*.

Ijtihad *Ijtihad* or independent judicial reasoning is the exercise of interpreting scriptural texts. The traditional schools of jurisprudence established standards for determining which scholars were suitably trained to engage in *ijtihad* (such a person would be designated a *mujtahid*).

Imam Religious leaders within Islam. In Sunni Islam, imams typically lead worship services, serve as religious leaders, and provide religious guidance. In Shiʿi tradition, the imam refers to the leader of the community (as in Imam Ali).

Imam Hatip School Religious vocational schools (middle schools and high schools) intended to train imams and religious workers.

Mecelle The civil code enacted by the Ottoman Empire in the late 19th and early 20th centuries.

Mevlevi A Sufi order commonly found in the early territory of the Ottoman Empire. The *Mevlevi tariqat* was founded by Jalal ud-Din Rumi in the 13th century. It was patronized by the early Ottoman court. Its training tended to emphasize spiritual practices as opposed to *fiqh*.

Mukkhtassar An abridgment or summary of legal rules of a specific Islamic legal guild. These rules would be applied by low-level jurists without need for any scriptural justification.

Ottoman Empire An empire founded in 1299 by Oghuz Turks under the rule of Osman I, centered in the Anatolia region. The Ottoman Empire, which ended in 1922, directly preceded the Republic of Turkey.

Qiyas The use of analogical reasoning to apply the underlying efficient cause for a rule (the text's *illa*) to a new situation or fact pattern and create a new rule. Certain restrictions, such as appropriateness (*munasaba*) or necessity (*darura*), limit the scope of new rules derived via *qiyas*.

Quran The central religious text of Islam as purportedly revealed to the Prophet Muhammad. An individual chapter is called a *sura*, and a verse is referred to as an *ayah*.

Shariʿa A term of art referring to the ideal of God's law. *Shariʿa* is considered by some to be a fixed corpus of rules established by God, but it raises very complex questions of meaning addressed throughout this book.

Sufi An esoteric, ascetic aspect of Islam, consisting of spiritual practices and beliefs that in some cases trace back to the first generations of Muslims.

Sunna The *Sunna*, as preserved in *Hadith* collections, is the Prophet's example. It was generally accepted as a model of correct behavior as the formal tradition of Islamic jurisprudence developed. It is one of the root sources of *fiqh*.

Taqlid In Islamic jurisprudence, the act of precedential reasoning. *Taqlid* entails accepting the view of a recognized leading jurist without scriptural proof of its correctness.

Tariqat A school or order of Sufism for teaching and practicing the methods of the Sufi order. Examples include the *Naqshbandi*, the *Qadiri*, the *Mevlevi*, and the *Bektashi*.

Ulema Recognized scholarly authorities of Islamic jurisprudence within a community.

Zina Unlawful sexual relations in Islamic jurisprudence. This includes adultery and fornication.

Preface

I returned from Istanbul in the summer of 2013, having recently completed the data collection for this project.[1] I have studied Turkey for nearly 30 years and first lived there in 1990. Since then, I have visited regularly to teach and to conduct research. In the spring of 2013, I stayed in the *Taksim* district of Istanbul, where I often stay during my visits. However, something was different this time. On May 31, in response to the use of police force against a small group of nonviolent demonstrators, massive protests broke out. It was not the first time in recent weeks that riot police used tear gas and water cannons.

At 7:30 a.m. on May 18, I was walking to a café on *Istiklal* to meet with a graduate student I was mentoring. Hundreds of police blocked the street and thousands of people were trapped, trying to move away from the riot police. Like many locals with places to be, I used side streets to avoid both the mob and the police attempting to herd it. At one point, the police blocked every direction. Tear gas enveloped the crowd. People began to panic. I started to cough and my eyes watered from the gas. I took shelter in a nearby restaurant. Locals were unsurprised by the riot tactics deployed against a Saturday evening crowd made up mostly of tourists, young people, and families. There were no reports of the incident in the local media, and I still do not know what prompted such an intense police response.

I ventured out for dinner on May 26 and stumbled upon hundreds of police lining *Istiklal*. I thought eating at home would be safer, so I bought takeout and returned to my apartment. At 7:15 p.m., I heard explosions and screaming. From my apartment window, just two blocks off *Istiklal*, I saw packs of police chasing civilians in the street. Tear gas seeped through the closed windows into my apartment. I retreated to the bathroom and ran hot water in an attempt to keep the gas at bay. For 30 minutes, I held my position, hoping the gas would dissipate. My neighbors were irritated, but unsurprised. Again, no one knew what had prompted this intense response by police.

There are constant demonstrations of one variety or another in the *Taksim* area. In May 2013 alone I saw Kurdish protests, anti-Russian protests, and a host of leftist and environmentalist demonstrations. Most were small and typical, frequently consisting of university students. This has been the state of affairs for decades, but the response this year lacked the restraint of the past. Once this type of police power exercised against earnest students and environmentalists, something more easily done in *Gezi* Park than in the narrow paths of *Istiklal*, was documented in social media, it tapped into deep anger and frustration directed at the government. This massive and spontaneous grassroots reaction reflects a deep alienation of those who are likely to be the next generation of Turkish leaders.

I interviewed many people who expressed frustration and concern at the ongoing consolidation of power by the ruling party. Even religious supporters of then Prime Minister Recep Tayyip Erdoğan expressed concerns about the use of excessive police force, the concentration of wealth in the ruling party's supporters, the prospect of enforced religious norms, and constitutional reform. Although the protests that escalated on May 31, 2013, included religious individuals and supporters of the ruling party, the anger focused on Erdoğan and what some believed to be his agenda of Islamization. Some viewed changes to laws regulating alcohol and the ban on public displays of affection as clear evidence of this program. The story took another dramatic shift in December 2013 when religious leader Fethullah Gülen, who had provided legitimacy to the ruling party, was recast as an enemy of the state. Institutions affiliated with him have been under attack ever since, culminating in the government takeover of the largest daily newspaper in Turkey, *Zaman*, in March 2016. This shifting landscape is emblematic of the complexity of Turkish law, politics, and religious identity that this research attempts to address. I am deeply thankful for the support of my family over the past four years as I have worked on this book.

Russell Powell

Note

1 A version of the Preface along with small portions of the Introduction and Conclusion were published as an essay intended to introduce the empirical research for this book. Those portions are reprinted with permission from *Pepperdine Law Review*, Volume 41, Issue 5, Copyright 2014 by the Pepperdine University School of Law. Russell Powell, "Does Shari'a Play a Role in Turkey." *Pepperdine Law Review* 41.5 (2014): 1101.

Note on transliteration, names, and dates

Terms from classical Islamic jurisprudence are transliterated in Arabic using standard transliteration rather than by using Turkish cognates. Terms from explicitly Ottoman or Turkish contexts are transliterated in their modern Turkish form. Surnames were adopted by law in Turkey in 1934, and I will generally include adopted surnames for Turkish citizens unless they are commonly known by some other name. Dates are presented according to the Gregorian calendar.

Introduction

Religion is one of the most contested realms of meaning in human interaction. Although disagreement is evident within internal communal discourses, conflict is perhaps sharpest in negotiating the role of religion, religious symbols, and religious meanings in the pluralist context of secular states and legal systems. This book attempts to provide historical and empirical contexts for understanding fragmented meanings in religion, secularism, and law by exploring the traditional and contemporary meanings attributed to "*Shari'a*" in Turkey. ***Shari'a*** is a term of art referring to the ideal of God's law, and I will attempt to unpack important historical perspectives and provide greater breadth by exploring my empirical research on the range of Turkish views of religion, *Shari'a*, and secularism.

Perhaps the single greatest challenge to considering the meanings of *Shari'a* is the widely held assumption that it carries universal and undisputed meaning within Islamic tradition and Muslim communities. While as a theological and ontological matter, *Shari'a* may be considered a fixed corpus of rules established by God, the legal and linguistic reality has been that rules and the words that express them have been and continue to be plural and fragmented. Islamic jurisprudence is not immune to post-structural semiotic critiques based on metalanguage (as in Barthes)[1] or power structures (as in Foucault).[2] In fact, the experience of legal realism and its resulting pluralism in the early centuries of the development of Islamic jurisprudence may support postmodern linguistic claims more naturally than the evolution of Christian theological and legal tradition.

This book will consider the historical meanings of religion, as a frame for exploring the formal articulations of *Shari'a* and secularism, all within the Turkish context. This is then juxtaposed with the range of meanings attributed to these words by Turks who participated in my empirical research, as well as the research of others. The historical analyses do not support univocal meaning, but they do indicate processes or methods that shared broad consensus within theological and legal communities of authority. These highly nuanced meanings contrast with the diverse and polarized understandings, often detached from the historical tradition, expressed by participants in my research. Because the word *Shari'a* is both presumed to contain fixed, unchanging norms and because it is so bitterly contested as a source of law, it is an ideal subject for exploration. Ultimately, it might be that this project sheds more light on common understandings of the relationship between religion and law than on *Shari'a* or the Turkish experience.

My research for the past seven years has focused on the dynamic relationship between religion and law in contemporary Turkey. Many polls, including my own, indicate that a notable percentage of Turks want "*Shari'a*" to be enforced by the state. However, my evidence shows that Turkish people seldom consider what implementing *Shari'a* might mean in terms of its effect on civil law. In other words, there is often a disconnect between supporting an adoption of *Shari'a* and supporting the regulation of everyday behavior through civil codes. It is clear from research conducted by myself and others that even religious people do not want Turkey to become more like Iran or Saudi Arabia (using the language of some participants). In fact, many of the religious people I interviewed believe that the robust protection of religious freedom enhances their own religious experience by making it more meaningful and more authentic. This attitude, held by many in present-day Turkey, suggests that religious belief and individual choice are not only valued but may also enhance each other. Based on my research, I believe that forcing Turkish law to conform to *classical* Islamic legal norms will likely provoke far greater public opposition, even from many people of faith, than did the response evoked in June 2013 during the *Gezi* protests.

One goal of this book is thus to describe the landscape of popular Turkish views on *Shari'a* and to evaluate the likely factors that shape those views. The operating hypothesis is that education is the most likely causal factor. The empirical study was designed to collect data to explore the general assumption that religiosity determines attitudes toward *Shari'a* and to provide a deeper understanding of Turkish views of *Shari'a*.

Turkey is a very religious country, and polling consistently indicates that a significant majority of Turks identify as religious. In this regard, it is not so different from the United States. Both countries are home to religious politicians who propose to bring state law into greater conformity with ethical and religious norms rooted in their faith. Further, in both nations, when the actions of religious politicians are viewed as overreaching, there is public outcry. The tradition of Kemalist secularism (*laiklik*) is often cited to distinguish Turkey as an exceptional case among predominantly Muslim countries. However, while it is true that the Turkish Constitution, laws, and legal opinions treat the relationship between the state and religion differently than do Iran, Saudi Arabia, Egypt, and even Indonesia, it would be wrong to underestimate the role of religion in the formation of Turkish legal norms and in citizens' understandings of those norms.

There is a wealth of literature describing the evolution and nature of Turkish secularism.[3] For example, a number of quantitative and qualitative studies question and analyze Turkish voters' preferences for *Shari'a*.[4] Such studies ask whether respondents favor the establishment of a *Shari'a* state or not.[5] Over the past 15 years, these surveys have indicated that support for a *Shari'a* state ranges from 5% to 25% of the total population.[6] However, these results are extremely problematic because they do not explore what respondents – whether they are for or against the change – mean by "the establishment of a *Shari'a* state." In response to this discrepancy, this study unpacks the range of possible meanings attributed to *Shari'a* among Turkish voters. The research also serves as a framework for future empirical studies and as the basis for a deeper understanding of the role of Islam within Turkish law and politics.

The first half of the book provides historical context for the ideas and terms considered in the empirical studies. These include concepts of religion in general, *Shari'a* in particular, and secularism in the Turkish state. Specifically, Chapter One considers competing theoretical approaches to the concept of religion, and it places emphasis on the need to understand both the formal theology of religions as well as the lived experience of religious people. It also begins to consider the relationship between religion and the state. Chapter Two considers meanings attributed to *Shari'a*. Here, I discuss the methodologies of classical Islamic jurisprudence and the rise of complex interpretive tools and the transition to rules of precedent. The use of codification is evaluated within both the colonial and Ottoman contexts. These discussions form the basis for considering modernist appropriations of the Islamic legal tradition (in general and in the explicitly Turkish context), the impact of Turkish constitutional secularism, and the role of the contemporary Turkish state in mediating the tradition. Chapter Three considers the landscape of forces shaping popular religion in Turkey today. These include a number of religious, political, and media leaders, as well as the influence of newspaper and television outlets. Religious scholars Fethullah Gülen and Yaşar Nuri Öztürk bridge the gap between formal jurisprudence and popular religion, and this chapter considers the implications of their work in some detail. Chapter Four provides historical and scholarly context for the various meanings attributed to "secularism" in Turkey. This section pays particular attention to constitutional, statutory, and case law rules that govern the relationship between religion and the state. The chapter concludes by considering prior empirical research attempting to evaluate popular views regarding the appropriate role of Islam in Turkish law.

The second half of the book examines my empirical research designed to describe contemporary Turkish understandings of religion, and of *Shari'a* in particular, to test the popular thesis that education predicts views toward *Shari'a* and to provide a more thorough description of Turkish views on law and religion than is currently available. The empirical research also explores the modernist claim that personal religiosity is predictive of preference for a religious state. Chapter Five reviews my quantitative research in order to provide more helpful and specific understandings of Turkish views related to *Shari'a*. It problematizes the conventional assumption that religiosity tends to influence policy preferences related to secularism more than factors such as education. Further, the chapter dispels the notion of a binary division among those who favor Islam and those who favor secularism. Chapter Six reviews my qualitative research, which asked Turkish citizens to explain why they hold particular views related to secularism and *Shari'a*. This chapter identifies some surprising overlaps that transcend economics, education, political preferences, and religious ideology. Turks, including "secularists" and the very religious, seem to share a strong preference for traditional moral values while at the same time embracing a libertarian approach to law and religion. Chapter Seven considers my qualitative research related to the formation of views of *Shari'a*. These narratives tend to refute the assumption that legitimacy is equated with adherence to classical jurisprudence, an assumption that might be truer in other, predominantly Muslim, countries, but which in any event overshadows much contemporary scholarship. Instead, it appears that charismatic leaders, thinkers, and the media play critical roles in forming religious views and conceptions of *Shariʿa*.

The analyses in the first half of the book fit within their own linguistic, jurisprudential, and historical disciplinary contexts. However, the empirical studies analyzed in the second half require some additional explanation since they are referred to throughout. The first large-*n* survey was a 37-question national telephone poll that used standard representative polling strategies. The questions probed for preferences and perceptions of *Shariʿa*. Across the country, 935 random phone numbers were called, controlling for population distribution. A far more extensive survey was posted online via SurveyMonkey, and the links were distributed via Facebook in Turkey. Three hundred and one subjects participated in the online survey. Many survey questions were based on studies by Pew,[7] the World Value Survey (WVS),[8] Ali Çarkoğlu,[9] and Ersin Kalaycıoğlu[10] in order to make valid comparisons with similar polls conducted in Turkey and in other countries.

The telephone poll and the online survey established demographic status through background questions regarding age, gender, residence, religion, employment, and other factors. The chief independent variables (education and religiosity) were based on self-reporting questions. The dependent variable (preference for *Shariʿa*) was based on responses to the statement, "I would like to have a *Shariʿa*-based religious state founded in Turkey." Questions presented to respondents were formed using Turkish wording very similar to that used in prior studies in order to enable statistically significant comparisons with prior polling.

According to Pew and the WVS, an overwhelming percentage of Turks – more than 80% of the population – identify as "religious" or "very religious."[11] This number has remained fairly stable in studies spanning the last two decades. Surveys on wealth and education are vague on allocation, but there is a general trajectory toward greater wealth and access to education. There is movement over time in the percentage of those who prefer a strong secular state – both up and down, with a general downward trend as the possibility for "softer secularism" becomes more plausible.[12] There is similar movement among those who express a desire for an Islamic state (numbering around 10%–15%). These are extremely important surveys, despite their methodological problems.[13] Although I refer to many previous studies, my primary objective is not analyzing or documenting trends in secularism. Rather, I am interested in looking at factors that influence understandings of *Shariʿa* and the impact on discourses related to law.

Most analyses of Turkish law and Islam presume that strong religious commitment and identification tend to result in a view of traditional Islam that is incompatible with Kemalist secularism.[14] Using the variables in this study, this view would anticipate that a low score in religiosity would correlate with a preference for strong secularism, a middle score would indicate a preference for softer secularism, and a high score would indicate a preference for a theocratic state.

One study by Yılmaz has examined class and preferences for secularism, and it indicates that the middle class tends to prefer secularism.[15] While I do not dispute this conclusion, it is not specific enough to be helpful in explaining actual policy preferences. Using increasingly explicit questions, particularly in regard to preferences for *Shari'a*, this study provides a more satisfying explanation for the causes of preferences for *Shari'a* and for which forms of secularism are preferred (in terms of effect on policies). The main problem with the Yılmaz study that I would like to explore is that "secularism" is a largely untheorized variable with little concrete meaning. As a result, it has been used as a proxy for a preference for strong Kemalist secularism, when in fact it may indicate a preference for a *soft* secularism that emphasizes free exercise and antiestablishment values.

The ability to perform process tracing is one of the main advantages of adding in-depth case studies. For the qualitative portion of the study, I conducted screening interviews with hundreds of people, primarily in the *Beyoğlu* neighborhood of Istanbul. I also conducted detailed, open-ended interviews with four groups of Turkish citizens, including two groups representing the range of independent variables,[16] a third group consisting of ten university students and recent university graduates, and a fourth group of six people active in the **Hizmet** Movement (sometimes called the Gülen *Cemaati* or simply the *Cemaat*).[17] The range of interviews allowed me to develop a thicker description of religious experience relating to law, and to consider possible causal mechanisms existing between religious belief and law, than would be possible with a more limited interview population. Participants completed hard copies of the survey, which I reviewed before the interviews. At that point, the telephone poll had already been completed, and the online version of the survey was in place, so I had some sense of the correlation between variables and possible causal mechanisms.

I then worked backward from preferences for *Shari'a* (my dependent variable). In the interviews, I asked which factors influenced these preferences in order to illuminate causal relationships. I was most interested in tracing these connections to elements of education, but I also tested for religiosity and the more granular elements of identity mentioned in the survey. I asked interviewees open-ended questions to provide explicit details about causal connections. Perhaps the most interesting questions relate to religious instruction and experience.

To the extent that the analysis confirmed the working hypothesis, the data was placed in a context that explains results in prior studies. The main sets of studies in this area have focused on education, class, religiosity, and views of secularism, and they have generally assumed a thin and binary view of secularism (hard secularism as it exists in the Turkish Republic versus a religious state). This study thus provides a more nuanced picture of the influence of these factors. Political secularists might object to the characterization of soft secularism as authentic secularism, arguing instead that it is a pretense for the creeping influence of religion into the public sphere. This is a somewhat problematic position because the same critique could be made in the U.S., where soft secularism is the constitutional norm.

Placing the empirical data within the context of the linguistic, jurisprudential, and historical analyses presented in the first half of the book provides compelling insights into the fractured meanings attributed to *Shari'a* in contemporary Turkey. Even for traditionalists in Turkey, Islamic jurisprudence is not generally conceived of in classical or medieval terms. It has become a symbol of faith and piety for some and of oppression for others. But regardless of the meanings attributed to it, *Shari'a* impacts public discourse around law. This is hardly surprising; the role of scripture and "natural law" play a similarly polarizing role in U.S. legal discourse. However, *Shari'a* in Turkey must be considered within its own religious, historical, legal, and political contexts.

Notes

1 *See generally*, Roland Barthes, *Elements of Semiology*. New York: Hill and Wang, 1968.
2 *See generally*, Michel Foucault, *The Order of Things: An Archaeology of the Human Sciences*. London: Tavistock, 1970.
3 *See, e.g.*, Feroz Ahmad, *The Making of Modern Turkey*. London: Routledge, 1993. Zeyno Baran, *Torn Country: Turkey Between Secularism And Islamism*. Stanford, CA: Hoover Institution Press, 2010; Sibel Bozdoğan and Reşat Kasaba (Eds.), *Rethinking Modernity and National Identity in Turkey.* Seattle: University of Washington Press, 1997; Soner Çağaptay, *Islam, Secularism, and Nationalism in Modern Turkey: Who Is a Turk?* London: Routledge, 2006; Alev Çınar, *Modernity, Islam, and Secularism in Turkey: Bodies, Places, and Time.* Minneapolis: University of Minnesota Press, 2005; Andrew Davison, *Secularism and Revivalism in Turkey: A Hermeneutic Reconsideration.* New Haven & London: Yale University Press, 1998; Carter Vaughn Findley, *Turkey, Islam, Nationalism, and Modernity: A History, 1789–2007.* New Haven & London: Yale University Press, 2010; Ahmet Kuru, *Secularism and State Policies Toward Religion: The United States, France, and Turkey.* Cambridge: Cambridge University Press, 2009; Yael Navaro-Yashin, *Faces of the State: Secularism and Public Life in Turkey.* Princeton: Princeton University Press, 2002; Esra Özyürek, *Nostalgia for the Modern: State Secularism and Everyday Politics in Turkey.* Durham: Duke University Press, 2006; Brian Silverstein, *Islam and Modernity in Turkey*. New York: Palgrave Macmillan, 2011; Berna Turam, *Between Islam and the State: The Politics of Engagement.* Stanford, CA: Stanford University Press, 2007; Hakan Yavuz, *Islamic Political Identity in Turkey*. New York: Oxford University Press, 2003; Erik Zürcher, *Turkey: A Modern History*. London & New York: I. B. Tauris, 2004.
4 *See, e.g.*, Ali Çarkoğlu and Binnaz Toprak, *Religion, Society and Politics in a Changing Turkey.* Trans. Çigdem Aksoy Fromm. Istanbul: TESEV, 2007.
5 *Id.* at 33.
6 *Id.*
7 *The World's Muslims: Religion, Politics and Society.* Pew Research Religion & Public Life Project, April 30, 2013, available at http://www.pewforum.org/2013/04/30/the-worlds-muslims-religion-politics-society-beliefs-about-sharia/.
8 World Values Survey 2005. Official Data File V.20090901, 2009. World Values Survey Association, available at www.worldvaluessurvey.org.
9 Ali Çarkoğlu, "Religiosity, Support for Şeriat and Evaluations of Secularist Public Policies in Turkey." *Middle Eastern Studies* 40.2 (2004): 111–136.
10 Ersin Kalaycıoğlu, "Party Identification, Islam and Secularism in Turkey." *Sabanci University Research Database* (2008), available at http://isanet.ccit.arizona.edu/sanfran2008/PreliminaryProgram.pdf.
11 *See e.g.*, World Values Survey Data for Turkey 2011, WV6_Data_Turkey_2011_spss_v_2014_04_28.zip. In this particular survey, 82% of respondents identified as "religious."

12 Softer secularism will be used in this paper to refer to something akin to U.S. secularism as expressed by the first amendment religion clauses and the case law interpreting them. Harder or strict secularism will be used to refer to traditions such as French laïcité or Turkish *laiklik*, in which the state plays a much greater role in regulating religion. This distinction is described in greater detail in Chapter Four.

13 *See* Chapter Four for a detailed discussion.

14 *See e.g.*, Bernard Lewis, *Emergence of Modern Turkey*. London: Oxford University Press, 1968, 2002.

15 *See* Hakan Yılmaz, *In Search of a Turkish Middle Class: Economic Occupations, Political Orientations, Social Life-Styles, Moral Values: Summary of the Basic Findings*. Istanbul: Bogazici University, 2008.

16 Education and religiosity are the two main independent variables, each with a value of lower, middle, or higher, for a total of nine combinations. There were two full sets of nine.

17 *Cemaat* was the term used by most people in the study to describe groups or institutions with some connection to *Gülen*. Most of the people actually active in those organizations preferred the name *Hizmet*, but some did refer more generally to "The *Cemaat*" (or The Community).

1 Religion in context

From the Latin, "*religare*," religion refers to "binding back," usually in the sense of connecting with the divine. However, not all scholarly definitions of religion imply divinity or even spirit. Three of the principal categories of theories defining religion are first, religion in its metaphysical or theological sense (e.g., the underlying truth of the existence of God, the dharma, etc.); second, religion as it is psychologically experienced by people (e.g., the feelings of the religious believer about divinity or ultimate concerns, etc.); and third, religion as a cultural or social force (e.g., symbolism that binds a community together or separates it from other communities). Definitions of religion typically begin by assuming one of these approaches, although some blend aspects of two or three. While understanding the first category, the metaphysical or theological, is important for context and is addressed by the data analyzed in Chapter Five, the qualitative data discussed in Chapters Six and Seven focus on the second and third categories (the personal and the social experiences of religion). This first chapter also addresses the relationship between religion and the state and the idea of secularism, which is explored further in Chapter Four.

Religion as the metaphysical or theological

In the first category, religion as metaphysical or theological, William James defines religion as "the feelings, acts, and experiences of individual men in their solitude, so far as they apprehend themselves to stand in relation to whatever they may consider the divine."[1] James's emphasis on the individual is distinguished from religion proper and is sometimes defined as "magic" or "asceticism." However, this definition does address religion as a matter of the human heart, providing a helpful starting place for considering the movement from the individual to the political.

In *The Idea of the Holy*, Rudolf Otto develops a vocabulary to define the aesthetic dimensions of religion.[2] He describes human engagement with the "numinous," which is "wholly other," indescribable, terrifying, fascinating, and characterized by dread and awe.[3] He refers to the *numen tremendum*, which indicates a sense of awe or the uncanny. It could be argued that such an experience is not necessarily "religious" but is instead "spiritual," i.e., it does not imply a supernatural being or force.[4] Regardless, like James, Otto begins with the individual's response to the numinous, whether in the form of the divine, the spirit, or of transcendence.

One of the most influential approaches to understanding religion is proposed by Max Weber. He identifies elements and expressions of religion ("ideal types"), demonstrating development towards higher orders of organization (e.g., magic to polytheism, to pantheism, to monotheism, and, finally, to ethical monotheism).[5] His taxonomy and explanatory project are helpful but are also fraught with over-generalizations and biases that favor German culture and Protestant religion.[6] Despite these shortcomings, Weber remains an extremely impressive comparativist who seriously considers the role of the divine or the numinous in the development of religion, as well as the relationship between religion and other social phenomena (economics in particular). Weber asserts a causal connection between ascetic Protestantism, in the context of his taxonomy of ideal types, and developmental superiority.[7] In one sense his schema attempts to explain German cultural and economic success, providing an apologetic to justify German superiority. Although Weber shows concern for cultural formation and knowledge production, economic competitiveness seems to serve as a default measure of religion's "success" throughout Weber's work.[8] Weber could thus be read, and usually is, as understanding religion to be primarily a social phenomenon, but I include him in this section because of his appreciation for the substance of German Protestantism, which takes on a pronounced theological character.

Although Weber is helpful for understanding the idea of religion in general, his view of Islamic jurisprudence and the role of its judges is deeply problematic and has perpetuated Orientalist biases with regard to Islamic law and society. In *Essays in Sociology*, he refers to Islamic legal tradition as one of "*kadijustiz*" or *qadi* justice, in which judges exercise unbridled discretion.[9] According to Weber, such judgments do not follow general principles and are fundamentally arbitrary. As unstructured opinions rooted in religious belief and intuition, this sort of justice is presumed to be the antithesis of the rational formalism found in Weber's ideal, i.e., Western, legal systems. However, Weber's view of Islamic jurisprudence does not comport with the classical tradition or with the bulk of contemporary scholarship on Islamic jurisprudence, as will be explained in Chapter Two.

Mircea Eliade's work is similarly comparative and historical in that it considers the wide breadth of human religious experience.[10] His model of archetypes seems concrete and prosaic; however, unlike much religious studies scholarship, he engages the mythological and the divine as legitimate subjects, rather than assuming a veneer of scientificity.[11] In other words, Eliade, unlike many of his colleagues, seriously considers the role of the divine or the numinous in the development of religion. Like Weber, he considers the relationship between religion and other social phenomena such as economics.[12] In Eliade's view, mythological and divine archetypes act as ideal Platonic forms upon which religious practices are modeled. In this sense, the numinous is real. In terms of social theory, Eliade shows little regard for politics per se, but he does make the argument that archetypes determine, and in some sense are determined by, specific forms of human social organization.[13] He thus rejects the study of religions solely from psychological or sociological perspectives and seeks to examine individual patterns or forms of religious expression on their own terms.[14]

Religion is often presumed to be a source of values, as in Ames definition of religion, "participation in the ideal values of the social consciousness."[15] However, values arise from sources other than those that might be defined as "religious." Similarly, religion provides a source of meaning. Joseph Gaer describes it as a thoughtful response to the "why" question.[16] As with values, other disciplines – philosophy, for example – also provide answers to this question. The Protestant theologian, Paul Tillich, writes of religion in terms of "ultimate concern" within which he would include secularism: "For secularism is never without ultimate concern."[17]

Although Islam could be understood on psychological and social grounds that are important for explaining religious practice and belief in predominantly Muslim societies like Turkey, I would argue that Islam is *internally* understood – i.e., within practicing Islamic cultures – as primarily metaphysical and theological. In terms of metaphysics, Sufism in particular has created a rich discourse on the nature of being and on the role of the transcendent.[18] Similarly, Islamic jurisprudence takes on a deeply theological character in much the same way that Weber viewed German Protestantism. This is not to say that Islam is merely theological. Historically, it has been embedded in political, economic, and social structures. However, it is arguably the authenticity of the numinous or transcendent experience that legitimizes those structures.

Psychological definitions of religion

The second category of definitions for religion, the psychological approach, is best exemplified by Freud's incorporation of psychoanalysis into his discourse on religion. His dialogue in *The Future of an Illusion* is both a refutation of religion in the modern context and a justification for its import – at least in a transitional sense.[19] Freud describes religion as the principle force for impulse restraint within society. However, he also presumes that it is an illusion and a force of socialization – a perspective not wholly inconsistent with the view of other scholars, such as Berger[20] or Bourdieu.[21] Like Durkheim, who will be discussed later, Freud finds the origin of religion in totemism. For Freud, religion is a response to human helplessness and anxiety:

> The gods retain the threefold task: they must exorcize the terrors of nature, they must reconcile men to the cruelty of Fate, particularly as it is shown in death, and they must compensate them for the sufferings and privations which a civilized life in common has imposed on them.[22]

Ultimately, science and human reason provide a suitable substitute, though not without peril. Although the insight that religion addresses fundamental human anxieties is powerful and is observably true, the assumption that it will ultimately be replaced by science has not been demonstrated over the past one hundred years of history. Furthermore, if religion is simply a coping mechanism for anxiety, it is not easily distinguishable from other comforting explanatory systems, including those of philosophy and science.

Like Freud, Victor Turner describes religion as a social or historical response to anxiety, locating it in liminality, which provides a social space to wrestle with that anxiety.[23] Turner's consideration of liminality as a focal point for the creation of *communitas*, which may serve as a proxy for religion in his work, is key.[24] The rites of passage he describes engage critical psychological and social anxieties with rich symbols and continue to impact human communities even when they are completed. Turner thus avoids Freud's bias toward a secular scientific worldview while maintaining the importance of religion's role in comforting people, providing meaning, and creating community (moving to the third approach – understanding religion as the social). With regard to Islam, there is a body of literature that considers religion from a psychological perspective, particularly within **Sufi** mysticism.[25]

Religion as the social

Consistent with the third approach to describing religion, religion as the social, William Newman indicates that "regardless of what else may be said of religion, it is also a social phenomenon – it is something that people do in groups."[26] This move toward social and scientific understanding characterizes most contemporary religious studies scholarship. For example, Durkheim assumes that religion is a definable and appropriate subject of scientific inquiry.[27] For Durkheim, religion is characterized by totemism, symbols representing and creating community (whether in the context of totem animals, symbols, or even flags).[28] He thus understands religion in a social context ("God is society writ large"). In this view, religion is constructed by society, and its expressions have a number of common forms – e.g., a division of the world into sacred and profane; a belief in souls and the spiritual world; and a faith in some form of divinity, asceticism, or rites/liturgy. The identification of these forms allowed Durkheim to analyze commonalities across religious traditions in order to make generalizations about "religion." In addition to characterizing religion as "the social," Durkheim made a connection between religion and religious community:

> A religion is a unified system of beliefs and practices relative to sacred things, that is to say, things set apart and forbidden – beliefs and practices which unite into one single moral community called a Church, all those who adhere to them.[29]

This is arguably the most influential approach to understanding religion in the social sciences.

Berger provides a description of the dialectical role of religion in mediating between society and individuals.[30] He identifies three steps in this process: externalization, objectivation, and internalization.[31] Externalization is the physical and mental outpouring of human beings into the world. Objectivation is the phenomenon of these outpourings coalescing around and confronting the original producers (in his terms as a "facticity").[32] Internalization is the reception of this reality by human beings, transforming "the structures of the objective world into structures of the subjective consciousness."[33] This process creates a meaningful order that, when well established, may be described as religion or "the human enterprise by which a sacred cosmos is established."[34] Religion reinforces the power of internalization by legitimating social institutions as sacred.[35] However, beyond legitimation there continues to be a reciprocal relationship as individuals continue to impact objectivation through their ongoing externalization.[36] I am reasonably comfortable with this description as a way of understanding the mediating role of religion, even if it is not entirely comprehensive.

In "Genesis and Structure of the Religious Field," Bourdieu attempts to use a market analysis in his description of religion.[37] In addition to harmonizing Marx, Weber, and Durkheim, he tries to describe a market of religious capital in order to explain the dialectical relationship between religious institutions, which may even serve as a proxy for society and individuals.[38] Though interesting, Bourdieu's analysis stretches the market analogy beyond its usefulness. Unlike works of art and books (referring here to Bourdieu's broader concept of social capital), religious capital is not clearly quantifiable or priced; its influence or "value" may not be described in terms of the creation of supply and demand. Furthermore, even if we assume that there is a market dynamic governing religious capital, that conclusion is not useful if potential market failures cannot be clearly identified (e.g., monopoly, information imbalances, externalities, collective action problems, etc.). However, a "market of religious capital" does explain the creation of the social in terms of the economic and has been helpful in religious studies scholarship.

James Wellman's definition of religion as "the social enactment of a desire for the ultimate, usually related to a spirit or god, spirits or gods"[39] relates to Durkheim's understanding of religion as the social and seems to incorporate something like Berger's understanding of its formation in the "enactment." However, it also appears to synthesize elements of the psychological and the theological. The role of "desire," for example, acknowledges a fundamental psychological need for order and explanation as a defense, presumably against anxiety. Looking to the "ultimate" and a relationship with the "infinite" evokes a sense of the numinous and makes space for metaphysical and theological understandings of religion. This synthesis may provide a more satisfying description of religion, even if it creates some degree of ambiguity by considering the numinous.

Also in the tradition of Durkheim, Clifford Geertz provides a helpful definition in the context of social science:

> A religion is a system of symbols which acts to establish powerful, pervasive, and long-lasting moods and motivations in men by formulating conceptions of a general order of existence and clothing these conceptions with such an aura of factuality that the moods and motivations seem uniquely realistic.[40]

Drawing on Foucault, Talal Asad critiques this definition for failing to identify the disciplinary role of religion as a creation of power.[41] The creation of order in Geertz, and the role of power in Asad, provide insight into the relationship between the religious and the political that may help to explain the sort of "mischief" religion has been blamed for.

Clifford Geertz and Talal Asad have been particularly important in shaping an anthropology of Islam within their consideration of religion more generally. Geertz's comparative study of Islam in Morocco and Indonesia concludes that the Islamic conception of life carries different meanings in those two cultural contexts.[42] Thus, Geertz argues that Islam, as a subject for research, must be understood in the context of local experience, history, and custom. In contrast, Asad pushes back on Geertz's generalizations regarding Islam and proposes that, "Islam as the object of anthropological understanding should be approached as a discursive tradition that connects variously with the formation of moral selves, the manipulation of populations (or resistance to it), and the production of appropriate knowledges."[43]

Religion and politics: Boundaries and interactions

A number of scholars engage the relationship between religion and politics in order to consider the overlap and influences between the two. In considering the religion–state interaction, as well as the role of the "secular," I consider five of the most influential theses regarding religion and politics. All five theses wrestle with the relationship between the nation-state and religion in the modern period, particularly in the context of political liberalism, which is usually characterized by a commitment to some sort of secularism.

Ernest Renan was a French philosopher and writer best known for his political theories and influential historical works on early Christianity. In "What Is a Nation?" Renan describes the nation as "a soul, a spiritual principle," with two distinguishing characteristics – a common legacy of memories and present consent by its members.[44] He dismisses arguments that nations are based on race – or, perhaps more precisely, on common descent – or that language, which he does identify with nations, relates to race or to genetic affinity.[45] He notes the phenomenon of conquerors adopting the religion of the conquered, which seems at first counterintuitive.[46] His identification of the national with the spiritual is not entirely clear. On the one hand, he may be anticipating the identification of the religious with the social, as in Durkheim. However, it is more likely that his thesis anticipates the development of civil religion in modern nations. In fact, it may be that the need for both a "common legacy of memories," and "present consent" in societies of diverse groups requires the creation of some sort of communally acceptable worldview, which might best be described as "religious." In other words, for Renan, the nation must either draw upon a common tradition or find overlap among a plurality of traditions to create something new. Within the liberal state, that overlap might be described as the secular because it does not draw upon a single source.

Robert Bellah was a sociologist best known for his work related to "American civil religion." He argues that Americans embrace a common civil religion with certain fundamental beliefs, values, holidays, and rituals parallel to or independent of their chosen religion.[47] Descriptively, this seems to be accurate and consistent with the observations made by Renan, Durkheim, and Rawls. Bellah identifies three critical stages of civil religious tradition in the United States. The first stage is established by the leaders of the revolution, and it is closely identified with the experience of the Hebrews' flight from Egypt to the Promised Land.[48] The second stage occurs at the time of the American Civil War and establishes President Lincoln as a civil Christ figure who sacrifices himself for the community.[49] The third stage is characterized by America's wrestling with its political, economic, and military dominance in the world.[50] This seems to raise the sorts of question that faced the Davidic Kingdom of Israel or the early Christians who sought the "reign of God."

Once the third stage is established, a new question emerges: How is power to be righteously exercised by the faithful? This stage is analogous to the Roman Empire after Christianity became the official faith: The mélange of American civil religion incorporates elements of major religious traditions – including elements of Protestantism, Catholicism, and Judaism, in particular – as well as various patriotic symbols used to connect people from other traditions not noticeably represented. However, "faith" in such a religion is likely to be tenuous in nature, since the new conglomeration of symbols and traditions maintains a religious character but also invites secular themes as the public image of religion is stripped of clear identifications with any particular tradition (other than through general references to God, which invoke ideas of monotheism). In this sense, "civil religion" is neither truly religious, since it does not reflect the actual spiritual beliefs of any one person, nor is it truly secular, since it cannot be entirely neutral.

Francis Fukuyama is an American philosopher and political economist. He is best known for his essay "The End of History," in which he argues that the progression of human history as a struggle between ideologies is largely at an end, with the world settling on liberal democracy after the end of the Cold War.[51] Using a Hegelian framework, he posits that the tension between thesis and antithesis ends with the development of liberal democracy – a view consistent with Hegel's own understanding of 19th-century Germany.[52] Fukuyama argues that liberal democracy results in a system of rights and distribution that defuse class tension, is copied across cultures, and is stable over time.[53] This view is consistent with and is the basis for some neoconservative thought. Implicit within Fukuyama's argument is the assumption that religious tension and distinction become irrelevant in liberal democracies because of their commitment to secularism in law and government. However, there are a number of problems with Fukuyama's views on the universality and superiority of liberalism – many of which even he acknowledged in the context of the American experience in the occupation of Iraq.[54] Liberalism, and perhaps more importantly, secularism, developed in very particular historical, economic, and cultural contexts in Europe and North America, and, as an overlay or imposition in other contexts, it has not been easy to reproduce. This is not to say that some sort of governmental neutrality, or commonly held civil religion we might call "secular," cannot not develop in other contexts. However, in order to reproduce itself in other contexts, such secularism must have local legitimacy. The legitimacy of liberalism is an ongoing question in Turkey as discussions of the empirical study in Chapters Five through Seven will demonstrate.

Samuel Huntington was an American political scientist who gained prominence through his Clash of Civilizations thesis of a post–Cold War new world order.[55] He argues that the nation-state is not the primary force around which human beings organize themselves. Instead, he maintains that culture acts as this center.[56] He specifically identifies seven (or eight) discrete cultures (Western, Confucian, Japanese, Islamic, Hindu, Slavic-Orthodox, Latin American, and possibly African).[57] He further maintains that "[t]he most important conflicts of the future will occur along the cultural fault lines separating these civilizations from one another."[58] Although he identifies these civilizations by culture, it is more than coincidence that the main distinguishing factor between them is religion. Instead of dismissing traditional religion, as liberalism often does, Huntington reifies religion and establishes an expectation – or perhaps a self-fulfilling prophecy – that it will be the basis for future struggle.[59] Huntington's essay also establishes the justification for Western, primarily American, efforts to protect liberal secular democracy from the onslaught of hostile cultures, even preemptively.[60] Like Fukuyama, Huntington is confident in the superiority of "Western" culture; however, he does not seem as optimistic about its potential to achieve global hegemony or about the eschatological end of history – at least not yet. He is particularly concerned by the new axis of Sino–Islamic cooperation that could ultimately threaten liberalism.[61] Although the tragedy of 9/11 was used to promote Huntington's thesis in order to justify military force in Afghanistan and Iraq, his characterization of particular cultures and nations – China and Turkey in particular – is simplistic, essentialized, and extremely problematic. In the context of the relationship between nations and religion, both Turkey and China have developed forms of secularism within their own cultural contexts that continue to evolve outside of the "Western" culture that Huntington presumes is the only one capable of producing a stable, secular, and civil society.

Slavoj Zizek is a Slovenian continental philosopher and critical theorist working in the traditions of Hegelianism, Marxism, and Lacanian psychoanalysis.[62] His essay "The Clash of Civilizations at the End of History" critiques both Huntington and Fukuyama.[63] This piece uses the film *Children of Men* as an allegory for the modern world, which is ironic since the film is set in a dystopic future.[64] The film describes a world in which human beings are no longer able to reproduce. The privileged have fallen into profound self-indulgence and have imposed an oppressive political and military order to protect their power. Refugees and marginalized religious groups are held in camps that are beset by violence – but it is only these groups that maintain spirit, drive, and desire. Zizek compares the privileged in the film to liberal democracies, where people have become passionless consumers living in fear of terrorism, consuming fat, and smoking tobacco.[65] It is the poor, the oppressed, and those who refuse to be colonized who preserve the human spirit.[66] It is not surprising then that, in the film, it is among the outcasts that the miracle child is born. Through this allegory, Zizek critiques the ostensible neutrality, objectivity, and fairness of liberal democracies, including their view of secularism. He finds more real human passion in believing Muslims – both in the film and in the real world.[67] However, it is not clear whether this is meant as a critique of pluralist attempts at coexistence and creation of civil society or of secularism, which seeks to strip all spirit, honesty, and integrity from public life. Although he is critical of the ideological agendas of Huntington and Fukuyama, he does wonder whether the clash of civilizations is the end of history, leading inexorably to the tragic and apocalyptic vision of *Children of Men.*

In the context of exploring the relationship between religion and politics, then, religion may be (a) the core of political identity, (b) an idea to be adapted by the political in order to provide social cohesion, (c) a force tamed by politics, (d) the source of ongoing human conflict which politics (i.e., Western liberalism) must defeat, or (e) a source of identity and inspiration that must be free of political control. Renan and Bellah acknowledge a positive role for religion in informing politics, though both seem to view this relationship as a dynamic ultimately shaped by political power, even if it began as a dialectical relationship. Similarly, although Fukuyama and Huntington may have positive views of the religious traditions that influenced the development of political liberalism, both consider the need for political power in the form of liberalism to displace competing worldviews. All four authors consider religion a potential source of division and a threat to national political order. Only when it is domesticated and homogenized does religion cease to cause mischief. However, I would argue that such "religion" ceases to be religion because it no longer addresses the human heart. This is the insight and criticism offered by Zizek.

Religion and politics: The dynamic of competition

Liberal denominations' attempts to conform to secularism or civil religion have been largely unsuccessful in retaining members, let alone garnering the sort of devotion traditionally attributed to "religious fervor."[68] Instead, untamed religion, which engages the human heart and challenges political power, has filled ideological voids created by such dynamics as the fall of the Soviet Union and the decline of mainline Protestantism. American Evangelicalism, *Salafi* Islam, and even liberation theology have all benefited from the failure of state attempts to tame religion. This may be further demonstrated by the crises created within these religious movements once they attain political power, shifting focus toward consolidation, discipline, and control and away from finding meaning, purpose, and the numinous.

An alternative explanation for this dynamic can be found in feminist scholarship. Pamela Sue Anderson considers the construction of the self and the role that theistic religion plays in that process.[69] She applies a feminist critique, and her argument is related to standpoint theory in that the failure to incorporate the lived experience of women inevitably results in "corrupt aspiration" – such as the male inclination to aspire to be infinite – which she views as the hallmark of theistic religion.[70] Thus, the role of religion in the construction of selves must include the feminine, which is in fact a solution to the traps set by male theistic religion. Perhaps the male aspiration to be infinite explains the tendency to fuse religion with political power.

Similarly, though in an explicitly Catholic context, Mary Daly wrestles with describing the phenomenon of religion.[71] Although she is a feminist theologian and philosopher, her work uses an anthropological lens in considering the origin and deconstruction of patriarchy as a human dynamic. She describes religion as a social or historical response to anxiety.[72] Daly finds authentic religion in the "confrontation with the experience of nothingness."[73] Symbols are extremely important in her analysis. Daly problematizes the Father God as the central symbol and justification for patriarchy and the oppression of women.[74] Although not all religious systems are as explicitly patriarchal in their symbolism, both Anderson and Daly would likely conclude that most religions, including Islam, are patriarchal in practice.

Although he is not explicitly concerned with gender oppression, Feuerbach criticizes the "false or theological essence of religion," i.e., the view that regards God as having a separate existence from humankind – a view consistent with the feminist critiques above.[75] Mistaken beliefs such as revelation not only injure the moral sense, but also "[poison], nay [destroy], the divinest feeling in man, the sense of truth."[76] Invoking a social view of religion, Feuerbach claims that man surrenders his identity to God, whom he describes as a selfish being.[77] This selfishness shapes man, corrupting him.[78] More generally, Feuerbach asserts that creation remains a part of the creator, while the creator remains greater than the creation. He develops what he calls the "true or anthropological essence of religion."[79] He treats God in his various aspects "as a being of understanding," "as a moral being or law," or "as love."[80] God is nothing other than man.[81] He is the outward projection of man's inward nature (a view consistent with Durkheim's).[82] In this view, religion contains the seeds of morality and meaning, but it also provides a powerful impetus to exercise control.

The tendency to divide, to assert control, and to cause mischief can be identified with fundamentalism:

> [F]undamentalists would reject the suggestion that they are doing something radically new; a crucial element of their rhetoric and self-understanding is the assertion that their innovative programs are based on the authority of the sacred past, whether that past be represented in a privileged text or tradition, or in the teaching of a charismatic or official leader.[83]

Almond, Sivan, and Appleby go on to describe a family resemblance test for identifying fundamentalism, which includes tests for reactivity to the marginalization of religion, selectivity, moral Manichaeism, absolutism/inerrancy, millennialism/messianism, election, sharp boundaries, authoritarian organization, and behavioral requirements. Religious movements with these traits are often associated with excess and aspirations to political power in contexts as varied as the Iranian Revolution, Wahhabi Saudi Arabia, the Bharatiya Janata Party, and the Moral Majority.

Whether the source is patriarchy, fundamentalism, or an inherent aspect of religion, its propensity for asserting coercive political control is problematic. Modern states have had three approaches to preventing such excesses. Some have forced religious conformity as a practical matter (more in the sense of Saudi Arabia than in the state churches of Western Europe). Others have attempted to quash religion.[84] But the most common approach, even outside of liberal democracies, is some form of secularism.

The role of secularism

The medieval origin of the word "*seculare*" distinguishes parish priests who were "in the world" ("*in saeculo*") from vowed religious men and women. In the 19th century, the term "secularism" was coined by George Jacob Holyoake to refer to those (nonreligious) things he believed lead to human happiness, such as well-being, science, and doing good.[85] One of the more common meanings refers to state neutrality.[86] Perhaps the most popular formulation conceives of secularism as the separation of "church and state."[87] The French, the Turks, and other nations use cognates of the word "laicism" to refer specifically to a barrier between religious and state institutions. In one sense, secularism is intended to protect individuals from coercive social pressure (though this is clearer in French or Turkish laicism). Thomas Jefferson in the Virginia Statute for Religious Freedom writes: ". . . No man shall be compelled to frequent or support any religious worship, place, or ministry whatsoever . . ."[88] Although secularism has been offered as a solution to curbing religious excess and division, it is often criticized as a tool of Western control and has been relatively unsuccessful at supplanting religion. However, it may still provide a theory for tolerating diversity at the level of the state.

The idea of separating church and state is generally considered an Enlightenment principle effected by the French and American Constitutions, but both medieval Islam and Christianity developed complex doctrines defining separate political and religious spheres (*siyasa* and *Shari'a* in Islam and state and church in Christianity). The most influential theoretical model of secularism today is probably that provided by John Rawls and is rooted in his theory of justice. He posits that *justice* must fundamentally be *fairness* and proposes that rational persons, not knowing the circumstances into which they were born, would choose a system in which they would be in the best possible position if they were born into disadvantage.[89] That is, if we knew that we might be born into a marginalized group – whether discriminated against because of class, race, ethnicity, gender, religion, orientation, or disability – we would choose a system that would provide opportunities comparable to those who were not disadvantaged. Rawls proposes that fair legal rules can be developed as a social contract negotiated from the "initial position."[90] The initial position is a notion similar to the classical "state of nature";

however, it is an artificial position that requires ignoring the actual state of privilege and/or disadvantage into which one is born. It assumes that one cannot make a fair decision regarding the distribution of social goods knowing a priori what advantages or disadvantages he or she will actually be born into. So, in order to negotiate a fair social contract, we make distributive decisions pretending not to know. This is called the "veil of ignorance." As opposed to some other theories of social contract, Rawls' veil of ignorance is thick in that it denies knowledge of any details of life such as religion, gender, race, ethnicity, intelligence, health, disability, or orientation.[91] Presuming human rationality and risk aversion, Rawls asserts that a person in the original position, and reasoning behind the veil of ignorance, will choose to live in the best possible situation if born into disadvantage even if it means sacrificing economic or social privilege if born into advantage.[92]

In this context, Rawls argues that religion should play little or no overt role in what he calls public reason.[93] The idea of public reason proposed by Rawls is intended to regulate political discourse and decision-making in the liberal state. He distinguishes between "public reasons" and "nonpublic reasons." Public reasons are truths that are widely accepted, premises rooted in a society's conception of political justice, and "guidelines of inquiry" that establish standards for evaluating competing arguments.[94] Nonpublic reasons comprise those that do not fit into these categories – most notably of these are religious reasons – which are often the basis for moral and policy preferences.[95] Instead, theological arguments must be made using plausible, independent, and secular grounds. In this context, political power is exercised in response to the marketplace of nonreligious ideas (implying elements of free speech theory) and on the basis of overlapping consensus. Rawls posits that law, particularly international law, has legitimacy when there is overlapping consensus among peoples with different beliefs and traditions.[96] So, in a sense, Rawls describes an approach to developing legal rules with legitimacy in a pluralistic world. This is likely the dominant normative understanding of secularism in the United States.

However, this view is subject to criticism, particularly from those who argue that religion and religious reasons cannot be either repressed or "translated." For example, Michael Perry argues for the inclusion of religious premises within public discourse on liberal grounds rooted in individual liberty, authenticity, and the common good.[97] This argument goes beyond the argument for softer, American-style secularism. In addition to strong protection of the free exercise of religion, Perry argues that there is a proper place for religious premises within public discourse.[98] Although this argument is in part one in favor of authenticity, it arguably opens the door to "mischief" by conflating religion and politics.

The most extensive recent treatment of secularism is Charles Taylor's *A Secular Age*, in which he makes a strong case for the presence in ordinary moral life of something like Plato's idea of the good.[99] Taylor engages the question of the role of religion in constituting a person's identity. He explains the prerequisites for faith in the absence of any equivalent to the intellectual, cultural, and imaginative surroundings in which premodern religion was embedded.[100] This is what he calls our "social imaginary": how we collectively sense what is normal and appropriate in our dealings with one another and with the world around us.[101] Taylor considers secularism a response to pluralism rather than to religion per se. This distinction is helpful when considering the neutral role of the state, but it misses something in the assumption that religion is like any other identifying trait or social phenomenon. If religion is somehow distinct, and powerfully so, then treating it is a single element of social identity might create new opportunities for "mischief."

Talal Asad explicitly challenges the dominant discourses of American secular theory. He borrows from Rawls the idea that "there can be no universally agreed basis, whether secular or religious, for the political principles accepted in a modern, heterogeneous society."[102] Rather than trumpeting the "triumphalist history of the secular" or anticipating religious revival, Asad is more interested in understanding the positions from which such narratives originate and what makes them possible under particular conditions.[103] Although he is skeptical of the secularism rooted in the Enlightenment and political liberalism, he offers a number of bases for harmonizing orthodox understandings of Islamic tradition with elements of secularism.[104] In this regard, his position may not be so far from that of Taylor in that he advocates state neutrality toward its citizens. His insights are particularly helpful because they acknowledge the role of power and discipline within religion generally, as well as the problematic links between Western liberalism and colonial oppression. Asad's comparative paradigm and deep engagement with Islamic tradition also make his generalizations more persuasive.

For Asad, secularism is not simply the division between public and private realms. Instead, secularism can become a source of exclusions. It redefines religion as private and eschews ritual and discipline from the public space, which stands in stark contrast with the development of religious traditions, including both Christianity and Islam. European and North American secularism claim to be facially neutral with regard to Islam, and yet, as a non-Christian cultural group, they are either tolerated or restricted.[105] Thus, Asad is quite critical of European conceptions of secularism, which are often used as tools to isolate and marginalize Muslims and thus increase the religious antagonism they ostensibly intend to defuse.[106] The specific topic of Turkish secularism will be discussed in Chapter Four.

It is not clear whether secularism is intended to domesticate religion or to prevent religion from exercising coercive political power, or whether it achieves either. The experience of the U.S. and Turkey would seem to suggest that state secularism is unable to domesticate religion and may even give rise to new, reactive religious movements. Nor does it prevent religious groups from exercising political power. However, it may blunt the extremes of division and abuse attributable to religion by shifting the assumptions regarding the appropriate use of state power. For example, in Turkey, avowedly religious political leaders have been in power for fourteen years (the impact of which will be discussed in Chapter Four and in the analysis of the empirical study). Although many have argued for more public expressions of Islam (as in the case of the proposals to lift the Turkish ban on headscarves for women in universities), almost all public discourse is framed by the assumption that the principle of secularism is necessary as a limitation on governmental power and for either political or social cohesion.

Perhaps Weber was right and human societies are moving toward more complex and successful forms of religion along an evolutionary path. Durkheim had a similarly optimistic and developmental understanding of religion. Alternatively, if Freud is right, religion will continue to divide and cause mischief, and we merely need to hold out until science displaces religion altogether.[107] However, it is more likely that the dialectical relationship between religion and politics described in the last two sections will continue unabated. There is no doubt that religion per se is largely a social construction that addresses fundamental human needs (particularly psychological needs). Durkheim, Berger, and others make compelling arguments explaining the dynamic of this construction. Even so, perhaps it is the sense of the ultimate or the numinous which distinguishes religion from other social constructions. This might explain how it serves as a compelling source of meaning and values distinct from science, politics, or economics. When religion is conflated with these other structures and loses its sense of awe, it ultimately loses its persuasive and cohesive force *as* religion.

In exploring the relationship between religion and the state in Turkey, using the data from the empirical study presented in Chapters Five through Seven, it is important to provide context both for the established normative theological understandings of Islam (*Shari'a* in particular) and the personal and social experiences of Islam described by participants in the study, which may exist in tension with formal teachings. Chapter Two will provide context for understanding *Shari'a* as part of the formal, theological teaching of Islam, while Chapter Three will explore some important elements of popular religion in Turkey as it is experienced personally and socially.

Notes

1 William James, *The Varieties of Religious Experience: A Study in Human Nature*. New York, NY: Penguin Books, 1982 at 42.
2 Rudolph Otto, *The Idea of the Holy: An Inquiry into the Non-rational Factor in the Idea of the Divine and its Relation to the Rational*. Oxford: Oxford University Press, 1936.
3 Otto at 5–7.
4 *Id.* at 12–13.
5 Max Weber, "Objectivity in Social Science and Social Policy," in *The Methodology of the Social Sciences*. Ed. and Trans. E.A. Shils and H.A. Finch. New York: Free Press, 1949. "[A]n ideal type is formed by the one-sided accentuation of one or more points of view" according to which "concrete individual phenomena . . . are arranged into a unified analytical construct"; in its purely fictional nature, it is a methodological "utopia [that] cannot be found empirically anywhere in reality" at 90.
6 *See e.g.*, Max Weber, *The Protestant Ethic and the Spirit of Capitalism*. New York: Oxford University Press, 2011 at 24–25.
7 *Id.* at 180–183.
8 *Id.*
9 *See* Max Weber, *Essays in Sociology*. Oxford: Oxford University Press, 1958.
10 Mircea Eliade, *The Myth of the Eternal Return: Cosmos and History*. Princeton, NJ: Princeton University Press, 2005.
11 *See e.g., id.* at 34–48.

12 *Id.* at 159–162.
13 *Id.* at 43–44.
14 *See e.g., id.* at xxvii–xxix.
15 *See* Edward Ames, "Non-Religious Persons." *American Journal of Theology* 13 (1909): 541, 542.
16 Joseph Gaer, *How the Great Religions Began.* New York: Dodd Mead, 1981.
17 Paul Tillich, *The Dynamics of Faith.* San Francisco: HarperOne, 2009 at 52.
18 *See e.g.*, Annemarie Schimmel, *Mystical Dimensions of Islam.* Chapel Hill: University of North Carolina Press, 1975.
19 Sigmund Freud, *Future of an Illusion.* Mansfield Centre, CT: Martino Pub, 2010.
20 Peter Berger, *The Sacred Canopy: Elements of a Sociological Theory of Religion.* New York: Anchor Books, 1990.
21 Pierre Bourdieu, *The Field of Cultural Production: Essays on Art and Literature.* New York: Columbia University Press, 1993.
22 Freud at 30.
23 Victor Turner, "Liminality and Communitas," in *The Ritual Process: Structure and Anti-Structure.* Ithaca, NY: Cornell University Press, 1969, pp. 94–130.
24 *Id.* at 94–113.
25 *See e.g.*, Idries Shah and Doris Lessing, *Learning How to Learn: Psychology and Spirituality in the Sufi Way.* New York: Penguin, 1996; or Javad Nurbaksh, *The Psychology of Sufism.* New York: KNP, 1993.
26 William Newman, *The Social Meanings of Religion: An Integrated Anthology.* Chicago: Rand McNally, 1974.
27 Emile Durkheim, *The Elementary Forms of the Religious Life.* Mineola, NY: Dover Publications, Inc., 2008.
28 *Id.* at 310–311.
29 Durkheim at 46.
30 Berger at 25–28.
31 *Id.* at 4.
32 *Id.* at 14.
33 *Id.* at 4.
34 *Id.* at 24.
35 *Id.* at 32–39.
36 *Id.* at 10–20.
37 Bourdieu at 7–13.
38 *Id.* at 22–31.
39 James Wellman (Ed.), *Belief and Bloodshed: Religion and Violence across Time and Tradition.* Plymouth: Rowman & Littlefield Publishers, 2007 at 4.
40 Clifford Geertz, "Religion as a Cultural System," in *The Interpretation of Culture: Selected Essays.* London: Fontana Press, 1993 at 90.
41 Talal Asad, *Genealogies of Religion: Discipline and Reasons of Power in Christianity and Islam.* Baltimore, MD: Johns Hopkins University Press, 1993 at 29–53.
42 *See* Clifford Geertz, *Islam Observed: Religious Development in Morocco and Indonesia.* Chicago: University of Chicago Press, 1968 at 56–89.
43 Talal Asad, "The Idea of an Anthropology of Islam" at 10, document available at http://ccas.georgetown.edu/story/1242687906497.html
44 Ernest Renan, "What Is a Nation? Modern Political Doctrines," London, 1939, available at http://archive.org/stream/ernestrenan00barruoft/ernestrenan00barruoft_djvu.txt.
45 *Id.*
46 *Id.* Note however that this is perhaps a gross generalization. In the case of the early spread of Islam, it was generally the reverse. However, in periods of occupation, it was fairly common for invaders to adopt Islam (as in the case of Turkic tribes and the Mongols).
47 Robert Bellah, "Civil Religion in America." *Daedalus* 117.3 (1988): 97–118.

48 *Id.*
49 *Id.*
50 *Id.*
51 Francis Fukuyama, *The End of History and The Last Man*. New York: Free Press, 2006.
52 *See* Georg Wilhelm Hegel, *The Philosophy of History*. New York: The Colonial Press, 1899 at 455–457.
53 *See* Fukuyama.
54 *See e.g.*, "Interview with Ex-Neocon Francis Fukuyama: 'A Model Democracy Is not Emerging in Iraq.'" *Der Spiegel Online*, March 22, 2006, available at http://www.spiegel.de/international/interview-with-ex-neocon-francis-fukuyama-a-model-democracy-is-not-emerging-in-iraq-a-407315.html.
55 Samuel Huntington, "The Clash of Civilizations?" *Foreign Affairs* 72.3 (1993): 22–49.
56 *Id.*
57 *Id.*
58 *Id.*
59 *Id.*
60 *Id.*
61 *Id.*
62 Slavoj Zizek, "The Clash of Civilizations at the End of History." *Cultural Inquiry* (2007), available at https://www.scribd.com/doc/19133296/Zizek-The-Clash-of-Civilizations-at-the-End-of-History.
63 *Id.*
64 *Id.*
65 *Id.*
66 *Id.*
67 *Id.*
68 *See e.g.*, James Wellman, *Evangelical vs. Liberal: The Clash of Christian Cultures in the Pacific Northwest*. Oxford: Oxford University Press, 2008.
69 Pamela Sue Anderson, "Gender and the Infinite: On the Aspiration to Be All There Is." *International Journal for Philosophy of Religion* 50.1/3 (2001): 191–212.
70 *Id.* at 196.
71 Mary Daly, *Beyond God the Father: Toward a Philosophy of Women's Liberation*. London: Women's Press, 1986.
72 *Id.* at 13–18.
73 *Id.* at 64.
74 *Id.* at 19–22.
75 Ludwig Feuerbach, *The Essence of Christianity*. Mineola, NY: Dover Publications, 2008.
76 *Id.* at 137.
77 *Id.* at 24.
78 *Id.* at 24–25.
79 *See id.* at Part I.
80 *Id.* at 147.
81 *Id.*
82 *Id.* at 26 and 51.
83 Gabriel A. Almond, Emmanuel Sivan, and R. Scott Appleby, *Fundamentalism: Genus and Species*. Chicago: University of Chicago Press, 1995. 399–424.
84 Clearly this is the case in the Soviet Union and the People's Republic of China; some would argue that it is also the case in the Republic of Turkey during certain periods. I would contend that the Turkish experience has had more to do with creating a single religious narrative that strengthens national identity rather than quashing religion per se.
85 George Jacob Holyoake, *Origin and Nature of Secularism*. London: Watts & Co., 1896 at 50.

86 *See e.g.*, Charles Taylor, *A Secular Age*. Cambridge, MA: Belknap Press of Harvard University Press, 2007.
87 Thomas Jefferson, Letter to the Danbury Baptist Association 1802, in relevant part, "Believing with you that religion is a matter which lies solely between man and his god, that he owes account to none other for his faith or his worship, that the legitimate powers of government reach actions only, and not opinions, I contemplate with sovereign reverence that act of the whole American people which declared that their legislature should make no law respecting an establishment of religion, or prohibiting the free exercise thereof, thus building a wall of separation between church and state."
88 Virginia Statute for Establishing Religious Freedom (1786).
89 *See generally*, John Rawls, *A Theory of Justice*. Cambridge: Belknap Press, 1999.
90 *Id.* at 10–11.
91 *Id.* at 118–123.
92 *Id.*
93 John Rawls, *Political Liberalism.* New York and Chichester: Columbia University Press, 1993 at 222–254.
94 *Id.* at 223–224.
95 *Id.* at 220.
96 *Id.* at 134–149.
97 Michael Perry, *Under God? Religious Faith and Liberal Democracy.* Cambridge, UK & New York: Cambridge University Press, 2003.
98 *Id.*
99 *See* Taylor.
100 *Id.* at 13–15.
101 *Id.* at 164–165.
102 Talal Asad, *Formations of the Secular*. Stanford, CA: Stanford University Press, 2003 at 2.
103 *Id.* at 46.
104 *See* e.g., *id.* at 32.
105 *Id.* at 168–169.
106 *Id.* at 252–256.
107 This does not appear to be the general trend in Turkey or the United States, both of which have had multiple religious renewals over the past century.

2 Historical meanings of *Shariʿa*

"Islamic law" is such a problematic term that some scholars refuse to use it.[1] It is a broad and imprecise term. *Shariʿa*, which is often translated as "Islamic law," refers to the ideal of God's law as understood within Islam and is similar to the ideal of divine law found in medieval Christian jurisprudence.[2] Since divine law is not knowable with certainty, human attempts to apprehend it are subject to error. Thus, there are multiple approaches to understanding *Shariʿa*.[3] The human exercise to ascertain *Shariʿa* is referred to as ***fiqh***, or Islamic jurisprudence.[4] Approaches to understanding are divided into three general categories: (1) orthodox classical, (2) nontraditional modern interpretations, and (3) unorthodox approaches. This discussion addresses primarily the orthodox classical and the nontraditional modern interpretations.

Within Sunni Islam, four historic schools of jurisprudence (*madhab*) ultimately survived: the *Hanafi*, the *Maliki*, the *Shafi'i*, and the *Hanbali*.[5] Each of the Sunni schools, functioning as guilds,[6] developed a separate body of legal rules reflected in treatises and in collections of legal opinions (*fatwa*, pl. *fatawa*).[7] According to the conventional view, the "Gates of ***Ijtihad***" (allowing jurists to interpret directly from the canonical sources) were closed within Sunni *fiqh* by the 11th or 12th century BCE such that the methodology of legal decision-making shifted from the interpretation of the jurist to following precedent created by prior legal decisions within the school.[8] The dominant school of Shiʿi *fiqh* is the *Ja'fari* school, which emphasizes the interpretation (*ijtihad*) of the **imams**.[9]

Classical tradition and *fiqh*

The sources of *fiqh*[10] are the **Quran**, the ***Sunna*** (as recorded in ***Hadith*** collections), *ijma*, and ***qiyas***.[11] *Ijtihad* is reasoning from scriptural texts – a direct interpretation. For this reason, *Ijtihad* is inherently subjective.[12] It is applied to fact patterns, which vary from the patterns described in scriptural texts and consequently creates ambiguities that must be resolved.[13]

The Quran

The Quran is a record of divine words revealed to the Prophet Muhammad but does not address all behaviors and is the source of relatively few legal rules.[14]

Even when the text does provide rules, they sometimes appear ambiguous or in tension with other passages, requiring an interpretive framework such as contextualization or abrogation.[15]

The Sunna

The *Sunna*, as preserved in *Hadith* collections, is the Prophet's example. Sunni Muslims accepted it as a model of correct behavior when the *madhabs* formed.[16] In order to interpret these reports, jurists would have to isolate and interpret texts, placing rulings into four categories: (1) with certain respect to both authenticity and meaning; (2) derived from texts whose authenticity was unquestionable, but whose meaning could not be established with absolute certainty; (3) probable authenticity and certain meaning; and (4) presumptive with respect to both authenticity and precise meaning.[17] Rulings that fit into the first category are absolutely certain, while rulings that fit into the second and third categories are binding unless the jurist discovered a more secure ruling to contradict it.[18] Only rulings in the last category were sufficiently uncertain as to be discounted as a guide to correct action.[19]

Ijma

The third *fiqh* source is *ijma*, or consensus, based on a *Hadith* indicating that the community would not reach consensus on a mistaken interpretation of the law.[20] It "was not a . . . source from which rulings were derived. Rather, it was a source through which the certainty of a ruling that had already been derived could be definitively established."[21] Traditionally, "consensus" was defined by that generation of legal scholars, but broader and narrower understandings have been advocated.[22]

Qiyas

In the absence of clear rules in the texts or *ijma*, jurists examined existing rules for application to a new situation. Derived rules are merely probable unless ratified by consensus. A jurist would look for absolutely clear rules in the Quran and the *Sunna* (or ratified by consensus). Presuming that none were directly applicable, a jurist would use *qiyas* (sometimes translated as analogical reasoning) to look for clear analogies in previous rules by identifying a text's *illa* (the underlying efficient cause of the rule). A rule derived by *qiyas* must serve the same *illa* as the text supporting it. Utilitarian methods were introduced to narrow the range of possible rulings (most importantly by al-Ghazali).[23] Appropriateness (*munasaba*) narrows the range of analogies by requiring that a rule derived by *qiyas* further the *muqasid al-Shariʿa* by promoting one of the five (or six) "necessaries."[24] The doctrine of necessity (*darura*) dictates that a law should never be applied in cases where following it would cause overwhelming harm to one of the *muqasid al-Shariʿa*.[25] Other scholars set the bar lower than massive harm to the community.[26] Various other subordinate interpretive methods were used within the schools at different times. For our purposes, another important subordinate interpretive method in Turkish tradition (here meaning Ottoman *Hanafi fiqh*) is the use of local custom (*urf*) as a basis for reaching a ruling.

Ijtihad *and* taqlid

By the time the schools were firmly established and had developed extensive bodies of legal rules and commentaries, individual *ijtihad* was displaced by ***taqlid*** (precedential reasoning) – deriving laws based on understanding texts as interpreted by earlier members of a chosen guild, the result of group interpretation that provided an objective basis upon which legal decisions and rulings could be described.[27] *Taqlid* entails accepting the view of a recognized leading jurist without scriptural proof of its correctness,[28] stabilizing the legal system with more regular and predictable legal outcomes.[29] The process of *taqlid* developed in part because jurists (*mujtahids*) came to believe that none among them had the requisite skill set to derive rulings through *ijtihad* alone; however, precedential reasoning was sufficiently flexible that jurists had some room to reason creatively.[30]

The system of *taqlid* created a three-tiered hierarchy of jurists.[31] The lowest-level jurists can only apply formalized rules contained in a ***mukkhtassar*** text (an abridgment or summary of the legal rules of the guild).[32] The middle-level jurist can choose from disputed rules found in guild commentaries and *fatawa* collections.[33] The highest-level jurist can perform a type of *ijtihad* by answering the question: "What would the founder(s) of the school do in this unaddressed situation (*takhrij*)?"[34] *Takhrij* must be compatible with broad-based legal precepts (*qawa'id*) derived from rulings of early imams.[35] On this basis, al-Qarafi argued that it requires more than *ijtihad* because the jurist must be knowledgeable in both *usul al-fiqh* and early precedent.[36] Thus, *taqlid* created a hierarchy of texts: the *mukkhtassar* containing straightforward rules of the guild, commentaries,[37] and *fatawa* collections (actual rulings).[38]

Statutes and edicts of rulers

Although classical texts describing Islamic law include the Quran, *Hadith* collections, *mukhtassars*, commentaries (which would indicate *ijma* of the scholars), and *fatawa* collections, the statutes and edicts of rulers might also be considered a textual source in the context of *siyasa-Shari'a*, a theory developed by Ibn Taymiyya that remains influential to this day.[39] The theory narrowed the range of fixed rules to clear rules found in the Quran, *Sunna*, or *ijma* and gave leaders flexibility to enforce norms in the interest of public welfare (*maslaha*).[40] Thus, rulers could require judges to draw rules from a single school such as *qadi fiqh*[41] or draft Islamic statutes in the interest of public good.[42] Therefore, Islamic statutes like those developed in North Africa[43] or in the **Ottoman Empire**[44] also serve as textual sources of Islamic law.

Although unorthodox classical sources from mystical or millennial perspectives exist, they tend to be persuasive exclusively in cultures that broadly accept them. While *Surwardi* or *Mahdist* texts might have influence in Pakistan or Sudan, respectively, they do not fit within well-established frameworks in other communities. In Anatolia, Sufi traditions, such as the ***Mevlevi***, *Qadiri*, *Naqshbandi*, ***Bektashi***, and others, influenced both doctrine and practice. As will be described later, modernists have generated a number of texts that provide alternatives to classical *fiqh*. These can include Rida's utilitarian neo-*ijtihad*,[45] Sanhuri's comparative new-*taqlid*,[46] or the Indonesian experience of proposing a new *madhab* incorporating its *adat* tradition.[47] In addition to methodological study, examples of modern methods used to apprehend and codify *Shariʿa* are readily identifiable through inspection of constitutions and statutes in jurisdictions incorporating Islamic law such as Egypt, Pakistan, or Malaysia. These modernist expressions provide a contemporary basis for understanding the current debate in Turkey surrounding the nature of the Turkish state and its relationship to Islamic jurisprudence.

The classical tradition of Ottoman jurisprudence

Ottoman jurisprudence developed within the broader context of the *fiqh/taqlid* tradition that had flourished within the Abbasid Caliphate. Some of the distinctions emerged in the early period of Ottoman expansion. However, the structural and methodological innovations considered particularly Ottoman emerged as court and judicial institutions matured in the 15th and 16th centuries.

The fledgling Ottoman state differed from the Seljuk Turkish state from which it emerged in a number of ways that likely influenced jurisprudence. Ottoman territory was on the border between Muslim-controlled territory and Byzantine territory. The Ottomans identified themselves in opposition to the Byzantine state and committed to *ghazi* military campaigns that resulted in the displacement of Byzantine authority in western Anatolia and later in the Balkans.[48] Thus, the role of non-Muslim minorities, religious identity, conversion, taxation, and membership (later citizenship) were arguably more important than they were in the more central Muslim lands. The early territory of the Ottoman state included a number of Sufi communities, most importantly the *Mevlevi* Order, that undoubtedly influenced Ottoman religious practice. As the successor to the Sultanate of Rum and as the inheritor of large numbers of former-Byzantine subjects and institutions, it is likely that Byzantine law and institutional structure influenced Ottoman jurisprudence. Evidence of centralization and establishment of harmonizing legal structures is clearer beginning in the 15th and 16th centuries.

The 15th century witnessed the consolidation of Ottoman power in the eastern Mediterranean and in the Balkans, culminating in the occupation of Constantinople in 1453. It was during this period that the Ottomans adopted the *Hanafi* school of Sunni jurisprudence. Guy Burak identifies four interrelated developments in this period that distinguished Ottoman law.

(1) the emergence of the institution of the state-appointed jurisconsult (*mufti*);
(2) the rise of an imperial educational system;

(3) the emergence of an imperial jurisprudential canon; and
(4) the systematic reconstruction and recording of the school's genealogy.[49]

The state appointment of *muftis* differed from Abbasid, and later Mamluk practice, in which *qadis* were appointed by the state and *muftis* obtained authority from teachers empowered to grant a permit to teach law and issue legal opinions (an *ijaza*), a system independent from the state.[50] This included appointment of the chief imperial *mufti*, the Sheikh al-Islam.[51] A centralized system of madrasa training was instituted to standardize training and to appoint jurists.[52] Under Süleyman the Lawgiver (*Kanuni*), texts and curricula used in the imperial system of madrasa education, as well as an organized imperial legal code (*kanun*), were established by the sultan.[53] Ottoman *kanun* may have even framed the understanding of *Shariʿa* rules.[54] Throughout the 16th and 17th centuries, there is evidence that the dynasty attempted to shape *Hanafi* jurisprudence by selectively including and emphasizing particular lines of legal thought and transmission within the *madhab*.[55]

In addition to centralizing legal education and the appointment of judges within the reimagined *Hanafi* tradition, Ottoman legal developments in the 15th and 16th centuries included at least two significant procedural innovations. First, Ottoman courts during this time began to keep records of proceedings that were publicly available.[56] Records of cases prior to this period were made, but they were not systematically maintained.[57] Second, the more formal structure of courts allowed an avenue of appeals to the imperial divan, at least in certain cases.[58] This formative period of imperial Ottoman legal development served at least two major functions. Most obviously, it provided for centralization and, ideally, greater efficiency and predictability. Contrary to the Weberian assumption that *Kadijustiz* was the product of "bargaining-for-relationships," *qadi* justice in the Ottoman Empire "was characterized by a substantial measure of real enforcement, rather than free floating bargaining" [59] and was quite predictable.[60] It is also clear that law played a role in creating an Ottoman *Hanafi* identity intended to promote social cohesion and stability. In this regard, the use of state power to create a national identity in Anatolia predates both the formation of the Turkish Republic and the Ottoman reforms of the 19th and early 20th centuries.

Although there is relatively little research indicating clear norms within the mystical traditions outside of the context of the *madhab*s, it would be remiss not to mention the importance of Sufi ***tariqats*** in forming much of the intellectual and social context for religious life and legal doctrine within the core of the Ottoman Empire. A variety of Sufi communities existed within the Empire, but I will focus on the *Naqshbandi*, the *Qadiri*, the *Mevlevi*, and the *Bektashi*, which I believe to be the most influential in the development of Islamic thought and jurisprudence.

The *Naqshbandi* trace their spiritual lineage to Abu Bakr, but the order was formalized in the 14th century by Bahaeddin *Naqshbandi* of Turkistan.[61] The *tariqat* existed within Anatolia, but the reforms led by Ahmad Sirhindi of India in the late 1500s and early 1600s contributed to the rise of the order's importance in the late Ottoman period.[62] As a result of Russian expansion, *Naqshbandi* immigration from Central Asia and the Caucasus also contributed to the growth of the order in Anatolia and Syria. Distinguishing traits generally associated with the *Naqshbandi* include a commitment to text and orthodoxy in jurisprudence, informality in that their organization did not require a lodge (*tekke*), and private and discrete devotional practices.[63]

The *Qadiri tariqat* was founded by the Hanbali jurist Abdul-Qadir al-Gilani in the early 12th century. His tomb is in Baghdad, and institutional hubs were founded in Damascus in the 16th century and in Istanbul in the 17th.[64] To the extent that Gilani preached as a Hanbali scholar rather than as a Sufi *pir* (guide or master), it is not surprising that the *Qadiri tariqat* would have some overlap with traditional Hanbali jurisprudence.

The *Mevlevi tariqat* was founded by Jalal ud-Din Rumi in the 13th century. Rumi was born in Balkh, but his family migrated to avoid the Mongol advances into Central Asia. He was trained as a *Hanafi* jurist and spent most of his life in Konya, where he established a school and a community under the patronage of the Seljuk Sultanate of Rum.[65] The order, sometimes called "the Way," was centralized in Anatolia and later in the core provinces of the Ottoman Empire.[66] It was patronized by the early Ottoman court, but its training emphasized spiritual practice as opposed to *fiqh*.[67]

The *Naqshbandi*, *Qadiri*, and *Mevlevi* orders all existed within the general ambit of Sunni tradition, but the *Bektashi* order, associated with Haji Bektash Veli, played a liminal role between Sunni and Shiʿi communities as it spread within the early Ottoman Empire. Haji Bektash Veli included veneration of Ali and other practices generally associated with Shiʿism into his spiritual teaching. Official Ottoman intolerance of overt Shiʿi doctrine and practice made the *Bektashi* community, which was nominally Sunni, a welcome place for those who had publicly or privately identified as Shiʿi. In addition to founding the order, Haji Bektash Veli is credited with forming the Alevi community, which incorporated elements of Shiʿism, Sufi thought, and Turkish shamanism. Identification of Alevi practice with the *Bektashi tariqat*, which became the official order of the Janissary Corps, gave it a sort of protected status that overt Imami Shiʿism, for example, did not have.[68]

Although Ottoman law developed within the broader continuum of Sunni *madhabi* jurisprudence, it was also distinctive. The geography of early expansion and the emphasis on centralization, order, and efficiency all had an impact on the practice of law and the understanding of *Shariʿa*. Though perhaps less concrete, the influence of Sufi thought and community also influenced jurisprudence within the Ottoman Empire. This was the setting for later Ottoman and Republican reforms that are typically considered "modern" or are at least engaged with the problems of the 19th and 20th centuries.

Range of modern approaches

The role of modernity in the creation and transformation of social and political domains remains a critical question for scholars studying Muslim societies. An interdisciplinary lens regarding perspectives oriented around historical and cultural forces will generate more compelling explanations for the development of Muslim civil society and an Islamic public sphere than will narrow analyses bounded by a specific discipline. For example, it allows for simultaneous evaluation of historical patterns, the evolution of institutions and cultural forces (particularly the influence of religion), and regional variations of political and social organization. Employing a range of approaches to consider complex legal and social questions also affords the opportunity to achieve additional depth of understanding from the use of a variety of disciplinary and methodological tools.

The central term for this analysis is "modernity," which I will define as the ostensibly rational political and social orders presumed to have arisen from the Enlightenment and the Industrial Revolution. Modernity produces new social forms and technologies of rule, and it creates subjects that vary according to geographic and cultural location. Here I define "Islam" in terms of its basic principles, practices, and historical legacy. This tradition engages modernity in various ways through a variety of outcomes and external perceptions.

The tradition may engage modernity in such a way that it manifests itself as "Islamic fundamentalism." This variety of response finds a number of forms, and it is characterized by a return to scriptural authority and a yearning for the unity perceived to exist within the early Muslim community; "Islamism," a religious answer to the secular state and a return to Islam's roots as a unified system; or as "political Islam" where political organizations are legitimized by adoption of cultural forms or traditions. One of the goals of much modernist discourse in the Muslim world has been to create a Muslim civil society[69] and an Islamic public sphere.[70] Although *Shari'a* is often mentioned in these discourses, the reference is typically vague, either by accident or design.

The doctrinal responses to modernity within Islamic law can be divided into four broad categories: (1) preservation of the medieval *fiqh*, (2) Islamic modernism, (3) the rejection of political expressions of Islam, and (4) the *Jihadist* approach.

The first approach attempts to preserve the connection between the medieval *fiqh* legacy and the traditional schools of jurisprudence (as described above).[71] Although this approach is nuanced by later developments, such as Ibn Taymiyya's *siyasa-Shari'a* theory,[72] it still relies on the guild-based training of traditional ***ulema***.[73] Elements of this approach can be found in many communities, including in Saudi Arabia and Malaysia.

The second response includes the broad category of Islamic modernism. Although their work varies significantly, I would include Afghani, Shah Waliullah, Abduh, S.A. Khan, Hassan al-Bannah, Iqbal, Mawdudi, Rida, Qutb, and Sanhuri in this group.[74] I subdivide this category according to method. Most forms of Islamic modernism argue for a form of renewed *ijtihad* and are characterized by some degree of rejection of the requirements of *taqlid*. As mentioned earlier, Rashid Rida proposed a method for narrowing the range of fixed legal rules to those from the Quran and the *Sunna* that are known with certainty or through consensus of the Companions.[75] Beyond this, traditional rules of *fiqh* could be replaced alongside rules tailored to best serve the public good.[76] This approach influenced the creation of statutes designed to enforce textual requirements of the *Shariʿa* (mostly in the area of personal status), alongside pragmatic legislation in other areas with no explicit connection to traditional sources of jurisprudence. Elements of this process bear a resemblance to *siyasa-Shariʿa*.[77] Sanhuri's approach would free the creation of law from traditional rules completely. He looked for consensus among the *madhab*s in order to extract legal and ethical principles.[78] In some senses, this move represents the privatization of religion. These principles were presumed to represent universal *Shariʿa*, which lawmakers were then bound to follow as a form of *taqlid*.[79]

The third category constitutes a rejection of explicit, political expressions of Islam in communal, near-monastic movements, such as the *Tablighi*.[80] The fourth category is the *Jihadist* approach, which considers religious expression as a product of a relationship with the individual and removes expression of faith from the constraints of the textual tradition entirely.[81]

Official Turkish policies represent a unique amalgam of the first three approaches (though all four approaches are represented in the population to varying degrees). Traditionalism remains an important basis for legitimacy, so reliance on the classical *fiqh* tradition is vital for the state's official religious rulings and for most theologians and jurists, including Fethullah Gülen.[82] The state and most public intellectuals – including Gülen and Öztürk, discussed in Chapter Three – employ modernist methods in order to adapt tradition to contemporary circumstances. However, interpretive moves are not always explicit. The influence of legal secularism in the Turkish Republic has made overt expressions of political Islam suspect, so that mainstream Turkish religious scholars tend to describe Islam as a moral system with implications for governance but that does not govern the state.[83] As such, the relationship between religion and law in Turkey arguably resembles that of Germany or Mexico more than that of most predominantly Muslim countries.

Ottoman and Turkish modernism

Although later Islamic modernist thinkers, such as Sanhuri and Sayyid Qutb, wrote after the context of the Ottoman Empire, pivotal early leaders, including Jamal ad-Din al-Afghani, Muhammad Abduh, and Rashid Rida, lived within and critically engaged official Ottoman policy, including its approaches to reform and Islamic political ideology. Their early *Salafi* approaches to reform had influence within the Empire, but they were generally in opposition to both the traditional Sufi institutions as well as to the centralized attempts to create an Ottoman national identity.[84] Religious thought and policy within the early Turkish Republic dismantled many of the core Islamic institutions, but in many ways the policies of the Republic were merely an extension of dynamics that began in the Ottoman period.

It is difficult to make generalizations about 19th-century reforms within the various Sufi communities inside the Ottoman Empire. Although they took varied approaches to modernity, jurisprudence, and spirituality, the *tariqat*s had widespread memberships and numerous lodges, particularly in key urban centers like Istanbul. The *Mevlevis*, *Qadiris*, *Rifa'i Khalwatis*, *Bektashis*, and others had influence within Ottoman Anatolia, but there is evidence that revival within the branches of the *Naqshbandi tariqat* made it the largest and most influential Sufi community in the late Ottoman Empire.[85] It was less hierarchical than were more monastic communities, thus allowing innovation and the incorporation of newer scientific and political ideas. Unlike some other *tariqat*s, the *Naqshbandi* opposed the possibility of foreign influence and the loss of Islamic lands to European powers. Historically, the *tariqat* had been actively engaged with affairs of Ottoman society rather than with retreating to a communal life of isolation and prayer (as was the case in some other traditions). By the late 1800s, *Naqshbandi* ideas were carried from provincial centers to more rural regions by the growing middle classes who found it relevant and meaningful.

Although notable *Hanafi* and *Shafi'i* scholars in the Ottoman period had affiliations with Sufi *tariqat*s, it would be difficult to elaborate a "*Naqshbandi*" jurisprudence. Instead, it might be appropriate to characterize official Ottoman jurisprudence as framed by the Caliphs, Sheikhs al-Islam, and the system of state-appointed or -sponsored *qadis* and *muftis*, as generally Sufi in character to the extent that religious practice and education within the Empire were deeply influenced by the various *tariqat*s. This is supported by the early *Salafi* reformers' critiques of Sufi influence within Ottoman jurisprudence that they believed required reform.[86]

Ottoman jurisprudence in the 19th century continued the tradition of centralized control and harmonization that had begun much earlier. Some of the *tanzimat* reforms may be understood as the exercise of appropriate political power by the Sultan (*siyasa*);[87] however, some reforms, such as the protection of religious freedom and other individual rights, were in tension with classical Islamic rules. For example, the Reform Edict of 1856, which provided religious freedom even in the case of apostasy from Islam, was criticized by some Muslim jurists and was blamed for the rise and influence of foreign missionaries in the late 1800s.[88] The drafting and enactment of the ***Mecelle*** was an attempt to regularize rules across the empire, which were inconsistent in many cases due to the use of local custom and had proven to be incompatible with global commercial norms (largely shaped by European practices).[89] As the early process of establishing the *Hanafi* school as the state approach to jurisprudence relied on the selective use of particular genealogies of legal rules believed to be useful to the Empire, drafters of the *Mecelle* attempted to reconcile emerging commercial norms with *Hanafi* jurisprudence to the greatest extent possible. At the very least, a simplified code of commercial law theoretically gave economic actors clearer notice regarding the rules that would apply to their transactions. As described earlier, codes had been used in Islamic jurisprudence; however, the centralized project of reconciling emerging norms with social welfare and the traditional rules within the classical tradition was an innovation.

Abdulhamid, whose reign lasted from 1876 to the Young Turk Revolution in 1908, explicitly attempted to create an Ottoman national identity rooted in

Islam.[90] He walked a fine line between liberal reforms (such as the 1876 Constitution) and the crafting of a new style of Islamic politics that challenged the tradition of cosmopolitanism (such as the millet system of relative autonomy for non-Muslim communities) and the earlier reforms of the *tanzimat* and encouraged piety through instrumentalities of the state.[91] Although these policies likely contributed to the persecution of religious minorities, particularly Armenians, there is evidence of a rising and educated Muslim middle class by the end of Abdulhamid's reign.[92]

Early Republican approaches to Islamic jurisprudence continued the dynamic of harmonizing traditional rules with contemporary European norms. Early work drafting the civil and criminal codes considered innovative approaches that would ostensibly include Islamic tradition, but drafters determined that borrowing and adapting existing European codes represented a more tested and reliable way forward. The project of the Republican leadership was to forge a new and sustainable Turkish identity that did not rely on traditional rules that might impede economic development. The sultanate was dismantled by the time independence was declared in 1923. In 1924, the Caliphate and *Shari'a* courts were abolished as part of constitutional reform.[93] In 1925, Sufi lodges were closed, and religious symbols and language were systematically removed from public life by the state. A secular civil code, based on the Swiss model, and a criminal code, modeled after Italy's, were passed in 1926. Much has been written regarding the secularizing policies of the early Turkish Republic. Although these reforms had a profound impact on public life, the private practice of faith continued. Elements of Islamic thought and jurisprudence were preserved in underground *tariqat*s and madrasas or by public figures like Said Nursi, who openly challenged Republican legal reforms.[94]

Traditional *tariqat*s such as the *Naqshbandi*, *Mevlevi*, *Qadiri*, and *Bektashi* were able to preserve their traditions underground during the early Republican period, but it is arguable that new communities arising from these formal traditions actually became more important than the original orders. The Süleymanlı, Nurcu, Hizmet/Gülen, and Milli Görüş movements all have roots in *Naqshbandi* tradition, and the Alevi community has historic connections to the *Bektashis*.

The Süleymanlı community was founded by Süleyman Hilmi Tunahan, a *Hanafi* jurist trained in the last years of the Ottoman Empire. He is considered by his followers to be the final link in the Golden Chain of Sufi masters in the *Naqshbandi tariqat*. The community maintains elements of traditional *Naqshbandi* practice, but they are most noted for their extensive network of Quran schools, which preserve a level of traditional Islamic education in the absence of the madrasa system.

The Nurcu community focuses less on the traditional elements of *Naqshbandi* practice and more on the writing of Said Nursi, whose *Risale-i Nur* is one of the leading Sufi works of the 20th century. Nursi also became a popular figure for his public objections to state interference in the practice of religion, particularly the Hat Law of 1925. The Nurcu movement flourished in a variety of locales and manifestations, including reading groups and social service organizations.

Although many Nurcu organizations focus solely on the legacy of Said Nursi, a larger number identify themselves as inspired by Fethullah Gülen (or as part of Hizmet).[95] This segment of the Nurcu community operates as its own distinctive movement, and it is arguably the largest and most influential spiritual movement in contemporary Turkey.

"Milli Görüş" (National Vision) operates within the context of the *Naqshbandi tariqat* and was the ideological basis for the Islamist political movements associated with Necmettin Erbakan, who coined the phrase in 1969. It has been explicitly political in its contribution to the formation of the National Order Party in 1970 and the National Salvation Party in 1972. The later Welfare Party and the Virtue Party were also led by Erbakan, but they were able to garner broader Islamist support from *Naqshbandi* communities and elsewhere.[96]

The Alevi community, which likely comprises 15% of the population of Turkey, claims Haji Bektash Veli as its leading early thinker. The Alevis did not adopt the formal organization of the *Bektashi tariqat*, but their heterodox practices may have been tolerated in part because of the privileged role the *Bektashi* order played within the Janissary Corps. Like many Anatolian Sufi communities, they have regular meetings, rituals, and musical practices, but their theology is also influenced by elements of Shiʿism and Turkic shamanism.[97] Having experienced marginalization under the Ottomans, Alevis tended to support the secularizing reforms of the early Republic as a guarantee of protection from religious persecution. Although there is a tradition of informal "*Dede*" courts within the Alevi tradition, there has been little scholarship on Alevi influences within traditional Islamic jurisprudence.

State Islam in secular Turkey

Although there is sympathy for the traditional *fiqh* approach among many Turkish Muslims, the most influential approaches to jurisprudence are modern in that they do not rely on *madhab* rules in a posture of *taqlid*. This might be more obvious within a civil law jurisdiction that is decidedly secular, but lack of *madhab* institutions and codification of *Shariʿa* make most contemporary approaches to Islamic jurisprudence "modern" in some sense. There is a range of views concerning Islamic law in Turkey, but it can be argued that the official state position plays a central role in shaping Islamic practice and understanding of religious jurisprudence. Although they have importance, I do not consider here the arguably more heterodox approaches of the *Naqshbandi*, the *Mevlevi*, or the Alevi.

The Turkish government plays an active role in shaping the structure of religious institutions and the content of religious teaching, which is quite unlike the U.S. doctrine of nonestablishment. According to the Turkish Constitution,

> The Directorate of Religious Affairs [*Diyanet*], which is within the general administration, shall exercise its duties prescribed in its particular law, in accordance with the principles of secularism, removed from all political views and ideas, and aiming at national solidarity and integrity.[98]

To American readers, this section of the Turkish Constitution is challenging, since it belies a completely different understanding of the relationship between religion and the state.

The Directorate (a position sometimes translated as "Presidency") of Religious Affairs (***Diyanet***) controls religious education, ordination/licensing, the construction of mosques, the appointment of imams, and even dictates the content of Friday sermons throughout the country.[99] It represents the highest Islamic religious authority in the country and is in some sense the successor to the Ottoman *Sheikh al-Islam*.[100] *Diyanet* has a budget approaching one billion dollars (USD) and plays an important role in – and for – Turkish society.[101]

Although there is no official content or method attributed to *Shariʿa*, the position of *Diyanet* implies a particular approach to law and theology, suggesting it can be interpreted as an alternative to traditional *fiqh*. *Diyanet* issues legal opinions that typically, but not always, reference the Quran, the *Hadith*, and the *Hanafi* texts.[102] However, its opinions are not limited by *Hanafi fiqh*. For example, in 2005, the head of *Diyanet* appointed two women as vice-*muftis*, an action which is arguably inconsistent with the traditional *Hanafi* position.[103]

In regard to the range of modern approaches to Islamic jurisprudence described earlier, *Diyanet* clearly manifests three. It relies on traditional *fiqh* rules and tends to refer to the *Hanafi* school for legitimacy. Even so, it is modern in its attempts to harmonize tradition with Turkish Republicanism and secularism and to provide religious counsel to Turkish citizens. This sometimes manifests itself in the selection of alternative classical rules (i.e., non-*Hanafi* rules). In other cases, rulings are based on new interpretations of texts or broad public policy arguments. *Diyanet* officials are very careful to acknowledge the legitimacy of the Turkish Republic and its secular constitution. Thus, Islam tends to be imagined as a religious and moral system that speaks to all aspects of life, but which is not imposed on the legal system. Although official Islam in Turkey, as understood by *Diyanet* officials, is not private per se, it is viewed as existing in a sphere insulated from politics and is separate from civil law.

I would tend to agree with scholars, such as İhsan Yılmaz, that the imposition of secular codes in deeply religious communities is likely to produce some sort of hybrid of religious law. Yilmaz observes that, in Turkey, the requirement that civil marriage ceremonies be devoid of religious content has created a parallel system of traditional Islamic *nikah* ceremonies (signing of the wedding contract). Although the civil ceremony is "legal," the religious ceremony is the one considered "legitimate," resulting in a hybrid and unofficial form of Islamic law developing in Turkey.[104] This is not so different from the legal separation and cultural conflation of civil marriage and religious marriage in many U.S. communities.

Conclusion

The meanings attributed to Islam, and to *Shariʿa* in particular, are complex and manifold in Turkey. Although there is a sophisticated community of religious scholars and jurists, some of whom are even trained in the traditional madrasa curricula, complex questions of theology and jurisprudence do not tend to percolate through the population. Instead, people are more concerned with questions that relate to their daily lives. For this reason, it is important to better understand the resources for religious knowledge and formation that Turks turn to in their lived experience.

Notes

1 *See e.g.*, Abdullahi Ahmed An-Naim, *Toward an Islamic Reformation: Civil Liberties, Human Rights, and International Law*. Syracuse, NY: Syracuse University Press, 1990.
2 Early versions of the background chapters on *Shari'a*, secularism, and religion in Turkey were presented at an Islamic Law Conference in St. Paul on September 28, 2012; Russell Powell, "Evolving Views of Islamic Law in Turkey." *Journal of Law and Religion* 28 (2013): 474–481.
3 Andrew Rippin, *Muslims: Their Religious Beliefs and Practices*. Ed. John Hinnel and Ninian Smart. New York: Routledge, 2005.
4 Lombardi, Clark B. *State Law as Islamic Law in Modern Egypt: The Incorporation of the* Shari'a *into Egyptian Constitutional Law*. Leiden: Brill, 2006 at 11.
5 *See* Rippin; Wael Hallaq, *A History of Islamic Legal Theories: An Introduction to Sunni Usul al-fiqh*. Cambridge: Cambridge University Press, 1997.
6 Lombardi at 15.
7 *Id.* at 13–17.
8 Haim Gerber, "Rigidity versus Openness in Late Classical Islamic Law: The Case of the Seventeenth-Century Palestinian Muftī Khayr al-Dīn al-Ramlī." *Studies in Islamic Law and Society* 5.2 (1998): 166; Mohammad Fadel, "The Social Logic of Taqlīd and the Rise of the Mukhataṣar." *Studies in Islamic Law and Society* 3.2 (1996): 194; Hallaq 1997 at 121–123.
9 Mohammad H. Kamali, *Shari'ah Law: An Introduction*. Oxford: OneWorld, 2008 at 155.
10 In Arabic, "*usul al-fiqh*."
11 *See* Lombardi at 13–17; Rippin at 75.
12 Sherman A. Jackson, "Islamic Law and the State: The Constitutional Jurisprudence of Shihab al-Din al-Qarafi." *Studies in Islamic Law and Society* 5.1 (1996): 77–78.
13 *See* Wael Hallaq, *Shari'a: Theory, Practice, Transformations*. New York: Cambridge University Press, 2009.
14 Fazlur Rahman, *Islam & Modernity: Transformation of an Intellectual Tradition*. Chicago: University of Chicago Press, 1982 at 42–48.
15 Lombardi at 22–26.
16 *See* Jonathan A. C. Brown, *Hadith: Muhammad's Legacy in the Medieval and Modern World*. Oxford: OneWorld, 2009.
17 Lombardi at 25.
18 *Id.*
19 *Id.*
20 *Id* at 26.
21 *Id* at 27.
22 *See id.* Rashid Rida, *Usr al-Islam wa Usul al Tashri al Amm*. Cairo: al-Manar Press, 1956 at 77.
23 Lombardi at 31.
24 *Id.* at 34–35.
25 *Id.* at 35–36.
26 *Id.* at 38.
27 Fadel at 193.

28 *Id.*
29 *See e.g.*, Fadel and Jackson.
30 *Id.*
31 Fadel at 200.
32 Jackson at 89–90.
33 *Id.* at 90.
34 *Id.* at 91–93.
35 *Id.* at 92.
36 *Id.*
37 Like that of Ibn Rushd on winedrinking (explaining the disagreements between the schools and offering opinions). *See* Ibn Rushd, *The Distinguished Jurist's Primer Volume I.* London: Garnet Publishing, 1994 at 571–577.
38 *See generally* Fadel and Jackson.
39 Baber Johansen, "A Perfect Law in an Imperfect Society: Ibn Taymiyya's Concept of 'Governance in the Name of Sacred Law,'" in *The Law Applied: Contextualizing the Islamic Shariʿa*. Ed. Bernard G. Weiss, Peri Bearman, and Wolfhart Heinrichs. London & New York: I. B. Tauris, 2008, pp. 259–261.
40 Lombardi at 49.
41 *Id.* at 50.
42 *Id.* at 51.
43 David Powers, "Four Cases Relating to Women and Divorce in Al-Andalus and the Maghrib, 1100–1500," in *Dispensing Justice in Islam: Qadis and Their Judgments.* Ed. Muhammad Khalid Masud, Rudolph Peters, and David Powers. Leiden: Brill, 2006, p. 383.
44 Engin Deniz Akarlı, "Law in the Marketplace: Istanbul, 1730–1840," in *Dispensing Justice in Islam*. Ed. M. Khalid Masud et al. Leiden: Brill, 2006, p. 245; Leslie Peirce, "State, Society, and Law in Islam: Ottoman Law in Comparative Perspective." *Studies in Islamic Law and Society* 2.3 (1995): 365.
45 Term coined by Lombardi at 83–92 (narrowing the range of fixed textual rules to the Quran, *Hadith* of certain meaning and transmission, and the *ijma* of the Companions).
46 *Id.* at 92–97 (extrapolating universal principles from the rules of the madhabs, which then become the basis for legal rules).
47 R. Michael Feener, "Muslim Legal Thought in Contemporary Indonesia," in *Islamic Law in Contemporary Indonesia: Ideas and Institutions.* Ed. Mark E. Camack and R. Michael Feener. Cambridge: Harvard University Press, 2007, pp. 14–25.
48 *See e.g.*, Marshall Hodgson, *The Venture of Islam Volume 2*. Chicago: University of Chicago Press, 1974 at 424–425.
49 Guy Burak, "The Second Formation of Islamic Law: The Post-Mongol Context of the Ottoman Adoption of a School of Law." *Comparative Studies in Society and History* 55.3 (2013): 579–602 at 584.
50 *Id.* at 584, 585.
51 *Id.* at 585.
52 *Id.*
53 *Id.* at 586.
54 *See* Leslie Peirce, "A New Judge for Aintab: Shifting Legal Environment of a Sixteenth-Century Ottoman Court," in *Dispensing Justice in Islam*, Ed. M. K. Masud, R. Peters, D. S. Powers. Leiden: Brill, 2006, pp. 86–87.
55 *Id.* at 586–587. Ottoman Hanafi scholars notably excluded jurisprudence developed in Arab provinces in favor of South and Central Asian traditions within the *madhab*.
56 *See e.g.*, Peirce 2006, Akgündüz 2009, and Ergene 2004.
57 Peirce at 72.
58 *See* Engin Deniz Akarlı, "Law in the Marketplace: Istanbul, 1730–1840," in *Dispensing Justice in Islam*, Ed. M. Khalid Masud, Rudolph Peters, and David Powers. Leiden: Brill, 2006 at 246–247.

59 Haim Gerber, *State, Society and Law in Islam: Ottoman Law in Comparative Perspective.* Albany, NY: SUNY, 1994 at 16.
60 *Id.* at 177.
61 *See* J. Spencer Trimingham, *The Sufi Orders in Islam.* Oxford: Oxford University Press, 1998 at 62.
62 Kemal Karpat, *The Politicization of Islam: Reconstructing Identity, State, Faith, and Community in the Late Ottoman State.* New York: Oxford University Press, 2001 at 110. *See also* Schimmel, *Mystical Dimensions of Islam* at 367–373 for a discussion of Ahmad Sirhindi's theological contributions.
63 *See* Ahmet Yükleyen, "Sufism and Islamic Groups in Contemporary Turkey," in Turkey in the Modern World, Ed. R. Kasaba. Cambridge, UK and New York: Cambridge University Press, 2008 at 382–384.
64 Trimingham at 43–44.
65 For the definitive biography of Rumi, *see* Franklin Lewis, *Rumi – Past and Present, East and West: The Life, Teachings, and Poetry of Jalâl al-Din Rumi.* London: Oneworld, 2007.
66 Trimingham at 60–62.
67 *See generally* Schimmel at 324–326.
68 Trimingham at 69, 80–83.
69 That is, institutions and relationships that organize social life between the state and family or individual, including guilds, associations, etc.
70 A social space fostering the ability to organize actions within collective discourses, with the aim of basing politics on reason rather than power alone.
71 Brown 2009 at 20.
72 Basheer M. Nafi, "The Rise of Islamic Reformist Thought and Its Challenge to Traditional Islam," in *Islamic Thought in the Twentieth Century.* Ed. Suha Taji-Farouki and Basheer M. Nafi. London: Institute for Ismaili Studies, 2004, pp. 30–32.
73 Brown 2009 at 20.
74 *See* Nafi.
75 Daniel W. Brown, *Rethinking Tradition in Modern Islamic Thought.* Cambridge: Cambridge University Press, 1996 at 41; Talal Asad, *Formations of the Secular: Christianity, Islam, Modernity.* Stanford, CA: Stanford University Press, 2003 at 219.
76 *See generally* Felicitas Opwiss, *Maslaha and the Purpose of the Law.* Leiden: Brill, 2011.
77 Lombardi at 93.
78 *See* Enid Hill, "Al-Sanhuri and Islamic Law: The Place and Significance of Islamic Law in the Life and Work of ʻAbd al-Razzaq Ahmad al-Sanhuri, Egyptian Jurist and Scholar 1895–1971." *Arab Law Quarterly* 3.1, 3.2 (1988): 33–64, 182–218.
79 *Id.*
80 Barbara Metcalf, "'Remaking Ourselves' *Ourselves*: Islamic Self-Fashioning in a Global Movement of Spiritual Renewal," in *Accounting for Fundamentalisms: The Dynamic Character of Movements.* Ed. R. Scott Appleby and Martin E. Marty. Chicago: University of Chicago Press, 1994, p. 706.
81 Faisal Devji, *Landscapes of Jihad.* Ithaca: Cornell University Press, 2005 at 15–32.
82 Thijl Sunier, Nico Landman, Heleen van der Linden, Nazli Bilgili, and Alper Bilgili. *Diyanet: The Turkish Directorate for Religious Affairs in a Changing Environment.* Amsterdam: Changing Environment at 88–102, Universities of Amsterdam and Utrecht, 2011 at 88–102, October 23, 2013, available at http://www.fsw.vu.nl/nl/Images/Final%20report%20Diyanet%20February%202011_tcm30–200229.pdf.
83 For Diyanet's view *see* Sunier et al. at 97–98. For Öztürk and Gülen *see* Chapter Three.
84 *See e.g.*, Karpat at 239; Rida's critiques were known within the Empire, and his Muhawaret al-Muslih wa'l-Muqallid was banned by Sultan Abdulhamid and was translated into Turkish in 1916.
85 *See e.g.*, Karpat at 89–116.

86 *See e.g.*, Karpat at 230 and 347.
87 Tax and military reforms, for example.
88 *See* Selim Deringil. *The Well-Protected Domains: Ideology and the Legitimation of Power in the Ottoman Empire, 1876–1909.* London: I. B. Tauris, 1998 at 112–134 on this "Missionary Problem."
89 *See e.g., The Mejelle: Being an English Translation of Majallah el-Ahkam-I-Adliya and a Complete Code of Islamic Civil Law.* Kuala Lumpur: Islamic Book Trust, 2001.
90 *See e.g.*, Karpat and Deringil.
91 *Id.*
92 Deringil at 107.
93 *See* Edward Mead Earl, "The New Constitution of Turkey." *Political Science Quarterly* 4.1 (1925), at 89–100 for an English translation of the Turkish Constitution of 1924.
94 Carter Vaughn Findley, *Turkey, Islam, Nationalism, and Modernity: A History, 1789–2007.* New Haven & London: Yale University Press, 2010 at 288–291.
95 Yükleyen at 385.
96 *Id.* at 386.
97 *Id.*
98 The Constitution of the Republic of Turkey November 7, 1982 Art. 136 (as amended).
99 Sunier et al. at 51–52.
100 *Id.* at 9–20.
101 *See 2006 Malý Yili Bütçesý*, October 18, 2005, available at http://www.alomaliye.com/ekim_05/2006_mali_yili_butcesi.htm.
102 Diyanet maintains a collection of its *fatwas* and even offers a phone service to answer religious questions. *See* Turkiye Cumhuriyeti Basbakanlik, Diyanat Işleri Başkanliği, 2013. *See* http://kurul.diyanet.gov.tr/sorusor/diyanet/default.aspx.
103 *See* the Diyanet website for a discussion of clergy and Islam. "Turkiye Cumhuriyeti Basbakanlik, Diyanat Işleri Başkanliği", 2013, available at http://www.diyanet.gov.tr/turkish/ingilizce/icerik.aspx?IID=310.
104 İhsan Yılmaz, "Secular Law and the Emergence of Unofficial Turkish Islamic Law." *The Middle East Journal* 56 (2002): 113.

3 Landscapes of popular religion in Turkey

Sources of influence in Turkish popular religion

There are numerous sources of popular religious views and conceptions of religion in modern Turkey. Television has become perhaps the most influential and ubiquitous of these sources, but print media and traditional publishing also remain important. This section will consider religious education, religious organizations, popular religious leaders, and the media in terms of their roles in shaping popular religion. Although this chapter considers these cultural influences on the formation of religious identity, it does not ignore the fact that family members are likely to have the most significant influence.[1] The leading qualitative study to consider influences on religious identity concludes that parents have substantial influence on the formation of religious identity; however, other social and cultural factors are important.[2]

> In addition to kinship, social networks, neighbours, and Imams, religious groups and organizations are also important in developing late adolescents' religious knowledge and attitudes. In some areas, female neighbours arranged home meetings to read the Quran together which developed a strong social network for the participants. Religious books and TV programs provide children and adolescents with knowledge, and their effect is as strong as that of parents, relatives and peers. We also have found that some religious groups and congregations such as "Süleymancılar" were important to several participants but little is known about these groups and how they operate. Although such religious groups are somewhat closed, they merit further study.[3]

This chapter is intended to introduce the landscape of factors contributing to religious views, including beliefs and opinions related to *Shariʿa*, as context for the data presented in Chapters Five, Six, and Seven. It is not intended to create a comprehensive model.

Education

Formal education plays a role in the formation of identities and in the transmission of knowledge, including religious identity and knowledge.[4] This was perhaps the chief aim of traditional madrasa education. Public education in Turkey has arguably formed religious views even during the periods when religious education was completely excluded from the formal curriculum. The rise of ***imam-hatip schools***, as a parallel public system that includes some traditional forms of religious education, has had increasing impact on religious discourse, particularly since graduates were allowed to take the university entrance exam. There are also important institutions that supplement formal education – most notably Quran schools and university exam preparatory classes.

Madrasa education

As discussed earlier, traditional religious training took place in the institution of the madrasa. Typically, madrasas in the Ottoman Empire were supported by *waqf* (a religious endowment) and were attached to mosques. Members of the *ulema*, who were authorized by *ijaza* to issue legal opinions and to teach, would follow the curricula of their particular *madhab*. However, as noted earlier, Ottoman adoption of the *Hanafi* school led to some reimagining of the tradition, which authorized some texts and denied others. Education in the later Ottoman period was divided into a lower level, which consisted largely of Arabic language, calligraphy, and Quran, and an upper level, which included *Hadith*, *qalam*, and *fiqh*.[5] Natural sciences and ethics also received some coverage.[6]

The *tanzimat* reforms of the 19th century were accompanied by an attempt to broaden access to education, particularly in the sciences. However, this reform of education did not extend to madrasa education, which was still quite extensive.[7] The government did interfere briefly by revoking the exemption from military service for a large number of students from the provinces, but popular backlash prompted a return to broad exemptions and a hands-off policy.[8] The number of madrasa students continued to grow after this failed experiment both in Istanbul and in the provinces (though there was an effort to cap the number of students in Istanbul at 10,000)[9] until after the Young Turk Revolution, when madrasa attendance was cut in half.[10]

In the core of the Ottoman Empire, madrasa education remained largely unchanged in the late 19th and early 20th centuries, while madrasa education in other parts of the Muslim world was reformed, primarily to incorporate modern scientific curricular elements.[11] Importantly, failure to reform madrasa education may have actually preserved the integrity of the traditional system. All madrasas in Turkey were closed by the government in 1924, and religious education came under the control of the state;[12] however, some members of the *ulema* continued to teach the traditional curriculum to a small number of students, mostly in the provinces.[13] This tradition continues today, and scholars receiving an *ijaza* from this system are acknowledged as authentic members of the *ulema*, even by some faculty members at the state-sponsored schools of theology.[14] A number of public intellectuals and religious leaders, such as Hayrettin Karaman and Yasin Aktay, were educated in this underground system.[15] However, there is virtually no scholarship regarding this informal and underground tradition, and it is unclear what impact it had on religious education and views in Turkey more generally.[16]

Religion in public education

Expanding state-sponsored general and scientific education was a priority for the Ottoman Empire in the latter 19th and early 20th centuries.[17] The basis for modern education in Turkey is the Regulation of General Education enacted in 1869 (the Regulation), which organized primary schools (*iptidai*) that in many cases displaced *sibyan* (locally supported schools emphasizing religious education), secondary schools (*rüsdiye*), and *idadi* schools (which filled a role between secondary schools and universities).[18] Prior to the Regulation, madrasa education was the dominant form of access to literacy. There were also non-Muslim religious schools, including schools founded by foreign missionaries. The model for "modern" education was Galatasaray, which was originally founded as a palace school in 1481 by Bayezid II and adopted French as a language of instruction in 1830, when it hired a number of French professors to staff its medical school. The school became the Lycée Impérial Ottoman de Galata-Sérai in 1868. The Regulation required Galatasaray to include some instruction in Turkish language instruction as an *idadi* school in 1876, and it became a model for educational reform.

Primary school education was centrally regulated. By 1906, there were 9,347 "modern" elementary schools within the Ottoman Empire, educating an estimated one million students out of a population of 37 million people.[19] They were intended to provide basic literacy, to create a common social identity, and to prepare students for high school. Religion and ethics remained core components of the curriculum, which typically covered three years.[20]

High school was primarily a pathway for the elite. By 1908, the Empire ran 619 high schools with approximately 40,000 students. The course of study typically lasted four or five years and emphasized secular subjects (except the first year, which emphasized Arabic, Persian, and religion). French was usually taught in the final two years.[21]

Idadi schools like Galatasaray were accessible only to the very elite, and by 1894 only 51 existed.[22] There was tremendous pressure on the government from prominent citizens throughout the Empire who wanted their children to receive this sort of education, which could open doors to higher studies and senior government positions.[23] As a result, there was a move to convert existing high schools to *idadi* schools.

This is largely the structure of the education system inherited by the early Turkish Republic, and the system of primary schools, secondary schools, and high schools bears some resemblance, structurally, to the Ottoman system. One of the sharpest contrasts is the role of religion in the curriculum. Over the past 90 years, religion has been included and excluded from the national school curriculum, which is heavily regulated. In 1927, religion was completely removed from public school curricula, but a single class was added to the fourth and fifth grades in 1949. Religious education was more broadly reintroduced in 1956 as part of Demokrat Parti reform, but parents could opt out.[24] In 1980 (after the coup), religion became a required class for every grade after primary school.[25]

Today, religion classes begin in the fourth grade and continue through graduation for a total of eight years.[26] The class is known as "Culture of Religion and Knowledge of Ethics" and includes ethics and comparative religion, in addition to instruction related to Islam, which makes up half of the national curriculum approved by the Ministry of Education.[27] The content and the ideological orientation of this course has been subject to substantial critique from both secularist and religious circles. It has also been a topic of concern for the European Union.

> ECRI [European Commission against Racism and Intolerance] notes that only Muslim pupils are required to follow these courses, while pupils belonging to minority religious groups can be exempted. ECRI considers the situation unclear: if this is indeed a course on the different religious cultures, there is no reason to make it compulsory for Muslim children alone, the report notes. Conversely, if the course is essentially designed to teach the Muslim religion, it is a course on a specific religion and should not be compulsory, in order to preserve children's and their parents' religious freedom.[28]

The arguments for a more pluralist and inclusive curriculum prompted the addition of Alevism and an increase in the coverage of non-Muslim faiths, but this move has also proved controversial.[29] Secular nationalists may object to this sort of instruction because a pluralist understanding of religion in Turkey could dilute Turkish identity – which is often presumed to be Sunni, Hanafi, Muslim, and Turkish speaking – and religious Muslims might similarly object to the notion of teaching nonorthodox views (due to a concern for traditional doctrinal instruction). The dominant political position seems to be to maintain the status quo, although there are factions that would prefer to make the class optional or to end state control over the content of religious education.[30]

It is not clear how effective the state curriculum of religious education is at forming a national consensus on religious identity or belief, even for Sunni Muslims who adhere to the *Hanafi* tradition, but it clearly has some impact.[31] However, given the polarization of political views related to religion – evidenced by the popular press, recent elections, and popular protest – it is clear that if religious education was intended to socialize students in a particular way, it has had varying results and some strong reactions against it. Some research considering the effectiveness of similar classes intended to socialize students in a particular way indicates that they have limited effectiveness.[32]

Higher education in religion is reserved for the theology faculties (*ilahiyat fakülteleri*) at public universities, and the entire system is subject to the Ministry of Education and *Diyanet*. This system trains religious scholars and imams, who lead religious communities throughout Turkey, including in *Diyanet*. Fields within Islamic Studies include Arabic, Quran, *Hadith*, *fiqh*, *qalam*, Islamic law, Islamic *madhab* history, and Sufism.[33] The impact of this centralized approach to theological training is perhaps best demonstrated by the positions taken by *Diyanet* in interpreting and mediating Islamic jurisprudence (as described in Chapter Two).

Imam-hatip *schools*

The Law of Unification of Instruction transformed madrasas into "*imam-hatip* schools" which no longer benefitted from pious endowments or the support of Sufi *tariqat*s.[34] As a result, there were only 29 existing in the country at the conversion in 1924, and they disappeared completely in 1930 when all religious education was banned in schools.[35] *Imam-hatip* schools were reopened by the Ministry of Education as religious vocational schools intended to train imams and religious workers in 1951 after the Demokrat Parti came to power.[36] By 1961, there were 19 middle schools, 17 high schools, and 4,545 students enrolled in *imam-hatip* schools.[37] Although the availability of these schools made religious instruction more widely available, graduates were not allowed to participate in the university entrance exam, which proved to be a significant limiting factor on enrollment. In 1971, there were more than 42,000 students in *imam-hatip* middle schools, but they were then closed for three years.[38] There was a sharp upturn in enrollments beginning in 1983, when graduates were first allowed to participate in the university entrance exam, reaching over 600,000 students in 1997.[39] However, in 1997 compulsory public education through eighth grade led to the phasing out of vocational middle schools, including *imam-hatip* schools, leaving only the high schools.[40]

In 2008, there were nearly 130,000 students in *imam-hatip* schools, and slightly more than half of them were female.[41] Historically, the majority of students came from rural areas or were the children of migrants from rural areas. They tended to be religiously traditional and politically conservative.[42] The distinctive part of the curriculum (vocational courses) includes Quran, *qalam*, *fiqh*, *hadith*, creeds (*aqaid*), life of the Prophet, history of religions, Arabic, and preaching and vocational training, while "cultural academic courses" include Turkish, math, science, history, social sciences, foreign language (English), national defense, "History of Principles and Reforms of Kemalism," and physical education.[43] Although the curriculum is designed to prepare students for traditional roles, such as an imam or a muezzin, only about 15% of graduates obtain employment in the religious sector.[44] This indicates that many students are enrolling not because they desire vocational training for religious work but because they desire a more explicitly religious education. This is particularly true for female students who have very narrow opportunities for work in the religious sector.

In a fascinating qualitative study of *imam-hatip* schools in Ankara, Soon-Yong Pak conducted in-depth interviews with 31 students, 19 teachers, and 11 parents.[45] He found that students came from a variety of socioeconomic backgrounds and that many had migrated from rural areas to the outskirts of the city. Some of the parents identified as Islamist (*İslamcı*) and expressed their preference for the *imam-hatip* school as a place to protect their children and encourage their spiritual development.[46] There was a general concern for preserving religious tradition as an inherent part of Turkish culture.[47] Teachers in the cultural academic courses tended to represent a variety of perspectives, but teachers in the vocational (i.e., religious) courses shared camaraderie around the religious identity of the school.[48] Among the vocational teachers, doubt or critique were not typically acceptable. Pak observes, "On many occasions, I found that the religious views of the teachers were aggressively impressed upon the students without much opportunity for reflection."[49] He concludes that instead of promoting an integrated view of state-sanctioned religion, the *imam-hatip* schools he studied

> Simply magnif[y] the fragmented splits between the Islamist ideal and the secular reality. The *imam-hatip* school is unable to provide students with a conceptual structure that subordinates the factors of implicit cultural divergence. Consequently, the students attending these schools must deal with a complex reality whereby intrinsic cultural valorization calls for the coexistence of competing outlooks on life.

This position might be a bit strong, but it does reflect the tension his subjects expressed between the values at school and those in broader Turkish society.

Quran courses

One form of religious education that is extensive and yet understudied in Turkey is the Quran course and schools. At various points in modern Turkish history, these have been underground, and in many cases they remain informal. A more formal model was promoted by Süleyman Hilmi Tunahan (who is discussed in greater detail later) in the form of after-school classes for schoolchildren, teaching Quran recitation, basic Arabic, and other religious topics not covered by public schools. Extracurricular Quran courses have provided one of the only opportunities for young people to gain proficiency in Arabic. However, educational programs on Arabic and Quran recitation are now broadcast extensively in Turkey. High school curricula were revised in 2012 to include an elective in Quran, which may also lower the demand for private courses.

There are also Quran courses intended for adults. State-sponsored courses offered at local mosques use essentially the same materials as the school-level religion classes, which many observant Muslims find inadequate.[50] Kim Shively has a fascinating study of her experience observing a women's Quran course offered informally in Sincan.[51] Although the young woman teaching the class used the standard state-approved text for basic religious practice, she used outside materials on the life of the Prophet and especially on moral teaching.[52]

University entrance exam prep courses

After-school preparatory classes (***hazırlık***) for the university entrance examination in Turkey (*sınav*) are offered across the country in private teaching centers (*dershaneler*).[53] The exam is perceived as being so expansive and difficult that students in every economic stratum enroll in these courses in order to improve their chances for obtaining admission into a limited number of slots for entering university students. A wide range of businesses offers these sorts of programs, but the most extensive network is affiliated with the Hizmet movement and Fethullah Gülen. FEM is the largest, but other individual schools or groups of schools are affiliated.[54]

The current university placement exam asks only five questions out of 160 on topics that might include religion, so this is not a major content area for these programs. In any event, religious content would be limited to the state curriculum for religion, and it is thus quite narrow and homogenized. However, religiously affiliated programs are often established with the aim of creating positive connections between teachers, who participate in the religious mission of the sponsoring organization, and students, which might ultimately lead to student interest and participation in the religious organization. Much of this work exists simply in the context of the teacher–student relationship, but study groups and discussion groups outside of the curriculum also create opportunities. Anecdotally, the increase in Hizmet participation has tracked the growth of its educational institutions, including prep courses. It is perceived as such a successful recruiting and business model that prep courses have been targeted by the government for nationalization in an effort to weaken the influence of Gülen-inspired institutions, which are now viewed as antagonistic to the ruling Adalet ve Kalkınma Partisi (or "Justice and Development Party" in English; hereafter "AKP").[55] The issue is so contentious that the Constitutional Court reviewed the issue for possible annulment of the law, which would close private prep courses by September 2015.[56] The scheduled closure of private **dershane** was halted by the Constitutional Court in July of 2015, but the ultimate legal impact of the law remains unclear.[57]

This issue has very publicly highlighted the role of educational institutions in shaping particular views of Islam, and the strong reactions on both sides seem to indicate agreement that access to students impacts their views, even when the majority of the formal curriculum is nonreligious. The AKP clearly views religious institutions affiliated with Hizmet as a threat to their political authority and vision of national identity, and they view prep courses as a venue that is subject to regulation and even nationalization (as opposed to the large network of private primary and secondary schools affiliated with Hizmet that are embedded within the educational landscape). Supporters of Hizmet consider this an attack on their ability to recruit and raise funds, which threatens its institutions more broadly.[58]

Religious organizations

Turkey hosts a large number of religious and religious-oriented civil society organizations. Some are informal and local, but many are highly structured and national, or even international, and exist within complex networks. Two of the largest networks of religious organizations are primarily, though not exclusively, committed to education. The Süleymancılar are best known for their network of

Quran schools, and the Hizmet movement has an international network of university exam prep courses (hazırlık) and high schools, as well as a handful of universities and other civil society organizations. Both organizations boast millions of members and have a notable impact on Turkish religious discourse. These two groups, along with the *Menzil Cemaati* and the *Nakşibendi Cemaati*, which are both nearly as active in Turkey as the Süleymanlı,[59] all trace their origin to the *Naqshbandi tariqat*.[60]

Süleymanlı

It is curious that the two largest religious organizations/communities (*Cemaat*) in Turkey have ties to leaders who were persecuted in the early years of the Turkish Republic, both of whom were renowned for their opposition to legal restraints on religious expression. In the case of Süleyman Hilmi Tunahan, his protest tended to emphasize religious education, whereas Said Nursi came to national prominence for his objections to the Hat Law of 1925. Süleyman Hilmi Tunahan was born in 1888 in the Ottoman village of Ferhatlar, which is now located in Bulgaria. He was trained as a *Hanafi* jurist at the *Medresetü'l-Mütehassisin* in Istanbul.[61] He remained a professor in the Istanbul madrasas until they were closed by the state, at which point he worked as a preacher and privately taught students in his home until the late 1940s, when religious education was again legalized.[62] He is regarded by his followers as the last in the chain of preeminent *Naqshbandi* sheikhs.[63] During his lifetime, he was a teacher and an advocate for Quran courses that provided for students religious education absent in the school system.

The *Süleymanlı Cemaat* or *Süleymancılar* refers, usually derogatorily, to the network of people and organizations inspired by Süleyman Hilmi Tunahan. It is regarded as the second largest community in Turkey,[64] and it is also very active within Turkish-speaking communities in Western Europe.[65] Although the community relies on some traditional *Naqshbandi* structures, it has also adapted in order to effectively train and organize its members in a variety of cultural contexts.[66] They are perhaps best known in Turkey for sponsoring Quran schools and courses for students. As with the Hizmet-affiliated prep courses described earlier, these programs give teachers the opportunity to mentor students, the main difference here being that the content of the instruction is explicitly religious. Their influence is important enough that they are mentioned by interviewees in empirical studies as significant in the formation of religious views, and they are sometimes criticized for being overly political.[67] However, these groups tend to be closed and difficult to study.[68]

Nurcu

Nurcu groups are so named because of their affinity for Said Nursi and his magnum opus, *Risale-i Nur*, an extensive work of Quranic commentary and spiritual exploration.[69] Discussed in greater detail later, Nursi attracted a large number of followers during his lifetime as a result of his writing, teaching, and public protest, for which he spent significant time in jail. *Risale-i Nur* became a theological model for many pious Turks as they attempted to appropriate their religious tradition in the face of aggressively secular social contexts. The work is an explicitly Sunni and Sufi attempt to communicate and make sense of orthodox tradition, theologically and in practice.[70] While there are certainly many Nurcu communities that adhere to Nursi as *Üstad* (master or teacher) and do not identify with other religious groups, by far the largest network of organizations in the Nurcu tradition is Hizmet, or those who follow Fethullah Gülen, who was himself inspired and influenced by Nursi. Today, the Hizmet-affiliated publisher, Tughra, is printing the entire corpus of *Risale-i Nur* in a variety of languages for sale in Turkey and around the world.[71] In many important ways, Hizmet has taken up the mantle of the Nur *Cemaati*, displacing it in terms of membership and activity.

Hizmet, often called the *Cemaat* by outsiders, is the largest religious network in Turkey. Estimates of the number of active participants vary, but news outlets typically presume millions.[72] In addition to the network of *dershane* prep courses, there are at least 300 Hizmet-affiliated schools in Turkey and over 1,000 worldwide.[73] The network had strong media outlets, such as the *Zaman* newspaper and the Samanyolu television network, as well as an extensive business network that has funded foundations throughout the world to support Hizmet's religious, educational, and charitable works. The growth and success of the movement was encouraged by the success of the AKP, whose leaders relied on good relations with Hizmet and Gülen for religious legitimacy until the relationship soured in 2013. Comfortable relations with the AKP gave Hizmet affiliates access to senior positions within the government, particularly in ***Diyanet***, the Ministry of Education, and the Interior Ministry.[74] This relationship also gave business people affiliated with Hizmet access to lucrative government contracts.[75] As a result, although many Turks are favorably disposed toward Gülen, or at least to his teachings, many are also deeply suspicious of the group's political agenda and economic power.[76] Thus, when Hizmet was no longer viewed as an unwavering supporter of the AKP and the prime minister, it was quickly cast as a threat by senior members of the government. In an ironic turn of events, Hizmet may now be perceived as a persecuted minority, lending it greater credibility in the eyes of those who considered it synonymous with the AKP. Although it is possible that new religious groups will step in to fill the gap left by Hizmet in the AKP in order to provide legitimacy for religiously oriented voters, Hizmet and the network of groups inspired by Gülen remain tremendously important in Turkey.

Religious leaders

In the late Ottoman period, religious leaders generally had influence and authority because they had gone through traditional madrasa training and were appointed by the crown to positions of authority, or they achieved popular support as charismatic writers, teachers, or preachers. The landscape today is arguably more chaotic. Some leaders considered to have religious authority have conventional training from the theology faculties of major universities, some are artists (poets, novelists, or musicians), some are trained in professions (such as civil law), and some are in politics. This section will first consider two of the most influential living Turkish theologians, Fethullah Gülen and Yaşar Nuri Öztürk.[77] Accounts will be given for a handful of other religious thinkers, both living and dead, who shape religious thought in Turkey. I will then give a brief acknowledgement that political leaders now play a role in the development of religious views.

Fethullah Gülen

Fethullah Gülen is a prominent Turkish religious leader and a leading scholar of Islam.[78] He is the inspiration for the *Hizmet* (service) Movement, sometimes referred to as the Gülen Movement. This movement claims millions of participants, primarily in Turkey.[79] It shares some ideas with the Nurcu Movement inspired by Said Nursi.[80]

Sufi movements, such as the *Naqshbandi* and the *Mevlevi*, influence Gülen's approach to Islamic jurisprudence, and he notes the specific influence of Mevlana Jelaluddin Rumi and Said Nursi on his thought.[81] Organizations inspired by Gülen emphasize education, interreligious dialogue, nationalism, and free-market capitalism; they now include hundreds of schools, a handful of universities, and numerous foundations around the world.

Although Gülen often writes and preaches on spiritual, ethical, and political topics, his jurisprudence is difficult to discern. His writing indicates a tension between a deep commitment to textual tradition and an impulse to validate modern technological, economic, and political innovations. Although he occasionally acknowledges the importance of classical *fiqh*, he argues that changed circumstances, such as the end of the Caliphate, the rise of the nation-state, and fundamental economic transformation, require new legal rules.[82] He does not explicitly reject *taqlid* as a methodology, inviting a new era of *ijtihad*. However, in the absence of a robust system of Islamic education in the classical mode of the *madhab*, his approach can be interpreted as justifying new methodologies for deriving authentic Islamic legal rules. İhsan Yılmaz observes that "[by] exercising *ijtihad* without flagging it as *ijtihad*, Gülen reinterprets Islamic understanding in tune with contemporary times."[83]

Gülen's discrete use of *ijtihad*, whether in a mode of *taqlid* or in a modernist sense, reflects a pragmatic approach to jurisprudence. Structurally, he legitimizes the idea of a secular state and democratic decision-making. In the absence of a unified Muslim community and historically legitimate legal institutions, Gülen views secularism as a product of, and as a requirement for, an authentic understanding of Islam.[84] As for many Islamic modernists, democracy is suitable as a pragmatic and just form of governance compatible with the principles of *ijma* (consensus) and *shura* (consultation).[85]

Substantively, Gülen's jurisprudence has profound implications in four areas. First, it necessitates strong protections for free exercise of religion in a secular, and likely pluralist, state. This position is clearly influenced by his negative experiences with Turkish limitations on free exercise. Even so, Gülen is careful to limit criticism of Turkish secularism so as not to impugn Turkish Republicanism or nationalism. Second, a major substantive innovation is Gülen's understanding of citizenship and rights for everyone, regardless of religion,[86] a view that arguably diverges from classical *fiqh*. This position relates to his third area of concern – that human rights are an authentically Islamic discourse – without the reservations typically attributed to classical jurisprudence. In particular, he expresses concern for the rights and agency of women, the fourth area of substantive innovation in Gülen's jurisprudence.[87] Although he might argue that women have defined roles within Islam, he is a zealous advocate of formal legal equality regardless of gender.

Gülen is distinct among most modern Muslim legal reformers in three ways. First, he has been careful to harmonize his jurisprudence with Turkish Republicanism and nationalism. This is likely a reason that his movements have been more successful than those that opposed the Turkish government externally rather than acting internally to reform it. Second, his reticence to cast jurisprudence as a departure from classical *fiqh* has allowed him to innovate without claiming a break from the past. Finally, his support for the secular state as authentically Islamic justifies civil laws based on public welfare (*istislah*) rather than on textual sources (*usul al-fiqh*).[88]

Like *Diyanet*, Gülen relies on classical *fiqh*, usually from the *Hanafi* school, as a basis for legal rules. However, in his moral and social teaching, he is willing to interpret the core texts in ways more compatible with modern sensibilities.[89] Gülen is familiar with modernist thinkers, so he refers to Abduh, Rida, Sanhuri, or even Rahman, but he does not identify himself as a modernist. Although he has a complicated relationship with the Turkish state, he is a strong advocate of democracy and free enterprise. His support of legal secularism is somewhat more circumscribed, at least in regard to state control of religion in Turkey, but he seems supportive of softer forms of secularism, as is found in the United States, for example.[90] Gülen exhibits elements of traditionalism, modernism, and privatization in his jurisprudence. This approach is similar to that adopted by *Diyanet*, so it is not surprising that Gülen's views might influence the state position on some religious issues. It is also unsurprising that scholars sympathetic to Gülen might find service in *Diyanet* meaningful and compatible with their approach to Islamic jurisprudence.

Yaşar Nuri Öztürk

Yaşar Nuri Öztürk is one of the most influential Turkish religious scholars to address the compatibility of Turkish secularism with Islam.[91] He embraces an explicitly Islamic worldview compatible with Turkish nationalism, as well as a structural commitment to secularism.[92] Öztürk assumes a modernist view arguing that contemporary Muslim jurisprudence need not follow classical *fiqh*. He explicitly allows for new *ijtihad* and views authentic secularism as a natural product of Islam.[93] This view is especially important because it demonstrates a break from the confrontational models used by earlier Nurcu leaders and the *Refah*

Partisi.[94] The translation of Öztürk's *Secularism in Terms of Quranic Principles* – one of the most straightforward attempts by a Turkish religious scholar to reconcile Islamic and Turkish secularism – provides unique insight into an important voice in Turkish Islamic thought. This is exactly the type of jurisprudential move derided by Wael B. Hallaq for abandoning the tradition of classical *fiqh.*[95]

Öztürk understands legal secularism as a product of, and a requirement for, an authentic understanding of Islam.[96] He is critical of both atheism and political Islam, instead arguing that justice must have roots in the Quran as written, rather than as interpreted in the formative period of *fiqh.*[97] He finds a basis for secular neutrality (the *laic* system) and democracy (rooted in an understanding of *shura*), contending that after the death of the Prophet theocracy was illegitimate;[98] the only legitimate exercise of political power is in the name of society rather than Allah.[99] Although the *Sunna* can play a role in deriving principles for just governance, Öztürk argues that legal and political innovations starting in the *Ummayyad* period are not binding in the Muslim community except to the extent that they reflect Quranic principles.[100] His approach shares some elements in common with Rashid Rida and others who argue for new *ijtihad.* His argument also shares some of the rhetoric with Quran-only movements, though the *Sunna* still plays a role in jurisprudence.

While his work contains theological and jurisprudential claims, Öztürk's primary rhetorical goal seems to be justifying a vision of Islam centered in the Quran and that is consistent with Turkish secularism and the constitutional state.[101] In particular, his work argues that Atatürk advocated a Quran-based Islam, requiring a form of secularism guaranteeing the free exercise of religion and state neutrality in the religious sphere.[102] He finds the strongest evidence for this in Atatürk's support for the translation of the Quran into modern Turkish by Muhammed Hamdi Yazır (also known as Elmalılı).[103] This project was intended to make core moral and legal principles available to all Turks outside of the context of Ottoman or broader *Hanafi* legal tradition.[104]

One constant challenge to both the innovative and the modern approaches to Islamic jurisprudence is the assertion that interpretation from the sources of *fiqh* ended by the 11th century with the so-called "closing of the gates of *ijtihad.*" In order to better understand the controversial claims of contemporary Islamic scholars like Öztürk or Gülen, this type of innovation must be considered in light of Wael Hallaq's approach, i.e., as one that is critical of abandoning traditional *fiqh.* Hallaq argues that *ijtihad* continued into the medieval period, where *mujtahids* continued to be trained, scholars openly applied rules conflicting with their *madhabs*, and at least some jurists insisted on the importance of independent *ijtihad.*[105] There is scholarship rooted in Hallaq's claims asserting there was never consensus about the closing of "the Gates of *Ijtihad*" – enough debate that individual *ijtihad* might be justifiable today.[106] Öztürk supports this position. However, his support is problematic for Hallaq, who observes that "none of these restorative options can be realized without the contaminating influence of the state, rendering extinct the distinctiveness of premodern *Shari'a* as a non-state, community-based, bottom-up jural system."[107] Hallaq would consider Öztürk a modernist for advocating inclusion of Quranic principles in the formation of the constitutional state and for rejecting classical *fiqh*. In this regard, Öztürk's thought shares elements with Abduh, Rida, and even with Rahman.[108] However, not only does Öztürk overtly reject the content of classical *fiqh*, he also rejects the method – except to suggest that it might be found in the text of the Quran without the overlay of texts originating in the *Ummayyad* period or later.[109] Hallaq might look even less favorably on Öztürk's attempts to define the core principles of the Turkish Republic and Atatürk as authentically Quranic and as consistent with a legitimate understanding of *Shari'a*.

In contrast to scholars who consider classical *fiqh* tradition, particularly its methodology, as the correct basis for legitimate Islamic jurisprudence, Öztürk represents an important group of Muslim religious scholars who argue for the compatibility of Islam with the modern nation-state, including related notions of secularism, constitutionalism, rule of law, and democracy. This approach validates elements of Turkish Republicanism and seems to be increasingly influential among Turkish Muslims, including among religious leaders.[110]

Although Öztürk is generally a modernist in jurisprudence, he advocates a view that legitimizes Turkish democracy and a version of legal secularism. However, with regard to the jurisprudential approaches described in Chapter Two, he differs notably from *Diyanet* in his rejection of the traditional *fiqh* tradition. It is possible that this creates an appearance of coherence that *Diyanet* cannot. However, the rejection of classical legal methods and rules poses challenges for legitimacy.

Hayrettin Karaman

Hayrettin Karaman was born in Çorum in 1934.[111] He studied Islamic jurisprudence in Istanbul and is a highly regarded scholar of Islamic legal tradition with a long list of publications. He is also a regular columnist and a public intellectual.[112] Due to the lack of access to state-sanctioned religious education, Karaman pursued madrasa studies privately.[113] This education was illicit, but it did continue the tradition and curriculum of the traditional madrasas. He reentered public education in 1952 at the age of 18 in an *imam-hatip* high school.[114] He speaks highly of both his traditional education and his formal education, and he is recognized as a vigilant defender of the system of *imam-hatip* schools. He has written extensively on the need for Islamization and is the author of perhaps the most important popular press account of the topic.[115] As a legal scholar, he has been a consistent advocate for *ijtihad* as a necessary and appropriate tool for "regulating contemporary social, economic, and political life."[116] In his writing, he notes that Turkish-Islamic discourse needs to include references to reform movements from the rest of the predominantly Muslim world.[117]

Ömer Tuğrul İnançer

Ömer Tuğrul İnançer was born in 1946 in Bursa, Turkey.[118] He is a Turkish lawyer, Sufi scholar, and musician.[119] He holds a law degree from Istanbul University and practiced law for 21 years.[120] Since 1991, he has been the Director of Istanbul Historical Turkish Music Ensemble, part of the Turkish Ministry of Culture.[121] Mr. İnançer is an international lecturer on Mevlana Jelaluddin Rumi and is particularly expert on Rumi's work, the *Mesnevi*.[122] Mr. İnançer has lectured on numerous TV programs and has authored multiple books on Rumi.[123] He is also a frequent commentator on Turkish television, and he recently sparked public outrage when he stated that it was immoral for obviously pregnant women to be seen in public.[124]

Zekariya Beyaz

Zekariya Beyaz is a prominent Turkish religious leader. Born in 1938, he was raised and completed his high school education at an *imam-hatip* school in Gaziantep.[125] He was trained as a preacher and theologian and studied at Istanbul University.[126] He was a professor in the sociology department at Istanbul University and then dean of the theology faculty at Marmara University.[127] Although he has retired, he still writes and appears occasionally as a religious authority on television.

He has written a number of books and articles, including the influential *Islam and Dress*, published in 2000. In this work, he synthesizes theology, politics, and social science analysis. He does not ascribe ontological value to hair itself (in the context of *hijab*), but he does criticize the political misuse of the headscarf, arguing that traditional Turkish folk dress addresses the theological concern with modesty without invoking a potentially inappropriate agenda.[128]

Beyaz has also been an outspoken critic of Christianity in Turkey, arguing that Islamic identity is an inherent component of Turkish identity. In responding to the question of whether missionaries are harmful or not to national unity, he said the following:

> Yes, our national unity will disappear. We will disappear entirely; we will be emptied out from inside out. Religion is always integrated with nationalism, patriotism, and cultural values. Religion is the keystone. When you pull it out, everything else will crumble. Then you cannot have dedication to Turkish culture, patriotism, appreciation of historical heroes, or literary characters. When you become a member of the Anglican Church, you will become their man. You will read their literature. When you become a member of the Greek Orthodox Church in Anatolia, this means you become a Greek.[129]

Dücane Cündioğlu

Dücane Cündioğlu is a writer, novelist, and columnist who was born in Istanbul in 1962.[130] Mr. Cündioğlu's career as a columnist began in 1980 when he started to write articles for various journals and newspapers.[131] In addition to publishing numerous books, from 1998 to 2011 Mr. Cündioğlu authored a column for the newspaper *Yeni Şafak*.[132] Although he did not complete an advanced degree, he is a prolific writer and delivers public lectures on the role of religion in

Turkey.[133] He is particularly critical of the privatization of religion in the pattern of European and U.S. secularism.[134]

Mevlana Jelaluddin Rumi

Two of the most notable historical religious thinkers in Turkey are arguably Rumi and Nursi. Mevlana Jelaluddin Muhammad Rumi, a Sufi mystic and Persian writer, was born in Balkh (in today's Afghanistan) in 1207.[135] In 1228, at the invitation of the Seljuk Sultan, Rumi's father moved his family to Konya, in present-day Turkey.[136] Rumi spent the majority of the rest of his life in Konya,[137] where he became a Sufi mystic under the mentorship of Shams ad-Din Tabrizi and composed the *Masnawi*, a six-volume poetic masterpiece of Sufi lore and spiritual teachings.[138] Rumi is also the founder of the *Mevlevi* Sufi Order (also known as the Whirling Dervishes), who embrace music and dancing as a part of their spirituality.[139]

Rumi's poetry and philosophy continue to influence thinkers in the Middle East and in Turkey, most notably, Fethullah Gülen.[140] Gülen frequently alludes to or quotes Rumi in his work, primarily for his views on interreligious tolerance and for his love of creation.[141] Rumi is often invoked by Gülen to advocate for a tolerant interpretation of Islam that should be preserved, and he supports this interpretation by referencing that Rumi's *Mevlevi* School was directly influenced by the Prophet Muhammad.[142]

Said Nursi

Said Nursi was born in 1877 in an eastern Anatolian mountain village in the province of Bitlis.[143] Nursi's life was dedicated to reconciling the Quran and traditional Islamic sciences with modern scientific knowledge and for asserting that these studies were consistent.[144] Although Nursi was strongly influenced by Sufism in his writings, he was firmly grounded in classical Islamic scholarship.[145] His writings and newspaper articles displayed an attempt to bring concepts of liberal thought – such as constitutionalism, freedom, despotism (as a force to be opposed), progress, civilization, and nationalism – to the Turkish populace, while also linking those concepts with Islam. Although he protested government restrictions on the free exercise of religion, later in his life he advocated a retreat from the public sphere in favor of the interior life. Today, the influence of Nursi's seminal work, the *Risale-i Nur* ("Epistle of Light"), is evident in the Hizmet/Gülen movement and in the writings of Fethullah Gülen.[146] The Hizmet/Gülen movement strongly identifies with Nursi's goal of enhancing knowledge, progress, scientific thought, and modernization while remaining within an Islamic context in an effort to avoid stagnation in the Muslim world.[147]

Recep Tayyip Erdoğan

Two of the most prominent politicians who play a notable role in Turkish religious discourse are Erdoğan and Gül. President (formerly Prime Minister) Recep

Tayyip Erdoğan is arguably Turkey's most influential politician of the past half century. In 2001, he co-founded the conservative Justice and Development Party (AKP), which shortly thereafter won two-thirds of the seats of parliament in the November 2002 elections.[148] At the time, Mr. Erdoğan was barred by a court order from participating in the election due to a 1999 arrest for reciting a poem that Turkey's generals considered to incite religious hatred – an act in violation of Turkey's constitutionally mandated secularism.[149] However, on March 9, 2003, after overcoming the legal obstacles against him, Erdoğan was elected to parliament and appointed to the post of prime minister six days later.[150]

Politically, Mr. Erdoğan's conservative religious views have contributed greatly to his populist appeal. He is a pious Muslim whose wife wears a headscarf, and he appeals to a large number of devout Turks throughout Anatolia who often feel condescended to by the secular elite in Istanbul. In addition, until the summer 2013 *Gezi* protests began, Erdoğan remained popular for his economic reforms with much of the urban working class.[151] Since 2002, when the AKP came into power, Turkey's rampant inflation has all but disappeared, and GDP growth has averaged 5% annually, contributing to Erdoğan's appeal.[152]

Despite his popularity, President Erdoğan is also viewed as a divisive figure in Turkish politics. He has been criticized for appearing to have a lackluster commitment to democracy. During his tenure as mayor of Istanbul in the 1990s, Erdoğan remarked, "democracy is a tram that gets you to your destination, and then you get off."[153] On some issues, he has been criticized by members of the Hizmet movement, which has a strong ideological base within certain Turkish media outlets, government institutions, and the electorate.[154]

After the *Gezi* protests, Erdoğan and other senior AKP leaders grew disturbed at the lack of support from Hizmet leaders and organizations, which had previously defended the administration fairly consistently. In the fall of 2013, then Prime Minister Erdoğan confirmed support for earlier proposals to nationalize university prep courses (*dershane*), a move which has harmed Hizmet in terms of prestige, recruitment, and finances.[155] This led to increasing tension, particularly after investigations of AKP-related fraud in December of 2013, which Erdoğan blamed on Hizmet and Gülen. By distancing himself from Hizmet, Erdoğan removed what had been his primary claim to religious legitimacy. It appears that his own personal charisma and authority may no longer require outside legitimation, and I would not be surprised if Erdoğan increasingly takes public positions on religious issues that represent his own evolving views.

Abdullah Gül

Abdullah Gül was elected President of the Republic of Turkey on August 28, 2007 and served until 2014.[156] A co-founder of the AKP,[157] President Gül was supported by then Prime Minister Erdoğan in the presidential election process.[158] Politically, Gül was perceived as "Islamist," and as pro-Western by some, and he quietly used his diplomatic efforts to encourage Iran to abandon its nuclear program.[159] President Gül's political career began in 1991 when he was elected to parliament as a member of the Welfare Party, led by Necmettin

Erbakan.[160] Throughout the 1990s, Abdullah Gül was a leading figure in the Reformist Movement,[161] and, like Erdoğan, he has his political roots in Turkey's Islamist movements.[162] Prior to his election as president, he was particularly distinguished for his personal piety and for defending his wife's right to cover. As a result, he is viewed as a leader with religious authority, at least with regard to matters of personal piety and public morality.

The media

As in most of the rest of the world, media has become a powerful shaper of public opinion in Turkey. Thirty years ago, daily papers were widely read in Turkey, and there were a handful of government-controlled television channels. Today, overall print circulation has declined, but privately owned cable networks have proliferated. This has resulted in some degree of fracturing along ideological lines. However, the tremendous variety of perspectives has not resulted in the sort of fragmentation and polarization identified in the United States. The newspaper *Zaman*, and to a lesser extent the Samanyolu television network, both affiliated with the Hizmet movement and Gülen, have attracted a diverse and devoted base, which is open to the inclusion of religious identity and ideas consistent with core principles of the Turkish Republic.

Zaman *newspaper*

The *Zaman Daily* is a Turkish-language newspaper,[163] with a circulation in excess of one million newspapers daily.[164] Founded in 1986, the *Zaman Daily* focuses on both national and international issues, with specific focus on Turkey and the region in its geographical vicinity.[165]

The *Zaman Daily* and its English language counterpart, *Today's Zaman*,[166] are linked to the Fethullah Gülen movement.[167] As a result, descriptions of the *Zaman* news network have ranged from "religious, rightist" and "mainstream Islamist" to "political, independent."[168]

Despite its importance, there is relatively little written on the rise and role of *Zaman*.[169] A senior editor noted that he will endeavor to encourage substantive research related to the newspaper and its affiliates when he is made aware of research proposals.[170] The editors at *Zaman* have been extremely adept at translating the languages of both Kemalist and Muslim identity in an effort to reconcile them.[171] For example, columnists justify a distinction between the private sphere of religious devotion and the secular and tolerant public sphere on religious grounds.[172] This translation is attractive to readers because it affirms their identification as "modern" rather than problematizing it.[173] *Zaman*, and similar religiously affiliated publishers, thus become both reporters and agents of social change. Alexandar Balistreri observes the following with regard to the role of *Zaman* in contemporary Turkish culture:

> The promotion of democratic and pluralist discourse by religious citizens is not only an important factor in promoting social reform, but also in promoting

> the health of multiply asserted identities and their compatibility with the society in which they are embedded. Those who believed that religious identities would simply cave in at the onset of modernity, have been forced to reevaluate their position with the rise of public claims to modernity by religious citizens around the world. In Turkey, this process has been woven in pious Muslims' struggle for recognition of a right to their identity and a struggle to reduce the role of the state in private life.[174]

Since, late 2013 the Turkish state has taken numerous actions to counter Gülen-inspired institutions. In March 2016, the Turkish government took control of Zaman and its affiliates, arguing that they were affiliated with a terrorist organization.[175]

Samanyolu television

Samanyolu is a Gülen-inspired television network in Turkey that provides a variety of programming, including news, dramas, religious content, and a variety of health and family-oriented talk shows. *The Fifth Dimension* (Beşinci Boyut) is arguably the most popular religion-oriented drama on Turkish television. It aired on Samanyolu between 2005 and 2011 and is still broadcast in reruns. It bears a strong resemblance to the U.S. television shows *Touched by an Angel* and *Highway to Heaven.* All three portray angels as they play a role in bringing ordinary people to deeper faith. However, more than its U.S. analogs, *The Fifth Dimension* was viewed as dramatizing true-life stories.

In late 2015, the channels owned by Samanyolu Media Group were turned over to a state-appointed trustee. They were also removed from the two leading satellite systems, Digitürk and Türksat as a consequence of their affiliation with Fethullah Gülen.[176]

Conclusion

A wide range of institutions and individuals influence religious views in Turkey, including views of *Shari'a.* Although the government, through *Diyanet* and the curriculum of religious education, provides a basis for a single national approach to Turkish Islam, the market for religious truth and legitimacy remains highly contested (even within the government). If the Republican reforms in the 1920s and 30s were intended to eradicate religion, they were a miserable failure since Turks privately preserved religious tradition. Today, it is one of the more observant Muslim nations in terms of practices such as fasting and almsgiving.[177] It is more likely that the goal was to homogenize and tame Islam as a core, but ideally nondisruptive, element of national identity. Islam is certainly a core element of identity in Turkey, but as in the Ottoman period, it is not homogeneous. The question of government control of religion is highly complex and requires a deeper exploration of Turkish secularism.

Notes

1 *See* Gözde Özdikmenli-Demir and Birsen Şahin-Kütük, "The Role of Parents, Siblings, Peers, Relatives and Other Agents in Turkish-Muslim Emerging Adults Religious Socializations." *Archive for the Psychology of Religion / Archiv für Religionspychologie* 3 (2012): 363.
2 *Id.* at 390–392.
3 *Id.* at 392.
4 *See e.g.*, Özdikmenli-Demir and Şahin-Kütük; Daniel Hungerman, "The Effect of Education on Religion: Evidence from Compulsory Schooling Laws." *NBER Working Paper Series*, available at http://www.nber.org/papers/w16973.pdf (2011); and Bruce Sacerdote and Edward Glaeser, "Education and Religion." *NBER Working Paper Series*, available at http://www.nber.org/papers/w8080.pdf (2001).
5 Halil İnalcık, *The Ottoman Empire: The Classical Age 1300–1600*. New York: Praeger, 1973.
6 *Id.*
7 Amit Bein, "Politics, Military Conscription, and Religious Education in the Late Ottoman Empire." *International Journal of Middle East Studies* 38 (2006): 283–284.
8 *See id.* Note that the need for recruits to serve in the armed forces prompted a number of policies that seemed to upend traditional religious and social norms, including the conscription of madrasa students (in this case) and attempts to conscript non-Muslims. The wars with Russia at the beginning of Abdulhamid II's reign made adequate defense an imperative that trumped many traditional norms.
9 *Id.* at 296.
10 *Id.* at 297.
11 *Id.* at 284–286.
12 *Id.* at 299.
13 From comments by Professor Dr. Osman Taştan from the Ankara University Theology Faculty made at an Islamic law conference hosted by the Journal of Law and Religion in St. Paul, Minnesota on September 28, 2012.
14 *Id.*
15 Zeynep Özgen, "From Madrasa to Underground and Back: Is Turkish Secularization Path-Dependent?" an unpblished draft article held by the author.
16 *Id. See also* Amit Bein, *Ottoman Ulema, Turkish Republic: Agents of Change and Guardians of Tradition.* Stanford, CA: Stanford University Press, 2014.
17 *See general* Benjamin C. Fortna, *Imperial Classroom: Islam, the State, and Education in the Late Ottoman Empire*. Oxford: Oxford University Press, 2002.
18 Karpat at 99–100.
19 Karpat at 100.
20 *See* Deringil at 94–96.
21 *See* Karpat at 100–101 and Deringil at 95.
22 Fortna at 124.
23 Karpat at 101–102.
24 Hadi Adanalı, "The Many Dimensions of Religious Instruction in Turkey," https://www.iarf.net/REBooklet/Turkey.htm (last viewed April 2016).
25 *Id.*
26 *Id.*
27 *Id.*
28 ECRI, *Third Report on Turkey* (2004), available at http://hudoc.ecri.coe.int/XMLEcri/ENGLISH/Cycle_03/03_CbC_eng/TUR-CbC-III-2005-5-ENG.pdf
29 Mine Yıldırım, "TURKEY: Changes in School Religious Education Fail to Resolve Fundamental Problems" from *Forum 18 News Service*, available at http://www.forum18.org/archive.php?article_id=1603 (August 23, 2011).

30 *Id.* "The Election Programmes of the ruling Justice and Development Party (AKP) and the Demokrat Party (DP) are silent about religious education, which implies that they are satisfied with the current practice and do not wish to introduce any changes. By contrast, the Emek, Demokrasi ve Özgürlük Blok (Labour, Democracy and Freedom Bloc), the Turkish Communist Party (TKP) and the Republican People's Party (CHP) oppose compulsory religion classes. The Bloc instead proposed history of religions and religious studies as optional lessons. The CHP proposed that the RCKE lessons cease to be compulsory, and be offered instead as optional in primary and secondary schools. The Nationalist Action Party (MHP), Felicity Party (SP) and People's Voice Party (HAS) defend the current practice of compulsory RCKE classes. In addition, they also propose the ending of the state monopoly over formal religious education."
31 *See* Özdikmenli-Demir and Şahin-Kütük.
32 *See e.g.*, regarding "national security" required courses, Tuba Kancı and Ayşe Gül Altınay, "Educating Little Soldiers and Little Ayşes: Militarised and Gendered Citizenship in Turkish Textbooks," available at http://www.srii.org/content/upload/documents/bd1b99e2–0bfc-450e-876c-247b49b1fd57.pdf.
33 *See e.g.*, Islamic Studies, Marmara University, available at http://ilahiyat.marmara.edu.tr/bolumler/temel-islam-bilimleri/.
34 Diren Çakmak, "Pro-Islamic Public Education in Turkey." *Middle Eastern Studies* 45 (2009): 825, 829.
35 *Id.*
36 *Id.* at 830.
37 *Id.* at 831.
38 *Id.* at 831–832.
39 *Id.* at 833–835.
40 Soon-Yong Pak, "Articulating the Boundary between Secularism and Islamism: The Imam-Hatip Schools of Turkey." *Anthropology and Education Quarterly* 35 (2004): 327.
41 Çakmak at 838.
42 *Id.*
43 *Id.* at 388–389.
44 Pak at 327.
45 Pak at 328.
46 *Id.* at 332–333.
47 *Id.* at 334 from one interviewee, "It is a matter of who controls curricular content. You cannot force the urban–secular lifestyle to become the norm through which every Turk's life is measured as success or failure. For instance, the life of a pious Muslim is governed by a different set of motivations and convictions. For this reason, the *imam-hatip* school provides a healthy alternative to the regular school."
48 *Id.*
49 *Id.* at 336.
50 Kim Shively, "Taming Islam: Studying Religion in Secular Turkey." *Anthropological Quarterly* 81 (2008): 699.
51 *Id.*
52 *Id.* at 699.
53 Note that a "*dershane*" may offer broad academic support throughout a student's time in school, as well as an intensive program near or after graduation. It is the near- or post-graduation intensive preparation that is usually referred to as "*hazırlık*."
54 According to news reports, over 900 of the total 3,690 *dershane* in Turkey were affiliated with Hizmet at the end of 2013. *See* "Gülen Cemaatinin Kaç Dersanesi Var?" *Haber Vaktım*, November 20, 2013, available at http://www.habervaktim.com/haber/351528/gulen-cemaatinin-kac-dersanesi-var.html
55 *See e.g.*, Mümtazer Türköne, "Dershane Posturing." *Today's Zaman*, November 13, 2013.

56 *See* Hasan Karalı, "Constitutional Court to Discuss Merits of Controversial Dershane Law." *Today's Zaman*, May 23, 2014. It is more than slightly ironic that the CHP, which has historically been antagonistic toward Hizmet and Gülen, has referred the case to the Constitutional Court in order to annul the law nationalizing prep courses.
57 *See* "Top Court's Dershane Ruling Comes as Relief, but Uncertainties Persist." *Today's Zaman*, July 15, 2015.
58 Note that this conflict began more than a year after data for this study was collected.
59 *See e.g.*, "Türkiye'nin en büyük *cemaati* hangisi?" *Haber Türk*, June 22, 2011.
60 There is an interesting critique of Naqshbandi influence in Turkey as Arab, puritanical, and foreign. This is sometimes contrasted with authentically Anatolian Sufi tradition, which is presumably more inclusive and maintains elements of Turkic shamanism. These critiques tend to rely on Rumi, Yunus Emre, and Haci Bektaş as the more authentically Turkish interpreters of Islam. *See e.g.*, Cahit Tanyol, "Nakşibendilik ve Ötesi," in *Laiklik ve İrtica*. Istanbul: Altin Kitap Yayinevi, 1989.
61 *See* Mustafa Ozdamar, *Hadim-ul Kur'an Ustaz Suleyman Hilmi Tunahan*. Istanbul: Kirk Kandil Yaynlari, 2013.
62 *Id.*
63 *Id.*
64 *See e.g.*, "Türkiye'nin en büyük *cemaati* hangisi?" *Haber Türk* June 22, 2011.
65 *See e.g.*, Ahmet Yükleyen, "Production of Mystical Islam in Europe: Religious Authorization in the Süleymanlı Sufi Community" *Contemporary Islam* 4 (2010): 269.
66 *Id.*
67 *See e.g.*, Özdikmenli-Demir and Şahin-Kütük at 390.
68 *Id.* at 392.
69 *See* Şukran Vahide, *Islam in Modern Turkey: An Intellectual Biography of Bediuzzaman Said Nursi*. Albany, NY: State University of New York Press, 2005.
70 *See* Şerif Mardin, *Religion and Social Change in Modern Turkey*. Albany, NY: State University of New York Press, 1989 at 227–231.
71 From a meeting with *Tughra* Editor, Yusuf Alan, at the Zaman headquarters in Istanbul, November 5, 2013.
72 *See e.g.*, "Profile: Fethullah Gulen's Hizmet Movement." *BBC News*, December 18, 2013, available at http://www.bbc.com/news/world-13503361. In my meetings with Hizmet volunteers and leaders, I usually heard that they estimated that there were between five and six million participants.
73 These are the numbers that have been represented to me in the past year, and they seem consistent with news reports. *See e.g.*, Alexandra Hudson, "Turkish Islamic Preacher – Threat or Benefactor?" *Reuters UK*, May 14, 2008.
74 *See* Joshua Hendrick, *Gülen, The Ambiguous Politics of Market Islam in Turkey and the World*. New York: NYU Press, 2013.
75 *Id.*
76 *Id.*
77 Emphasis on these two figures is not meant to dismiss the importance of other leaders, but it is my judgment that Gülen and Öztürk have been the most important Turkish Islamic thinkers over the past 20 years.
78 Russell Powell, "Evolving Views of Islamic Law in Turkey." *Journal of Law and Religion*, 28.2 (2013) at 484–486.
79 M. Hakan Yavuz, "The Gülen Movement: The Turkish Puritans," in *Turkish Islam and the Secular State: The Gülen Movement*. Ed. M.H. Yavuz and J. Esposito. Syracuse: Syracuse University Press, 2003, pp. 30–47.
80 Said Nursi (1876–1960), a prominent Islamic thinker in the early decades of the Turkish Republic.
81 *See, e.g.*, Fethullah Gülen, *Toward a Global Civilization of Love and Tolerance*. Somerset: The Light, 2004 at 133–168. (An extensive discussion of the role and applicability of Sufi thought for contemporary Muslims).

82 Ahmet Kuru, "Search for a Middle Way," in *Turkish Islam and the Secular State: The Gülen Movement.* Ed. M.H. Yavuz and J. Esposito. Syracuse: Syracuse University Press, 2003, p. 126.
83 İhsan Yılmaz, "*Ijtihad* and *Tajdid* by Conduct," in *Turkish Islam and the Secular State: The Gülen Movement.* Ed. M.H. Yavuz and J. Esposito. Syracuse: Syracuse University Press, 2003, p. 200. *See also* İhsan Yılmaz, *Muslim Laws, Politics and Society in Modern Nation States: Dynamic Legal Pluralisms in England, Turkey and Pakistan.* Aldershot & Burlington: Ashgate, 2005.
84 *Id.* at 224 ("In Gülen's philosophy, secularism is not understood as a non-Muslim way of life. The separation between sacred and profane and the projection of secularism onto social life are acceptable.").
85 *Id.* ("Gülen argues that democracy, in spite of its many shortcomings, is now the only viable political system and that people should strive to modernize and consolidate democratic institutions in order to build a society where individuals rights and freedoms are respected and protected, where equal opportunity for all is more than a dream.").
86 *Id.* at 224–228.
87 *See, e.g.*, M. Sait Yavuz, "Women in Islam: Muslim Perspectives and Fethullah Gülen." *Fethullah Gülen's Official Website*, April 13, 2009, available at http://en.fgulen.com/conference-papers/gulen-conference-in-washington-dc/3112-women-in-islam-muslim-perspectives-and-fethullah-gulen.
88 Yılmaz 2008 at 221–223.
89 *Id. See also* İsmail Acar, "Fethullah Gulen and His Legal Thought," in *Mastering Knowledge in Modern Times: Fethullah Gulen as an Islamic Scholar*. Ed. Ismail Albayrak. New York: Blue Dome, 2011, pp. 71–84.
90 Yavuz 2009 at 28.
91 Russell Powell at 481–484.
92 *See* Margot Badran, "The Religious Face of Secularism." *Al-Ahram Weekly On-line* 519 (2001), available at http://weekly.ahram.org.eg/2001/519/intrvw.htm.
93 *See* Yaşar Nuri Öztürk, *Reconstruction of Religious Life in Islam: Returning to the Quran.* Trans. Ali Hayrani Öz. Istanbul: Yeni Boyut, 1999.
94 *See* Cihan Tuğal, *Passive Revolution: Absorbing the Islamic Challenge to Capitalism*, Stanford, CA: Stanford University Press, 2009.
95 Wael Hallaq, *Shari'a: Theory, Practice, Transformations*. New York: Cambridge University Press, 2009 at 444–450.
96 *See generally* Yaşar Nuri Öztürk, *Kur'an Verileri Açisindan Laiklik*. Istanbul: Yeni Boyut, 2003.
97 *See* Yaşar Nuri Öztürk, *Kur'an'daki Islam*. Istanbul: Yeni Boyut, 1997.
98 Öztürk 1999 at 5–11.
99 *Id.* at 66–69.
100 *Id.* at 82.
101 *Id.* at 92.
102 *Id.* at 85.
103 *Id.* at 85–87.
104 *Id.* at 88.
105 Hallaq 2009 at 443–450.
106 *Id.*
107 Wael Hallaq, *Shari'a: An Introduction to Islamic Law.* New York: Cambridge University Press, 2009.
108 *See* Rahman (describing his "double movement" theory of Quranic exegesis).
109 Öztürk 2003 at 82.
110 *See, e.g.*, Dieter Bednarz and Daniel Steinvorth, "Muslim Martin Luthers: 'The Theologians Working Toward a Euro-Islam.'" *Spiegel Online International* April 22, 2008, available at http://www.spiegel.de/international/europe/muslim-martin-luthers-the-theologians-working-towards-a-euro-islam-a-548970–4.html.

111 İren Özgür, "Social and Political Reform through Religious Education in Turkey: The Ongoing Cause of Hayrettin Karaman." *Middle Eastern Studies* 47 (2011): 571.
112 *Id.*
113 Hayrettin Karaman, *Bir Varmış Bir Yokmuş, Vol. 1.* Istanbul: İz Yayıncılık, 2008 at 77–78.
114 Iren Ozgur, "Social and Political Reform Through Religious Education in Turkey: The Ongoing Cause of Hayrettin Karaman." *Middle Eastern Studies*, 47.4 (2011) at 572.
115 Hayrettin Karaman, "İslamcılık." *Yeni Şafak*, February 23, 2003.
116 Ozgur at 574.
117 *Id.*
118 Ömer Tuğrul İnançer, *Goodreads*, available at http://www.goodreads.com/author/show/5225274._mer_Tu_rul_nan_er.
119 Ömer Tuğrul İnançer, "A Lecture of Love (Aşk) on Rumi and His Masnawi". The Prince Alwaleed Bin Talal Islamic Studies Program. Cambridge, MA: Harvard University. March 1, 2013, available at http://www.islamicstudies.harvard.edu/event/a-lecture-of-love-on-rumi-and-his-masnawi/.
120 *Id.*
121 *Id.*
122 *Id.*
123 *Id.*
124 "Presence of Pregnant Women in Public is 'disgraceful,' says Turkish Lawyer." *Hurriyet Daily News*, July 25, 2013, available at http://www.hurriyetdailynews.com/presence-of-pregnant-women-in-public-is-disgraceful-says-turkish-lawyer-.aspx?PageID=238&NID=51380&NewsCatID=341.
125 Lutz Berger, *Ein türkischer Reformtheologe? Zekeriya Beyaz zwischen Tradition und Politik.* Leiden: Brill, 2005 at 74–75.
126 *Id.* at 75.
127 *Id.*
128 Klaus Kreiser, "Turban and Türban: 'Divider between Belief and Unbelief'. A Political History of Modern Turkish Costume." *European Review* 13 (2005): 457.
129 Esra Özyürek, "Convert Alert: German Muslims and Turkish Christians as Threats to Security in the New Europe." *Comparative Studies in Society and History* 51 (2009): 106.
130 "Who's Who in Turkish Culture and Art: Dücane Cündioğlu." *Turkish Cultural Foundation*, 2011, available at http://www.turkishculture.org/whoiswho/literature/ducane-cundioglu-2932.htm.
131 *Id.*
132 *Id.*
133 Brian Silverstein, "Islamist Critique in Modern Turkey: Hermeneutics, Tradition, Genealogy." *Comparative Studies in Society and History* 47 (2005): 150.
134 *Id.*
135 "A Short Outline of the Life of Rumi." *The Whirling Dervishes of Rumi*, available at http://www.whirlingdervishes.org/rumilife.htm.
136 *Id.*
137 *Id.*
138 "Jalal Ad-Din Rumi." *Columbia Electronic Encyclopedia*. 6th ed., New York: Columbia University Press, 2013.
139 *Id.*
140 Phillip Bruckmayr, "Fethullah Gulen and the Islamic Literary Tradition." *Fethullah Gulen's Official Website*, November 27, 2008, available at http://en.fgulen.com/conference-papers/gulen-conference-in-washington-dc/3117-fethullah-gulen-and-islamic-literary-tradition.
141 *Id.*
142 *Id.*

143 Şukran Vahide, "Toward an Intellectual Biography of Said Nursi," in *Islam at the Crossroads: On the Life and Thought of Bediuzzaman Said Nursi*. Ed. Ibrahim M. Abu-Rabi'. New York: SUNY Press, 2003, pp. 1–2.
144 *Id.*
145 *Id.*
146 Bruckmayr, "Fethullah Gulen and the Islamic Literary Tradition." 2008; Phillip Bruckmayr, *Fethullah Gulen and the Islamic Literary Tradition*. Fethullah Gulen's Official Website, November 14–15, 2008.
147 *Id.*
148 "Biography of Turkish PM." *Turkishnews*, July 7, 2011, available at http://www.turkishnews.com/en/content/2011/07/07/biography-of-turkish-pm/.
149 *See* Tuğal at 176; and Rana Foroohar and Pelin Turgut, "Turkey's Man of the People." *Time* 177.26 (2011): 36–40.
150 "Biography of Turkish PM." *Turkishnews*, July 7, 2011.
151 "Democrat or Sultan?" *The Economist*, June 8, 2013, available at http://www.economist.com/news/leaders/21579004-recep-tayyip-erdogan-should-heed-turkeys-street-protesters-not-dismiss-them-democrat-or-sultan.
152 *Id.*
153 Bobby Ghosh and Pelin Turgut, "Erdoğan's Moment." *Time* 178.23 (2011): 38–43.
154 "Lonely Command." *The Economist*, August 24, 2013, available at http://www.economist.com/news/europe/21583989-prime-minister-rules-roost-despite-setbacks-home-and-abroad-lack-serious.
155 *See* Mümtazer Türköne, "'Dershane' Posturing." *Today's Zaman*, November 18, 2013; and "No Back Steps in Education Reform." *The AKP Official Website*, November 22, 2013, available at http://www.akparti.org.tr/english/haberler/no-back-steps-in-education-reform/55778#1.
156 "Abdullah Gül." *Presidency of The Republic of Turkey*, available at http://www.tccb.gov.tr/pages/president/biography/.
157 *Id.*
158 "Turkey's President: A Family Quarrel." *The Economist*, April 15, 2010, available at http://www.economist.com/node/15913054.
159 *Id.*
160 "Abdullah Gül's Biography." *EbruNews*, available at http://news.ebru.tv/en/special/abdullahgul/106.
161 *Id.*
162 "Turkey's President: A Family Quarrel." *The Economist*, April 15, 2010, available at http://www.economist.com/node/15913054.
163 Zaman. *The Zaman Daily*, August 22, 2013, available at http://www.zaman.com.tr/haber.
164 "Zaman's Circulation Hits the 1 Million Mark." *Today's Zaman*. November 24, 2007, available at http://www.todayszaman.com/news-127814-zamans-circulation-hits-1-million-mark.html.
165 "Turkey: Any Information on Zaman Newspaper." *Immigration and Refugee Board of Canada*. Immigration and Refugee Board of Canada, June 12, 2001, available at http://www.refworld.org/docid/3df4beb310.html.
166 "About Today's Zaman." *Today's Zaman*, 2013, available at http://www.todayszaman.com/about-us. http://www.todayszaman.com/about-us.
167 William Armstrong, "Zaman's Circulation Figures – The Gülen Effect?" Turkish Press Review Blog. *Wordpress*, August 20, 2013, available at http://armstrongwilliam.wordpress.com/2013/01/09/zamans-circulation-figures-the-gulen-effect/.
168 "Turkey: Any Information on Zaman Newspaper." *Immigration and Refugee Board of Canada. Immigration and Refugee Board of Canada*, June 12, 2001.
169 A notable exception being Alex Balistreri, *Translating the Republic: Muslim Discourse on Modernity and the Rise of the Turkish Newspaper Zaman*. Doctoral dissertation, Princeton University, 2008.

170 From a presentation at Zaman headquarters on November 5, 2013.
171 Balistreri at 3.
172 *See e.g.*, Hilmi Yavuz, "İslam ve Demokrasi." *Zaman*, October 8, 2006.
173 Balistreri at 4.
174 *Id.* at 127.
175 "Trustees appointed to Zaman media group." *Hürriyet Daily News*, March 4, 2016, available at hurriyetdailynews.com.
176 "Gülen-linked TV stations removed from top satellite network." *Hürriyet Daily News*, November 15, 2015, available at hurriyetdailynews.com.
177 *See e.g.*, Riaz Hassan, "Giving and Gaining: Philanthropy and Social Justice in Muslim Societies." *Lahore Journal of Policy Studies* 1.1 (2007): 25–34.

4 Turkish secularism

Turkey has moved closer to Europe under the leadership of a party rooted in Turkey's Islamist politics, despite early Republican efforts to cut Turkish ties to Islam and to separate the politics of the new regime from religion.[1] The style of secularism in Turkey has ebbed and flowed since the founding of the Turkish Republic in 1923 – though it has roots in the structural reforms of the *tanzimat* period[2] – but the 2001 constitutional amendments increased the textual importance of strict secularism. Secularism (*laiklik*) is a core principle of Kemalist ideology from the founding of the Turkish Republic and appears throughout the Turkish Constitution. The preamble prohibits religious interference in state affairs and politics.[3] The Constitution defines Turkey as democratic and secular, with the strength of its language indicating the importance of secularism to its drafters. The establishment of state organs to control religion is consistent with French secularism, while giving authority to the state apparatus over religion is patently inconsistent with the U.S. tradition of separation of church and state.

A significant shift in the dynamic of Turkish secularism occurred in 2010 when, surprisingly, the Turkish Constitutional Court allowed proposed constitutional amendments to be decided by referendum.[4] These amendments, which were accepted, will have profound long-term impacts on Turkish law and may indicate a move toward more passive secularism that emphasizes free exercise and separation over government control of religion. The passage of the amendments was considered a great victory for the AKP, despite the fact that some consider it an Islamist party.

Although Necmettin Erbakan founded a precursor to contemporary Turkish Islamic parties in 1970,[5] beginning in the 1980s and 1990s, Turgut Özal, and to a lesser extent Süleyman Demirel, had greater influence through blending Islamic sentiment with market economics and conservative politics within center-right parties.[6] Ironically, these parties were not able to maintain the broad base created by the Welfare Party (*Refah Partisi*), which was more explicitly linked to Islamic sentiment than the center-right parties of the 1990s were. Nor were they as successful in integrating religious values with nationalism and liberal economics as was the later AKP. A 2002 survey of AKP voters indicated that a plurality self-identified as "Islamist" (27%), while the rest expressed a mix of seemingly unrelated ideological identifications.[7] This may be evidence that the AKP has been able to transcend its leaders' religious commitments and appeal to a broader segment of Turkish society. Both popular culture and literary expression reflect an increasing Turkish fascination with the country's Ottoman past and may indicate a broader integration with Turkish cultural history.[8]

Given the transformation of religious and political discourse, it is unclear whether leaders of religious parties, and religious leaders of social movements, have replaced deeply held religious convictions with parallel secular commitments. For example, expressing political conservatism, neoliberal economics, or libertarianism may serve as an acceptable secular vocabulary for restating familiar policy positions rather than for adopting a political identity defined by a religious system of belief. These leaders may have determined that more religious Turks are likely to understand political code words, while more secular Turks might assume that these religious leaders have tempered their religiosity in order to participate in the political arena.

Historiography

Five works stand out as important histories of the Turkish Republic and the role of Islam: those of Lewis, Zürcher, Findley, Ahmad, and Meeker. Lewis's *The Emergence of Modern Turkey* is the standard modernist and Orientalist Turkish history. This work reinforces the view that Turkey's development is linear and points toward development, modernity, and secularism. His work has been highly contested by critical, postcolonial, and postmodern scholars; however, some Turkish secularists have embraced Lewis's work because it reinforces Kemalist visions of progress within Turkey. A number of works within political science, anthropology, and sociology inform his study.

Zürcher's *Turkey: A Modern History* is a standard history of the Republic of Turkey. Perhaps the most interesting distinction of his work is his treatment of the period from 1908 to 1950 as a coherent period of transition from the Unionist period to the Republic, placing little emphasis on Atatürk and the formation of the Turkish Republic. This approach represents an important step toward acknowledging continuities between the Ottoman Empire and the Turkish Republic, rather than an approach that argues for their apparent rupture emphasized by other scholars.[9] However, Zürcher does not adequately explain increasing identification with Islam in contemporary Turkish culture and politics.

Findley's *Turkey, Islam, Nationalism and Modernity* consists of three parts. The introduction provides definitions for the terms in the title: Turkey, Islam, nationalism, and modernity. These definitions frame the arguments presented by Findley in the remaining parts of the text. He challenges Lewis's account of Turkey's linear march toward modernity and secularism. Findley proposes a Hegelian dialectical tension between Turkish expressions of modernity and Islamic traditionalism. The books analyzes seven periods of Turkish history. The core of each chapter consists largely of political history, but also addresses economic and social history. Perhaps the most interesting elements in the chapters are the discussions of major religious thinkers – particularly Mevlana Halid, Said Nursi, and

Fethullah Gülen – and the discussion of major literary works from each period. This approach is distinct from that of Lewis and provides a richer, more complex picture of Turkey's evolution. The conclusion is a detailed description and analysis of Orhan Pamuk's *Snow*, illustrating the main themes of the book – particularly the tension between religion and modernity. Findley, whose scholarship is largely of Ottoman history with an emphasis on social history and the development of bureaucracy, appears to have issued a literary response to existing histories of Turkey, such as *The Emergence of Modern Turkey*. He explicitly addresses perspectives beyond the political and engages questions of class, identity, colonialism, and power in a postmodern context as a way to push against the established narratives.

Like Lewis, Feroz Ahmad attempts to provide a thorough examination of the political, social, and economic processes that led to the formation of the Republic of Turkey. His book identifies five developmental periods in modern Turkey. Ahmad begins with a discussion of the Ottoman engagement with Europe, modernization, and the *tanzimat* as a legacy for reforms. The second period spans the revolution of 1908 to Turkish independence in 1923. The third period is the duration of single-party rule. The fourth period of development is the introduction of multiparty politics and the *Demokrat Parti* governments. However, he is primarily concerned with understanding the fifth period of coups – in 1960, 1971, and 1980 – in order to explore the role of the military and the martial character of Turkish culture and history. The book ends in 1989 with the election of Turgut Özal as a hopeful indicator of civilian rule and stability. Unlike Lewis, Ahmad emphasizes social and economic changes, rather than cultural or religious continuities, as the driver of politics. He identifies the upheavals between 1960 and 1983 as a challenge to the view that Kemalism had domesticated or transformed Islam. Further, he identifies modernity in the form of militarism (or perhaps more precisely, praetorianism) and polarizing left–right politics as a source of upheaval. While for Lewis modernity is the panacea for Turkey, for Ahmad modernity is a source of disorder.

Meeker's thesis on the continued importance of imperial social structures and discipline provides a compelling counter-narrative to the traditional model proposed by Lewis – i.e., that the Turkish republic was shaped by competing Turkish and Islamic identities, largely ignoring the legacy of the Ottoman state. His characterization of imperial structures may be overly simple to the extent that it underestimates local variation, opposition, and agency. That being said, Meeker extensively uses a variety of sources to create a rich description supporting his thesis.

The emphasis on continuing Ottoman influence must inform any consideration of Turkish modernity, which did not emerge in a vacuum but within the context of Ottoman reforms at least as far back as the *tanzimat* period.

Social science considering law and religion in Turkey

The contention that the AKP is no longer an Islamic party is supported by some of the most recent and rigorous social science research, including the ethnographic work of Jenny White. Scholars such as Silverstein, Yavuz, Çınar, Kuru, Navaro-Yashin, Çağaptay, and White would agree that the AKP tempered its policies in order to garner broader social support. Kuru and Yavuz, however, consider this shift an authentic endorsement of passive secularism, while Çağaptay remains more skeptical of the motives of the party's leadership. Yavuz and Çınar present optimistic views of religious parties' abilities to reconcile ideology with democracy for a new synthesis within the landscape of Turkish political discourses. However, it is possible that they both underestimate the external power of the military and the judiciary to moderate religiously motivated political positions, resulting in political discourse that might not reflect the actual desires of religious citizens or political parties.

Gülen and Öztürk are arguably the two most influential Turkish religious scholars to address the compatibility of Turkish secularism with Islam. Their influence, which is confirmed by my interviews, is discussed in greater detail in Chapter Three. Both appear to embrace worldviews compatible with Turkish nationalism and exhibit a structural commitment to secularism, but this is within the context of a more permissive position similar to Kuru's soft secularism. However, they take different approaches to integrating this view with Islamic jurisprudence. Öztürk is a modernist who argues that contemporary Muslim jurisprudence need not follow classical *fiqh*. He explicitly allows for new *ijtihad* and views authentic secularism as a natural product of Islam. Gülen does not completely dismiss classical tradition, but he does argue that the structures that make traditional *fiqh* workable no longer exist – and cannot exist. Thus, he implies that new *ijtihad*, along with a broad understanding of state power, makes secularism a reasonable system compatible with Islam when it allows for sufficient free expression. These views are important because they demonstrate a break with the confrontational models used by earlier Nurcu leaders and the *Refah Partisi*. All of these works demonstrate that something new is happening in Turkish political discourses, which has significant implications for understanding the interaction between religion and politics without relying on disputed assumptions of Turkish or Islamic exceptionalism.

A number of works bridge history, political science, and sociology. Soner Çağaptay, for example, studies the development of "Turkishness" in the early decades of the Turkish Republic and considers primary sources from the period. He posits that Turkish identity can be conceived of as three concentric circles: the outer ring consists of non-Muslims (who are only marginally included), the middle ring consists of nonethnic Turkish Muslims (primarily Kurds), and the inner ring consists of ethnic Turks. Therefore, the core of Turkish identity is ethnic and linguistic, the middle layer is religious, and the periphery is territorial. According to Çağaptay, secularizing Islam (Kuru's aggressive secularism entailing state control of religion) was important in defining Turkishness, citizenship, and power relations. Rather than viewing secularism as neutral and objective, he identifies a clear telos to enforce order and conformity. This approach is methodologically postmodern and resembles Edward Said's or Jenny White's approaches more than it does those of Hakan Yavuz or Ahmet Kuru. As a result, Çağaptay is concerned with those outside the core identity – Kurds, Christians, Jews, etc. – who are marginalized by the creation of a unitary Turkish form of Islam under the auspices of state secularism.

Focusing on developments in the 1990s, Çınar argues that Islamist ideology generated an alternative modernization project that applied the same strategies as the modernizing state to produce and institutionalize its own nationalist program. In this context, the covering of women's heads, rooted in the Islamic *hijab* requirements, symbolizes both gender liberation from the West and the struggle to reclaim a national culture. She incorporates elements of critical and postmodern geography, emphasizing the importance of Islamist parties and focusing their efforts on Istanbul, the economic and cultural center of Turkey, rather than Ankara, the political capital. She attributes the AKP's success to its incorporation, perhaps even cooptation, of key Kemalist values in order to transform itself into a broad-based conservative party.

Hakan Yavuz examines Turkish religious parties' experiences with explicit commitments to Islamic religious values. He creates a narrative for the rise of the AKP and its electoral victories in 2002 and 2007 that explains the AKP's ability to shift from dogmatic ideology to conservative yet democratic positions. More importantly, Yavuz examines the AKP electoral victories in 2002 and 2007 and the shift in Turkish political discourses from power sharing between the military and elected politicians to new discourses stressing human rights – and in particular cultural, religious, and property rights. He calls this transformation a "conservative revolution" because civil society led and shaped it, and because political changes followed the social and economic changes, "a bottom-up and gradual revolution in society to control the political language and society; and eventually the state."[10] Yavuz asserts that the newly emerging Turkey is based on three principles: (1) removing secularism as a source of polarization by reimagining "the meaning and function of authoritarian secularism"; (2) redefining political community on the foundation of Ottoman cosmopolitanism rather than on ethnic nationalism; and (3) empowering the democratic state by encouraging "a thickening of civil society" and reducing the role of the public sector.

A number of significant works by sociologists and anthropologists explore Turkey's development of secularism. Göle's *The Forbidden Modern* examines various forms of Islamic expression and imagination in the public sphere, especially those that create dispute. Her emphasis on body, place, space, and time invokes elements of critical and postmodern geography. She discusses the critical importance of urbanization and the strategic choice Islamists made when focusing their efforts on Istanbul. She identifies the strength of the AKP as its ability to relate to modern Turkish communities instead of defining itself as opposing Republican ideals, a stance taken by previous Islamist parties such as *Refah*.

Navaro-Yashin's book, *Faces of the State: Secularism and Public Life in Turkey*, is an anthropological study analyzing the production of the political state during the 1990s in the public sphere of people's lives in Turkey. She questions the use of secularism by making Istanbul the focus of her ethnographic study to demonstrate the distinction between spheres of power and resistance in public life. She evaluates and contextualizes the popular response to the *Refah* Party victory in Istanbul's municipal elections in 1994. Her book wrestles with the apparent division between secularists and Islamists. For Navaro-Yashin, secularism, and not religion, is the source of social tension. She cogently argues that there is a dialectic between the secular and the religious.

In contrast with much of the Muslim world, most Turks consider Islam to be a matter of personal choice and private belief.[11] Most observant Muslims in Turkey do not see this characterization of faith in an Islamic society as illegitimate. Silverstein's book is an ethnographic study of Islamic discourses and their articulation by Turkey's mass media against the background of late Ottoman and early Republican precedents. Like many of the works considered here, Silverstein observes a shift toward integration of Turkish expressions of Islam with a softer form of secularism that emphasizes free exercise of one's religious beliefs.

Although he takes a broader view of the relationship between religion and the modern state, going beyond Turkey alone, Wael Hallaq has wrestled with some of the challenges created by modernism, and secularism in particular, in Muslim cultural contexts.[12] He observes two options. Either Muslim societies

> must succumb to the modern state and the world that produced it, or the modern state and the world that produced it must recognize the legitimacy of Islamic governance, that is the Muslim conception of polity, law, and, most importantly, morality and its subordinated political and economic demands.[13]

The first option leaves little room for maintaining traditional religious identities, and Hallaq is skeptical that the second option is possible. It may be that evolving religious and political identities in Turkey problematize this binary and create new spaces for the reconciling of identities that could result in innovative and hybridized religious and political models.

Empirical studies considering preferences regarding *Shariʿa*

One area that indicates whether the Turkish polity has maintained its interest in secular politics, moved to embrace Islamist approaches, or forged a new understanding of the relationship between Islam and politics is in citizen responses to polls on this question (both quantitative and qualitative). In five major quantitative surveys, Çarkoğlu,[14] Çarkoğlu and Toprak,[15] the Pew Survey on Islam,[16] Kalaycioğlu[17] and Yılmaz,[18] social scientists conducted extensive polling in Turkey related to religious beliefs, party affiliations, and citizens' reactions to Turkish secular policies. Kalaycioğlu and Yılmaz explore overlapping concerns in their studies as well, particularly in regard to political preferences and class.[19] Three qualitative works by White,[20] Tuğal,[21] and Hart[22] are even more illuminating, as discussed below.

Quantitative studies

The existing studies on Turkish voter preferences suggest that, despite the Western concerns that the Turkish polity is significantly modifying its views toward traditional Islamist positions seen in other Arab nations, Turks continue to vote based more on secular concerns such as economic policy than they do on religious criteria. Although there are no detailed quantitative studies from the 1970s and 1980s, the periodical *Nokta* has claimed that the preference for *Shari'a* remained approximately 7% during the period.[23] Surveys by TÜSES in 1995, 1996, and 1998 indicated a spike to over 20%. Çarkoğlu's 1999 survey indicates a rate of 21%. Çarkoğlu and Toprak's 2007 study, *Religion, Society and Politics in a Changing Turkey*, captures the attitudes and preferences expressed by Turkish voters regarding issues such as religion, secularism, and democracy.[24] The authors gauge changes in respondent inclinations toward a secular society or theocratic state against the backdrop of political and economic reform in Turkey. Contrary to the expectations of some, the percentage of those who preferred a religious state declined from 21% in 1999 to only 9% in 2006.[25] Yet the report finds that there is a significant increase in the percentage of people who describe themselves as Muslim.[26] The authors suggest that identity politics have not swayed voters from democratic values or the secular system,[27] and that the gap in understanding between secularists and Islamists can be bridged through education.[28] The 2011 Pew survey included almost all predominantly Muslim countries and provided more detailed data related to understandings of *Shari'a*.[29] In that study, the percentage of people in Turkey desiring the application of *Shari'a* was 12%.

Kalaycioğlu's study, *Party Identification, Islam and Secularism in Turkey*, acknowledges that the current Turkish party system is only a few decades old and that some parties are even younger.[30] Therefore, Kalaycioğlu claims that scant evidence of psychological ties between voters and the political parties they support should be expected at the polls during Turkish elections.[31] As he documents, earlier research on Turkish parties and voting behavior indicated that Turkey often hosts a large number of political parties due to cultural and ideological divisions.[32] Prior literature indicated that the secular–Islamist divide is partly responsible for the sociocultural cleavages dividing the Turkish electorate.[33] However, Kalaycioğlu created and tested a causal model assessing the relative influence that ideological, economic, and psychological (party identification) factors exert in the political party preferences of Turkish voters, referencing national survey data from July 2007.[34] Kalaycioğlu's research suggests that macroeconomic policy and performance by ruling parties, as well as sociocultural preferences, play relatively large roles in determining party preferences of Turkish voters.[35] Although religiosity influences party selection, he argues that rational choice appears more important than dogma in Turkish electoral politics, at least in the case of the AKP.[36] One handicap for the AKP is that, as a new party, it does not have the benefit of family socialization enjoyed by more established parties.

Yilmaz's study is the most extensive survey of Turkish class differences and the preference for secularism.[37] Its main finding is that the Turkish middle class has a general preference for secularism.[38] His work is particularly helpful for delineating class boundaries, based on economic and social factors, in addition to boundaries generated by individual self-description of class and social rank.[39] Although it is an important study of class in Turkish society, it does not explore the contours of religious identity or preferences for secularism. The WVS, although less helpful than studies designed specifically for Turkey, provides extensive survey data gathered internationally and includes Turkey.[40] The study includes questions related to Islamic belief and practice that were only asked in predominantly Muslim countries and confirms similar domestic surveys concluding that religious identification among Turks is increasing,[41] though it makes no determination about the effect of that change on secular politics.

Qualitative works

Important qualitative studies by Jenny White and Cihan Tuğal show that political parties' appeals to class expectations may account for the uptick in voter identification with religion and religious parties. Kimberly Hart's study of religious practice and identity in rural western Turkey provides a helpful supplement to work focusing on major urban centers. Jenny White's book, *Islamist Mobilization in Turkey: A Study in Vernacular Politics*, is a rich ethnographic study on the role of political Islam in urban Istanbul neighborhoods where she conducted fieldwork from 1986 to 1998 (although her work focuses mainly on the mid-1990s).[42] Her primary tools – observations and interviews – offer a complex narrative that explain the appeal of Islamist parties, particularly the *Refah Partisi*, among poor and working-class city dwellers. She describes the Islamist strategy as "vernacular politics," which she defines as "a value-centered political process rooted in local culture, interpersonal relations, and community networks, yet connected through civic organizations to national party politics."[43] Although secular political organizers were active in the neighborhoods White studied, they were occasionally perceived as elitist, in part because they did not contextualize their messages in the language of the local community values discourse.[44]

Tuğal's *Passive Revolution* engages similar questions, emphasizing the transition from the *Refah* period in the 1990s to the rise of the AKP.[45] His study indicates that class plays a role in Turkish voters' visions of modernity and secularism, but he reaches a different conclusion than does White.[46] The divergent conclusions may be a consequence of the fact that his research, mainly in Sultanbeyli, engaged a different group of voters. Like White, Tuğal worked primarily in poor neighborhoods and acknowledged significant religious and political diversity within this community. However, he observed an overlap between traditionalist Islamic politics, particularly among *Refah* supporters, and pro-labor or even socialist sympathies among these voters.[47] In longitudinal studies, he identifies a shift to AKP support among many of the same individuals that parallels a shift toward pro-market liberal policy preferences and, in many cases, toward upward social mobility.[48] This may provide an explanation for similar shifts in the quantitative large-*n* studies, indicating an increased preference for secularism among respondents between the mid-1990s and the late 2000s.[49]

Hart's work provides a fascinating alternative example that both confirms observations made in urban settings and creates distinctions. Like White, she finds that religious activity creates spaces for education, leadership, and activism for women.[50] Although Tuğal notes the role of the AKP and Nurcu organizations among the urban working class and poor in Istanbul, Hart finds a rural corollary in the Süleymanli movement, which operates much more discretely. She observes the importance of Quran courses and discussion groups in providing religious training and community identity to a largely marginalized socioeconomic community, one where urban-based political and religious organizations do not invest significantly. That said, there is both a tension between the norms of secularism and religious identity and an attempt to reconcile them. For some people this means an internalization of official Islam as represented by *Diyanet*, but for others it means participation in a *tarikat* and membership in a *Cemaat* as a path for preserving their vision of authentic Islam.[51] Although villagers may participate in the political process, they tend to be marginalized as a matter of economics, so it is not surprising that groups active in these poor rural communities, like the Süleymanli, have operated to some extent at the margins.

Although White, Tuğal, and Hart describe key elements of class, religious, and political identities, they arrive at different conclusions. This creates the need for a new study that can resolve and contextualize their competing claims and to explore the role of religious and class identity in influencing preferences for secularism, which none of the authors specifically address.

The most striking aspect of contemporary empirical work on Turkish secularism is the voters' shift toward softer secularism and the increased favorability of the free exercise of religion, despite varying scholarly methods and theoretical perspectives. Although current research has not produced consensus regarding the reasons behind this shift, Tuğal is particularly helpful for uncovering the appeal of the AKP as it embraces elements of both Kemalism and economic liberalism in the context of religious conviction. Turkey polls as a very religious country.[52] Although the Kemalist elite suppressed many expressions of Islam early in the Republic, religious sentiments reemerged in the public sphere with the advent of multiparty politics. Religion was used to counter leftist strategies after the 1980 coup and was artfully linked to neoliberal economic thought.[53] The suppression of *Refah* in 1997 resulted partly from its opposition to the Kemalist narrative.[54] The AKP succeeded because it deferred to core Kemalist principles and characterized its distinctiveness in terms of Western rights discourse and liberal economics.[55]

It is clear from the theoretical and empirical studies of secularism and *Shari'a* in Turkey that views have shifted over the past 25 years. Orientalist scholars identified secularism with the Kemalist modernization project.[56] Lewis and others observed that lower religiosity and the preference for secularism likely correlate with education level (perhaps as a proxy for class) and government employment (particularly in the military).[57] White's work interrogated this commonly held assumption and presents convincing evidence that the urban poor and working-class Istanbul neighborhoods she studied in the 1990s defy this pattern, implying that religion, class, and political inclinations have a more complex set of interrelationships.[58] Tuğal's later study of similar neighborhoods indicates a shift in Islamic politics from an emphasis on social justice and communitarianism toward conservative market economics.[59] It remains unclear whether this shift reflects economic growth and changing boundaries of class or if it reflects other factors. However, it does invite a deeper exploration of the meanings attributed to Islam and Islamic law in Turkey.

Polls in Turkey over the past 25 years indicate shifting views of secularism, religion, and market economics.[60] The most recent elections, constitutional reforms, and proposed amendments indicate changes that deserve further empirical study. It is likely that views of secularism are influenced by multiple factors, including education, religiosity, and gender. The following chapters will consider the factors influencing views of secularism and *Shariʿa* based on my data, which was collected over the first five months of 2013.

Notes

1 Russell Powell. "Evolving Views of Islamic Law in Turkey." *Journal of Law and Religion* 28.2 (2013): 467–487 at 468–470.
2 *See, e.g.*, Findley 2010 at 91–106.
3 The Constitution of the Republic of Turkey November 7, 1982, preamble (as amended) ("The recognition that no protection shall be accorded to an activity contrary to Turkish national interests, the principle of the indivisibility of the existence of Turkey with its state and territory, Turkish historical and moral values or the nationalism, principles, reforms and modernism of Atatürk and that, as required by the principle of secularism, there shall be no interference whatsoever by sacred religious feelings in state affairs and politics . . .").
4 *See* "Turkish Key Constitutional Reforms Annulled by Court." *BBC News*, July 7, 2010, available at http://www.bbc.co.uk/news/10547710.
5 Cihan Tuğal, *Passive Revolution: Absorbing the Islamic Challenge to Capitalism.* Stanford, CA: Stanford University Press, 2009 at 42–49.
6 Ozal from ANAP (The Motherland Party) and Demirel from the Doğru Yol (The True Path Party) were the leading politicians in the transition from the 1980 coup to the end of the 20th century. Both held to a center-right political position, particularly with regard to market reforms and economic liberalization. Both also maintained a public piety that won support from some voters who desired a greater public role for Islam. By the mid-90's, their parties lost influence to expressly Islamist parties (Refah in particular), but their centrist political and economic positions were later adopted by former Refah leaders who formed the AKP. *See e.g.*, Findley at 351–359; Tuğal at 41–46.
7 Hakan Yavuz, *Secularism and Muslim Democracy in Turkey.* New York: Cambridge University Press, 2009 at 108.
8 *See generally* Özyürek; or Yavuz at 95 ("One of the key unifying factors among the leadership of the AKP is a powerful conviction that the Ottoman past holds the key to the future of Turkey . . . This reconstruction of Ottoman identity has been at work for the last three decades and has recently been articulated in art, literature, cuisine and politics.").
9 Lewis reinforces the narrative that a rupture exists between the traditions of the Ottoman Empire and the formation of a society as the Turkish Republic. This rupture is common within the more traditional histories of the Turkey.
10 Yavuz 2009 at 13.
11 *See* Çarkoğlu and Toprak.
12 *See* generally Wael Hallaq, *The Impossible State: Islam, Politics, and Modernity's Moral Predicament.* New York: Columbia University Press, 2013.
13 *Id.* at 162.

14 Ali Çarkoğlu, "Religiosity, Support for Şeriat and Evaluations of Secularist Public Policies in Turkey." *Middle Eastern Studies* 40.2 (2004): 111–136.
15 *See* Çarkoğlu and Toprak.
16 Pew Research Religion & Public Life Project, "The World's Muslims: Religion, Politics and Society." April 30, 2013.
17 *See* Ersin Kalaycıoğlu, "Party Identification, Islam and Secularism in Turkey." Paper presented at the annual meeting of the ISA's 49th Annual Convention, Bridging Multiple Divides, Hilton San Francisco, San Francisco, CA, USA, March 26, 2008, available at http://citation.allacademic.com/meta/p253518_index.html.
18 Hakan Yılmaz, *In Search of a Turkish Middle Class: Economic Occupations, Political Orientations, Social Life-Styles, Moral Values: Summary of the Basic Findings.* Istanbul: Bogazici University, 2008, available at http://hakanyilmaz.info/yahoo_site_admin/assets/docs/HakanYilmaz-2007-MiddleClassInTurkey-Summary.28470755.pdf.
19 Russell Powell at 470–474.
20 Jenny White, *Islamist Mobilization in Turkey: A Study in Vernacular Politics*. Seattle: University of Washington Press, 2002.
21 Tuğal.
22 *See* Kimberly Hart, *And then We Work for God: Rural Sunni Islam in Western Turkey*. Stanford, CA: Stanford University Press, 2013.
23 Nokta, October 17, 1986.
24 Çarkoğlu and Toprak.
25 *Id.* at 13.
26 *Id.*
27 *Id.* at 13–14.
28 *Id.* at 14–15.
29 Pew Research Religion & Public Life Project.
30 Kalaycioğlu 2008 at 5 and 17.
31 *Id.* at 14–16.
32 *Id.* at 4–6.
33 *Id.*
34 *Id.* at 2.
35 *Id.* at 17–18.
36 *Id.*
37 *See* H. Yılmaz, Although Yilmaz' study is extremely interesting, it does not address the inherently problematic theoretical and analytical problems raised by class as a category.
38 *Id.* at 6. This study found employment, salary, education, and residence to be critical self-indicators of class in Turkey. A salary below 750TL per month would presume a lower class in the study and a salary over 2,500TL per month would presume upper class. Government employment has typically been presumed to indicate middle class in previous studies, so that response might be associated with middle class.
39 *Id.* at 3–7.
40 World Values Survey 2005.
41 World Values Survey 1981–2008. Official Aggregate v.20090901, 2009. World Values Survey Association, available at http://www.wvsevsdb.com/wvs/WVSData.jsp.
42 White at ix–xi.
43 *Id.* at 27.
44 *Id.* at 242.
45 Tuğal at 95.
46 *Id.*
47 *See id.* at 60–77 and 137–144.
48 *Id.*
49 *See, e.g.*, Çarkoğlu and Toprak.

50 *See e.g.*, Hart at 11–12, explaining the training and role of female *hoca*'s within rural Süleymanci communities.
51 *Id.* at 195–222.
52 *See* World Values Survey 2009.
53 *See* Tuğal.
54 *Id.*
55 *Id. See also* Yavuz.
56 *See, e.g.*, Bernard Lewis, *The Emergence of Modern Turkey.* New York & Oxford: Oxford University Press, 2002.
57 *Id.*
58 *See* White.
59 *See* Tuğal.
60 *See, e.g.*, Çarkoğlu and Toprak.

5 Descriptive analysis of data

Descriptive claims are based on the telephone poll, which was conducted during February 2013. The data is a snapshot from the time directly before the *Gezi* protests and the subsequent political conflict. Although it may not accurately describe views today, it may provide context for the strong reactions to the perceived excessive use of police force, the alleged corruption, the mobilization of religious organizations, and the alleged government targeting of religious groups. According to the operating hypothesis of the study, we should expect a stronger (though inverse) correlation between education and views of *Shariʿa* than religiosity.[1] A correlation between an independent variable and dependent variable may allow an inference of causality that will inform the qualitative interview data.

A total of 935 voting-age Turkish citizens were interviewed using random sample techniques commonly used for political polling in Turkey (as described in the introduction). The sample differs from the actual distribution within Turkey in three areas: First, the rate of female respondents in the sample is approximately 2% higher than that of the population. Second, the average age and the distribution of age of respondents vary somewhat from the Turkish norm. For example, the percentage of respondents age 18 to 25 tended to be lower than the actual distribution among Turkish voters (15% in the survey versus 17.3% in the Turkish population). Third, perhaps as a result of the age of the sample, the employment numbers tend to vary somewhat from the Turkish population. It is also notable that the level of literacy and education in the sample is slightly higher than the general distribution within Turkey. Unless otherwise noted, all descriptive statistics are unweighted, and all correlational statistics are weighted to account for gender, education, and employment using propensity score matching.

The Internet survey is more difficult to situate, so it is much less informative than the telephone poll. As a result, I have limited its use in this chapter to checking the main correlations and providing speculative numbers using propensity weighting for questions that were not asked in the telephone poll.[2]

Table 5.1 Situating the telephone poll sample

Demographic Characteristics	*Unweighted Results*	*Turkish Norm*[a]
Rate of Female Population	51%	49%
Median Age	40 years[b]	30.1 years
Effective % under the Age of 30	49.5%[c]	51%
Unemployed	2.5%	8.2%
Rate of Illiteracy	2%	4.7%
Those with some Higher Education	24%	Minimum 16%[d]

a Demographic information is based on data from TUİK (The Turkish Statistical Institute).

b This number is provided for reference purposes, but it is not comparable to the median age for the entire Turkish population. The participants in the study were 18 and over, so the median age does not include anyone under 18.

c The percentage of the Turkish population under 18 is 29.7%, and 28% of the participants in the poll were between 18 and 30, giving a plausible effective rate of 49.5% under 30.

d 4% of the Turkish population has completed higher vocational education, 7% have completed university, 1% of the population has completed graduate school, and 4% are currently enrolled in higher education, for a minimum of 16%. There is no reliable source for specific percentages of adults who have received some higher education without completing a program, so the percentage meeting the criteria for the poll is presumably higher.

Preference for *Shari'a*

In response to the statement, "I would like to have a *Shari'a*-based state founded in Turkey," 2.4% strongly agreed and 17.2% agreed, for a total of 19.6% of the sample desiring *Shari'a*. When weighted, that number jumps to 23.1%. Even with the maximum margin of error[3] of 6.5%, this indicates an increase – perhaps a large increase – over the Pew survey from 2011, which was at 12% (itself an increase since 2006).

This polling question, or others quite similar to it, has been asked since 1995. Through the 1970s and 80s, *Nokta* reported that the rate of the Turkish population in favor of *Shari'a* was at about 7%.[4] The TÜSES Foundation conducted surveys in 1995, 1996, and 1998, indicating a rise to 19.9% in 1995.[5] By 1996, it had risen to 26.7% and then in 1998 dropped again to 19.8%.[6] The 1996 rise coincides with the rise of the first arguably Islamist government in 1996, which was led by the *Refah* Party and then Prime Minister Necmettin Erbakan. By 1998, the government was forced out by the military in the 1997 "Soft" or "Postmodern" Coup. In a similar study conducted in 1999, the rate of those desiring *Shari'a* rose to 21%.[7] The rate then drops to 16.4% in 2002[8] and then to 8.9% in 2006.[9] As previously noted, the 2011 Pew survey then shows a rise to 12%,[10] while the 2013 telephone poll indicates support increasing to between 19% and 23%. The passage of laws regulating the advertising and sale of alcohol and public displays of affection in May 2013 may reflect increasing comfort with conforming law with Islamic moral norms on the part of the AKP, even if they do not rise to the level of legislating *Shari'a* rules.

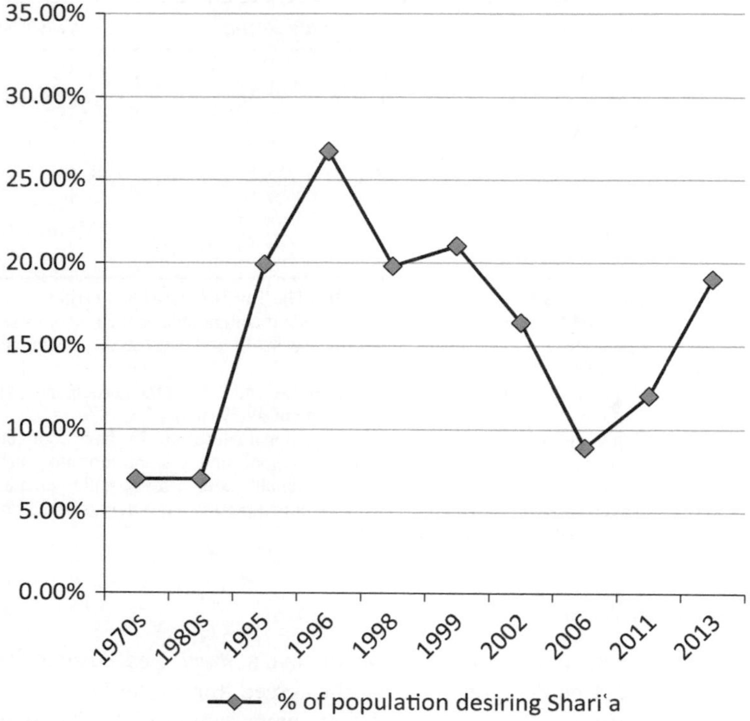

Figure 5.1 Percentage of population desiring *Shari'a*

At a time when mass protests against the government have largely been framed as secular, the increase in sympathy for the imposition of *Shari'a* may indicate an increasing polarization between religious and secular politics in Turkey. However, it also invites a deeper inquiry into the meaning attributed to *Shari'a* by Turkish citizens.

Religion

One key question motivating this study was the role of religiosity and education in shaping views toward *Shari'a*. The weighted results of polling indicate that 4.1% of respondents are very religious, 83.5% are religious, 5.3% are not very religious, 0.9% are not at all religious, and 6.2% were not sure or did not answer.[11] These numbers are fairly consistent with previous studies.[12]

Several studies have asked questions regarding religious freedom. There has been some variance in the perception of freedom to practice religion in Turkey.[13] More than 60% of those surveyed in the Internet survey indicated that religious people are able to freely practice their faith in Turkey.[14] When asked whether religious people are under oppression, 23% answered affirmatively, which is an increase from a 2006 study.[15] At 29%, more people indicated that religion itself was oppressed.

In response to the parallel question regarding whether secularism is under oppression, the Internet survey indicates a rise to 50%.[16] This might indicate further polarization between religiously and secularly identified people. Slightly more people indicated that nonreligious people are oppressed. As with the term *Shari'a*, using the term "*laik*" in Turkish raises significant questions of meaning. The Internet survey asked two questions regarding secularism: one regarding ideal secularism and one regarding Turkish secularism as it currently exists. In both questions, subjects were asked to choose any combination of the following: freedom of religion, freedom of expression, freedom from social pressure to be religious, separation of religion and state, government control of religious institutions, limits on public religious practice, prohibition on headscarves, government control of religious education, incorporation of religious symbols and discourse in public life, and removal of religious symbols and discourse from public life. Responses describing Turkish secularism tended to emphasize government control of religion, but the most commonly chosen traits for ideal secularism were freedom of expression (75%), freedom of religion (73%), and separation (70%). While 48% indicated that their ideal of secularism includes freedom from social pressure to be religious, only 33% indicated a belief that this is already a component of Turkish secularism. It is clear from the survey that a majority of Turks who participated desire less governmental entanglement with religion, a view that would seem to be at odds with the enforcement of *Shari'a* rules.

What is *Shari'a*?

Perhaps the most important question asked in this study is "what is *Shari'a*?" In the telephone poll, the online survey, and the face-to-face interviews, subjects were asked to "[b]riefly describe [their] understanding of *Shari'a*." Along with specific questions regarding the content and applicability of *Shari'a*, the responses to these questions provide greater context for political preferences related to law and religion.

Although responses in the Internet survey and interviews tend to correlate with responses in the telephone poll, for purposes of making descriptive observations, comments will be limited to the telephone poll unless otherwise noted. The most common answer to the question "what is *Shari'a*?" was "no comment" or "I don't know," which made up about 15% of the total responses. I would separate the remaining responses into three categories: descriptive, critical, and apologetic.

Descriptive comments

Descriptive comments were quite varied and bore the appearance of objectivity; however, it is possible that comments implying a negative feature represent a negative view of *Shari'a*, while comments implying a positive feature, such as justice, might represent a positive view of *Shariʿa*. Most descriptive responses in the poll tended to be quite broad. The single most common response in this category, and the second most common overall, was "Islamic law," or something similar such as "Islamic rules," "the law of God," or "religious law."[17] These responses capture the sense of *Shariʿa* as rules established by God, but they do not indicate the complexity of the systems of jurisprudence attempting to identify those rules. There are a number of related responses that addressed the question of the sources and interpretations of *Shariʿa*. The most common answer of this sort asserted that *Shariʿa* "is the Quran," "comes from the Quran," or "is based on the Quran." It was such a common response that it may actually have been influenced by Quran-only movements and by prominent religious leaders who adopt that view (such as Yaşar Nuri Öztürk).[18] Some respondents mentioned the *Sunna* along with the Quran, and a very small number of responses referred to classical jurisprudence or the *ulema*. These responses may indicate an understanding of the need for interpretation of the sources to discern the *Shariʿa* and leave space for the pluralism of the classical *fiqh* tradition.

A significant number of descriptive comments mentioned morality rather than law. It is possible that those respondents were simply emphasizing the moral content of *Shariʿa*, which may be more common in a secular legal system that does not intentionally enforce *Shariʿa* rules.

This could also indicate a naturalistic turn – conflating morality with law – or it might indicate a preference for privatizing religion and for relegating it to individual, moral choice. Where the latter is true, such comments might be viewed as critical of *Shariʿa*.[19]

A third category of descriptive comments identified a theory or historical source of *Shariʿa*. Several responses indicated that it means "reciprocity," or tit-for-tat, a very important underlying principle in the legal and moral thought of Islam, as well as in many other faith traditions. Some respondents simply noted that it comes from Arabia or Arab culture.

Critical comments

Overtly critical comments describing "*Shariʿa*" were common in the survey (more common than clearly apologetic comments, but less common than apparently descriptive comments). These responses tended to be longer and addressed multiple points. The three most common criticisms related to (1) *Shariʿa*'s presumed incompatibility with Turkish secularism (sometimes indicated by law, the Republic, or the system); (2) assertions that *Shariʿa* is harmful to women; and (3) general negative identifiers. Comments related to incompatibility with Turkish secularism were occasionally much longer than average and frequently appeared to reflect a strong emotional reaction to the question. There were numerous references to Atatürk, the Turkish Republic, and secularism. Many responses indicated concerns that *Shariʿa* is unfair or harmful to women, and there were several references to polygamy, rape, and the killing of women within these responses. Some responses noted legal inequity based on gender or religion. General negative criticisms included descriptors such as "authoritarian," "fundamentalist," "strict," "bigoted," "terrible," "insular," "denying of freedom," "oppressive," "discriminatory," "totalitarian," "imperial," "abnormal," "undesirable," etc. Perhaps the simplest sort of critical response was "We are against *Shari'a*."

There were a handful of interesting critical comments made from a religious perspective indicating that the enforcement of *Shari'a* would inevitably be arbitrary and that it would discourage authentic religion. This view may acknowledge the interpretive exercise and potential uncertainty in the *fiqh* tradition, but it is potentially at odds with the principle that following the rules of a *madhab* is good even when the rule is not actually God's rule. It implies the need for a new method for determining what religious rules are appropriate for the state to enforce – one that would presumably result in little or no enforcement, with the goal of maximizing individual freedom. Here the implicit argument for privatizing religion is not made for the benefit of freedom itself but because free choice presumably leads to a more meaningful and authentic religious experience.[20] It may also indicate concern regarding the enforcement of any "*Shari'a*" rule that is not certain. Some comments went so far as to describe *Shari'a* as secularism, that is, that secularism is the best approach to law and religion in a Muslim context.

Apologetic responses

There were two broad categories of apologetic responses. The first was prescriptive – "God requires it," or something similar. The second was rhetorical, presenting a case for the reasonableness of *Shari'a* in the Turkish context – e.g., good law, true freedom, justice, basic rights, clear rules, no cruelty, etc. Not surprisingly, those who provided such responses were more likely to indicate a preference for enforcing *Shari'a*. They were also more likely to agree with statements such as, "*Shari'a* requires legal equality regardless of gender, race, religion, or other difference"; "*Shari'a* requires that the basic health and educational needs of all be met"; "*Shari'a* provides religious freedom"[21]; "*Shari'a* is a path for living a moral life"; and "*Shari'a* provides economic freedom."[22]

It is clear that people bring different and multiple meanings to *Shari'a*. Those in Turkey who oppose it may understand it in terms of presumed negative attributes; those who support it are likely to understand it in terms of presumed positive attributes. However, a significant number of respondents indicated similar values – such as freedom, justice, equality, good governance, etc. – but differed as to whether they believed *Shari'a* diminishes or supports those values. This is further complicated by those subjects who reject the classical approach to jurisprudence, but not the ideal of *Shari'a*, and imagine compatibility between Turkish Republican political and legal structures and their vision of *Shari'a*.

***Shari'a* process**

Of those who imagine enforcing *Shari'a* – whether supportive of it or opposed to the idea – many have a particular view of what its enactment might mean. There is actually some consensus regarding some of the policy aims of *Shari'a*. However, even for those who desired it, there is little agreement regarding the process and parties necessary for enforcing *Shari'a* in Turkey.

The poll contained three questions regarding the way in which *Shari'a* might be enacted, as well as its content: The first referred to equality regardless of gender, race, religion, or other difference; the second referred to the economic rights of education and health; and the third referred to religious freedom. With regard to equality, 79.7% of respondents (80.8% weighted) agreed that it is a requirement of *Shari'a*. With regard to health and education, 74% (76% weighted) agreed that they are rights required by *Shari'a*. With regard to freedom of religion, 49% (50.1% weighted) agreed that *Shari'a* provides for it.

The Internet survey asked "whether *Shari'a* is a path for a moral life" and "whether it provides economic freedom." Forty percent agreed with the former and only 24% with the latter. The survey also asked respondents to identify "Islamic values" from a list of 28 options. The three most common choices were "charity" (71%), "justice" (70%), and "love" (68%). The next most common answers were "honesty" (65%), "family" (64%), "mercy" (64%), "prayer" (64%), and "tolerance" (64%). Presumably, those who support *Shari'a* would likely associate these principles with *Shari'a*, while those who oppose *Shari'a* would likely not identify these principles as the consequences of establishing a *Shari'a* state.

Each stage of the study asked whether *Shari'a* is "an individual moral obligation," "a state option," "a state requirement," or "neither a moral obligation nor a state option." In the telephone poll, 26.1% of respondents agreed that the state ought to, or could appropriately enforce, *Shari'a* (29.2% weighted). That group was then asked a number of follow-up questions regarding how enforcement might be achieved. The weighted percentage of those agreeing that the most influential *madhab* ought to have jurisdiction was 48.8%. Only 43.3% agreed that judges must follow the precedent of their *madhab* (an implicit rejection of *taqlid*). So, there does not appear to be agreement that the classical schools of thought ought to provide the rules or the process. However, 69.9% agreed that *Shari'a* rules ought to be memorialized in legal codes, which seems to indicate sympathy for the Ottoman experiments with codifying *fiqh* rules. The online survey also asked whether judges could interpret for themselves (*ijtihad*) as opposed to relying on precedent within a *madhab*: 45% agreed, 25% disagreed, and 30% were undecided. These numbers may indicate sympathy for modernist approaches to Islamic jurisprudence, which relieve jurists from the obligation of ruling according to precedent in the form of *taqlid* and allows them to interpret directly from the sources of *fiqh*. The telephone poll asked those who believe that *Shari'a* could be appropriately enforced to name the primary group responsible for determining how to enforce it. Responses fell into three categories. First, a number of respondents identified "the people" as the primary group tasked with enforcing *Shari'a*. This answer might reflect a commitment to democracy and may also reflect some degree of suspicion of governmental bodies, which is the second broad category. The part of the government that ought to be responsible for enforcing *Shari'a* was highly disputed. The most commonly mentioned organ was *Diyanet*. Many others simply indicated the government or the state. Some mentioned the parliament or even the prime minister. Some indicated judges or the courts. This diversity of opinion makes it difficult to imagine how government agencies or officials would choose to enforce *Shariʿa*. For example, statutes might be passed by the legislature, courts might be given broad power to interpret Islamic legal sources, or government agencies (*Diyanet*) might adopt an enforcement proposal. The poll and the survey results reflect the tension between reliance on experts in classical tradition and the need for nonexpert politicians and judges to provide legitimacy with statutes and legal decisions.[23] The third category of responses referred to religious scholars, Islamic jurists, or the *ulema*. There might be some overlap here with *Diyanet*, but it is also possible that these parties were preferred as nongovernmental actors with specialized knowledge in the field (like the classical *mufti*).

Previous studies asked relatively few questions regarding the process for including Islam in law. However, the question of whether Islam needs to be reinterpreted in the modern context was asked in a 1999 study and again in 2006; both times, approximately 35% agreed and 50% disagreed.[24] The 2006 study followed up with the narrower question of whether Islam needs to be reorganized in line with case law such that many parts must be reinterpreted within the modern context. There, 41% agreed and only 28% disagreed, indicating a broader acceptance of selective modernist reinterpretation to conform to Turkish law.[25]

One procedural question that has been asked in multiple studies is whether *Shariʿa* applies to non-Muslims. The 2011 Pew survey found that 5% of respondents favored applying *Shariʿa* to both Muslims and non-Muslims, while 6% favored applying it to Muslims only.[26] This question was only asked of those who indicated a preference for enforcing *Shariʿa*. The 2013 online survey asked the same question of all subjects: 20% agreed that *Shariʿa* applies to both Muslims and non-Muslims. The difference in results may be explained by agreement on the part of those opposing *Shariʿa* increasing the percentage in the online survey. After accounting for this difference in question methodology, the results are comparable (both below 10%). The most interesting aspect of this question is that a much higher percentage of Muslims in Southeast Asia, South Asia, and the Middle East–North Africa favor applying *Shariʿa* to all citizens, with approval ranging from 14% in Lebanon to 61% in Afghanistan.[27] Most European and Central Asian jurisdictions surveyed have rates comparable to Turkey (with the exception of Kyrgyzstan).[28] This may be explained by the tradition of legal secularism found in all of those jurisdictions, or it may be related to common Turkic cultures. In any case, there is a commonly held understanding that *Shariʿa* applies only to those who are members of the faith community. To that extent, there is an implicit privatization of religion and *Shariʿa*, which narrows its scope; only those who have consented by membership are considered subject to its jurisdiction. The classical approach to this question in Islamic jurisprudence is quite complicated, but there are clear cases when *Shariʿa* would apply to non-Muslims as a choice of law matter. The clearest example would be in disputes involving both Muslim and non-Muslim parties.[29]

The most important conclusion from this part of the study is that, even among those who express a preference for *Shariʿa*, there is no consensus regarding the sources, interpreters, scope, implementation, and method of effecting the enforcement of *Shariʿa*. Many respondents expressed skepticism toward government that would make any governmental move toward enforcing *Shariʿa* the likely subject of severe public scrutiny and criticism. This would appear consistent with the negative reactions to the 2013 codification of rules related to alcohol and public displays of affection.

Shariʿa rules

The question "what *Shariʿa* requires" is complex even for people who basically agree about methodology. In the interviews, a number of people commented that the question was easy because the rules were contained in books. By books, some meant the Quran, others meant the Quran and the *Sunna*, and others understood that classical *fiqh* manuals also contain rules. Most people did not seem to have a sophisticated understanding of classical methodology, which was historically pluralistic and developed far more rules than are contained in the Quran and the *Sunna*. Like many professors of Islamic law, I ask my students to study the various texts – the Quran, the *Sunna*, and the *fiqh* – related to winedrinking and intoxication. It becomes apparent to the students that the canonical sources contain tensions and apparent contradictions, and that the *fiqhi* jurisprudence results in competing rules. Each phase of this study included a number of questions asking what *Shariʿa* requires. A separate battery of questions addressed criminal punishment required by the canonical sources – ***hadd*** or ***hudud*** – which will be discussed later.

Gender

Four questions in the study related to *Shariʿa* rules regarding gender and the role and status of women. The first asked whether *Shariʿa* requires a woman to cover her hair. The issue of covering, or *hijab*, has been considered in several important books and articles,[30] and there is dispute among believing Muslims in Turkey as to what is actually required as a matter of faith and conscience. In the telephone poll, 49.3% of respondents agreed that *Shariʿa* requires that Muslim women cover their hair (50.8% weighted). The interviews indicated that people generally expressed what they believed to be the religious requirement, but there was also an indication that some answers may have reflected personal moral belief even if they believed that "*Shariʿa*" might require something different. Therefore, it is possible that the percentage agreeing is artificially low. However, the interviews indicated that some religious women believe that it is possible to comply with the Islamic requirement of modest dress without covering their hair. The Internet survey confirms that, regardless of the religious requirement or the legal prohibition, a majority of participants believe that women should be free to cover their hair, even in universities (85% in the Internet survey).[31] Of those who do cover their hair, nearly three-quarters do so because they believe that God requires it.[32]

The second question related to gender asked whether *Shariʿa* provides that daughters inherit half that of sons. Only 32% of those asked agreed.[33] Similarly, in response to the third gender-related question, which asked whether the legal testimony of a woman is worth half that of a man, 28% agreed. The final question related to gender asked whether *Shari'a* allows men to marry up to four wives, and only 18% of those polled agreed. The 2011 Pew survey asked whether the traditional practice of polygamy was "moral," and 13% of respondents agreed that it was moral. The lower approval rate in the Pew survey may be attributable to the fact that people may believe the practice is immoral, even if they understand it to be allowed by Islamic legal tradition. The 1999 TESEV survey asked whether respondents would approve of legalizing the traditional practice of polygamy, and 10.7% agreed.[34] Though not a clear gender equality issue, the Internet survey also inquired whether respondents preferred that high school boys and girls be educated in separate classrooms. Only 17% of those surveyed agreed. The interviews indicate that equality in inheritance, legal testimony, monogamy, and coeducation, as understood in contemporary Turkey, are viewed by most as being more faithful to the principles of Islam than are the traditional rules. The break with traditional rules reflected by these results is perhaps the strongest indicator of sympathy for a modernist approach to Islamic ethics and jurisprudence in Turkey.

Prohibitions

There are two questions in the study related to food. The statement that received the most consistent agreement was that "*Shari'a* prohibits Muslims from eating pork" (79.9%; 80.2% weighted). While 15% disagreed with this statement, it is not clear why. The interviews indicated that it was either because the respondent took a modernist approach to Islam that was not constrained by the textual tradition, or because the person was expressing a personal belief rather than an understanding of *Shari'a*. The other food-related question, whether or not *Shari'a* forbids Muslims from drinking alcohol, received slightly less agreement (72.4% raw and weighted). The interviews indicated less vacillation on the part of those who disagreed (21%). Disagreeing interviewees seemed confident that drinking alcohol was compatible with Islam. This result is not surprising given that alcohol production has been heavily promoted for decades, and drinking alcoholic beverages is deeply embedded in the culinary tradition of some Turks (as opposed to eating pork products).

Prohibitions against apostasy are problematic in many predominantly Muslim countries, since they tend to conflict with principles of religious freedom and international law. The percentage of respondents who agreed that *Shari'a* prohibits a Muslim from changing religion was 56.4%, with 33% disagreeing. Since apostasy is traditionally considered a crime carrying the death penalty – even if a school did not consider it a *hadd* crime – it is possible that some subjects disagreed largely because they oppose capital punishment in these cases and not because they believe that Islamic law is indifferent to apostasy.[35]

The prohibition against interest is often associated with Islamic law and ethics, and there are tremendous resources considering the issues.[36] In the telephone poll, just over 70% agreed that *Shari'a* prohibits interest, which is interesting in a country whose economy relies heavily on interest-bearing instruments and a variety of other financial mechanisms that might be prohibited according to a traditional view of Islamic jurisprudence. In the interviews, most respondents indicated that they believe "*Shariʿa*" prohibits interest, but after further questioning, it appeared they actually meant that *Hanafi fiqh*, and not God, prohibits it. No one argued that interest ought to be prohibited in Turkey, which may indicate a tacit acceptance of modernist approaches to Islamic jurisprudence.

Homosexuality is another difficult topic in many predominantly Muslim countries. In response to the question whether *Shariʿa* forbids homosexuality, 72.2% (68% weighted) agreed. As in the United States and Europe, approval of homosexuality in Turkey tends to correlate inversely with age. In the 2011 Pew survey, 85% of those interviewed indicated that homosexual behavior was morally wrong. It is possible that there has been some change in the perception of homosexuality in the course of two years, which might explain the difference. It might also be that subjects viewed the question of what *Shariʿa* prohibits differently from the question of moral wrong.

The questions asking about views on the content of *Shariʿa* pose a challenge to the extent that some people answer according to their own preference, as opposed to their view of Islamic jurisprudence. However, the interviews indicated that this might be a small minority. This study is helpful in demonstrating that a significant majority of Turks appear to take a modernist, or at least a revisionist, view of the classical legal tradition, particularly on issues related to gender. This seems consistent with important Islamic thinkers, including Gülen, Öztürk, and senior *Diyanet* officials.

Hadd *crimes*

One of the most contentious issues for states intending to conform contemporary law to *Shariʿa* is the requirement of specific punishments, which are often severe, for particular crimes mentioned in the canonical texts of the Quran and the *Sunna*.[37] Such crimes have expressly religious implications as "claims of God."[38] Theft, brigandage (highway robbery), illegal sexual intercourse (***zina***), false accusation of *zina*, and winedrinking, which in most schools includes intoxicants in general, are accepted as examples of such crimes by all four Sunni schools of jurisprudence, although the schools disagree as to the elements, evidentiary requirements, and punishments. Apostasy, which includes blasphemy in most classical jurisprudence, is typically included in the list of *hudud* offenses, but it has always been the subject of greater dispute – even more so today.[39]

The surveys asked respondents to identify which crimes on a list require the traditional *hadd* punishment. Seven of the options offered would typically be considered *hadd* crimes: adultery, highway robbery, theft, fornication, false accusation of adultery or fornication, winedrinking, and apostasy (with the caveat provided above). Five options were included as distractors, including potentially immoral or illegal activity that was not covered by *hudud* rules: treason, murder, kidnapping, arson, and homosexuality.

Table 5.2 Responses to *hadd* crime questions

Possible Hadd *Crime*	*% Agreeing*	*% Disagreeing*	*% No Response*
Adultery	82.8	10.7	6.5
Highway Robbery	68.4	20	11.6
Treason	69.5	19	11.4
Theft	82.6	11.9	5.6
Murder	82.2	12	5.8
Fornication	79.6	13.2	7.3
Kidnapping	65.8	20.9	13.4
False accusation of *zina*	78.4	13.9	7.7
Arson	69.6	18.1	12.3
Homosexuality	64.5	20.6	14.9
Apostasy	58.1	27.6	14.3
Winedrinking	64.8	24.5	10.7

a Percentages presented in this chart are weighted.

The 2011 Pew survey also asked questions related to *hadd* crimes, but it inquired into respondents' preferences for rather than knowledge of the traditional rules. For example, 88% of respondents in the Pew survey opposed the punishment of stoning people who commit adultery (the *hadd* punishment),[40] 85% opposed punishments like whippings and cutting off hands for crimes like theft or robbery,[41] and 89% opposed the death penalty for people who leave the Muslim religion.[42] These numbers – which contrast with the responses in the telephone poll – indicate a notable distinction between understanding of a crime in traditional Islamic jurisprudence and objecting to the punishment. Opposition to actual *hadd* punishments is much higher than in most predominantly Muslim jurisdictions polled by Pew.[43] Further, only a small minority of those polled who believe that *Shari'a* ought to be enforced supported the enforcement of *hadd* punishments for theft (35%), adultery (29%), and apostasy (17%).[44] This is an indication that most Turks reject punishments that are not considered fair, even if they are legitimated by Islamic tradition. The interviews in my study seemed to confirm this. Some interviewees acknowledged a dissonance between their preferences and their understanding of Islam. Others insisted that authentic Islam today no longer requires *hadd* punishments, either because the historical context within which they emerged has changed,[45] or because the guarantee of proper process and judgment cannot be ensured in most predominantly Muslim countries.[46] With regard to other *hadd* crimes, the Pew survey asked questions in terms of the morality of behavior: 66% indicated that drinking alcohol is morally wrong,[47] and 88% indicated that sex outside of marriage is morally wrong.[48] These numbers are more consistent with my study, though they likely differ somewhat because Pew asked about the morality of the behavior, while my study asked whether it constitutes a *hadd* crime.

The top two responses to my question regarding which crimes require *hadd* punishment were adultery and theft, which are generally considered to be *hadd* crimes. However, the third most common choice, murder, is not. This indicates a possible conflation of *hadd* crimes with serious, or perhaps capital, crimes. "Murder" in classical Islamic jurisprudence is actually treated somewhat like a tort from the point of view of Anglo-American jurisprudence. One way to interpret these responses is that crimes like murder are thought to require a strict and severe punishment even if they are not technically crimes with punishments prescribed by the canonical sources. Fornication and false accusation of *zina* also ranked highly, which is not surprising since they are indeed considered to be *hadd* crimes. Treason and arson ranked lower, which is also not surprising because they are not *hadd* crimes. Highway robbery, however, was considered by fewer people to constitute a *hadd* crime. Interviewees who admitted to not understanding the tradition of *hudud* found this particular question difficult. It also raises the question of legal terms of art; for example, many Americans would have difficulty distinguishing between theft, robbery, and burglary. Kidnapping also ranked lower, but it was included as a distractor, so this is unsurprising. However, winedrinking is a *hadd* crime in all of the Sunni schools and in the Shiʿi *Jafari* school of jurisprudence. Again, the interviews indicated that some people answered that it was not a *hadd* crime simply because they object to the rule, while others honestly believe that it is not an actual requirement. Also, as a complicated category within classical Islamic jurisprudence, it is not surprising that apostasy, a *hadd* crime, rated lower than the non-*hadd* crimes.

In the interviews, the question of homosexuality was vexing for a number of people, particularly those under the age of 30. Several people specifically mentioned it as an issue that challenged their faith. One interviewee called the *Diyanet fatwa* line and followed up by email in order to ask why Islam forbids homosexuality. In a detailed response, the expert at *Diyanet* indicated that the status of homosexuality is morally neutral, but that homosexual behavior is forbidden. He compared it to proclivities toward destructive activities like alcoholism or lying, an approach shared by some Christian communities. Others interviewed rejected this position and saw no problem with committed homosexual relationships.

It was somewhat surprising that all of the possible crimes in the list were believed to require *hadd* punishments by a majority of respondents, and that several non-*hadd* crimes were chosen more commonly than actual *hadd* crimes. There are inherent difficulties in asking knowledge questions in empirical research, and the quantitative data alone is somewhat problematic, if not interesting. The interviews, however, painted a picture of shifting values and a tension between legal sensibilities shaped within the Turkish Republic and traditional understandings of Islam. There were serious gaps in understandings of the *fiqh* tradition. Some people had a sophisticated and detailed understanding of these issues. Others did not, and relied on childhood education, media exposure, and intuition. Perhaps most significantly, every person I interviewed who supported the idea of enforcing *Shariʿa* objected to the imposition of most *hadd* punishments. This distinguishes Turkey from most countries in the Middle East.[49] It may also indicate a different sort of Islamic or Muslim politics, which embraces a religiously neutral legal system (at least facially).

Methodological approaches to *Shari'a*

While the quantitative elements of this study raise a number of interesting questions, they do not paint a consistent picture of popular understandings of *Shari'a* in Turkey that might form the basis for a coherent methodological approach to Islamic jurisprudence. Fortunately, the interviews provide some clarification, even if it may not be generalizable in the same way. Although it appears that the portion of the population that supports the enforcement of *Shari'a* is rising, it may not be assumed that this group agrees as to either the process for enforcement or the substance of the rules.

It appears that most Turks expect the state to play a role in enforcement, which would require constitutional amendment. Beyond that, it is not clear whether people would expect the executive to act through *Diyanet*, whether the parliament would play a role, or whether the existing court system would interpret the meaning of *Shari'a*. There does seem to be a consensus among those who support *Shari'a* that it ought to be codified. This would not be unique, but it is an innovation that arguably breaks with traditional jurisprudence. There remains debate as to whether the codification of commercial law in the Ottoman *Mecelle* was a modernist innovation or a development on earlier Islamic approaches to codification.[50] There is some expression that religious scholars in the state schools of theology, *Diyanet* officials, and traditionally trained *ulema*, who remain largely underground and outside of government regulation, might play a role similar to the classical *mufti*. There also appears to be an expectation that *Shari'a* rules would be enforced within the current legal framework of procedure, evidence, and rights.

With regard to content, there is a somewhat clearer picture. Although many people conflated *hadd* crimes with other sorts of crimes, there is a reasonably large consensus regarding the moral requirements of Islam. However, it is very clear that there is a trend to consider these requirements personal and private. Most Turks appear to reject the standards developed in the *fiqh* tradition, some of which might be considered by traditional jurists to be certain according to the canonical texts,[51] and particularly with regard to those cases involving disparate treatment based on gender. Even those desiring *Shari'a* generally do not want to be subject to its rules for crimes, family issues, or property disputes. This may indicate a privatization of religious rules in the form of personal morality. It does not mean that Turkey is no longer a religious country, or that its law will not in some ways reflect the morality of the dominant religious culture; but it may indicate that democracy, rule of law, and secularism have created the possibility for greater toleration of difference and dissent (though events since May 30, 2013, may challenge this indication).

It is unlikely that Turkey will move to enforce *Shari'a* in the near future, but it is clear that conservative religious politicians are interested in enacting laws that reflect Islamic values (as in the case of regulations on alcohol and public displays of affection). Even these early moves have proven to be destabilizing, but that does not mean that they will not continue. Although many secularists feel threatened in the current political environment, in one sense they have already won: The relatively minor act of legislating alcohol regulations, for example, is justified using nonreligious public safety arguments. As such, the arguments made by AKP legislators regarding legislation generally comport with the expectations of Rawlsian analysis, that is, they are secular arguments.[52] What is perhaps most interesting in the study is the self-conscious move to justify constitutional secularism (or at least neutrality) in explicitly Islamic terms.

Analysis of significant correlations in survey data

The operating goal of this analysis is to explore the factors contributing to the preference for enforcing *Shariʿa*, particularly education and religiosity. Ultimately, the preference cannot be explained by a single tested variable. However, the final model based on data from the telephone poll seems to create a plausible story for explaining some of the significant factors. This section will begin with a note regarding response rates and then turn to bivariate analysis, linear regression, and modeling based on binary regressions.

Response rates

Quantitative surveys in social science do not always report response rates. Historically, many journals, though encouraging response rates, do not have such a requirement and in fact publish many studies without response rates at all.[53] While it is suggested that response rates are required for validity, recent studies have called this into question. I note that the surveys from Turkey cited in this work do not report response rates (Kalaycıoğu, Çarkoğlu and Toprak, Yılmaz, and Pew). This approach is standard in some disciplines and is supported by a number of significant studies challenging the presumption that lower response rates mean lower survey accuracy.[54] Response rates were not tracked in the telephone poll software and are not available.

Introductory analysis

A key question driving this study is whether education is a more important predictor of views of *Shariʿa* than religiosity. Both the telephone poll and the Internet survey provide useful data for exploring this question and broader inquiries related to how *Shariʿa* is understood in Turkey. In general, there may be a more significant correlation between education and views of *Shariʿa* than religiosity and views of *Shariʿa*. That is, people with higher levels of education, particularly those with a university education, may tend not to prefer that *Shariʿa* become the law of the state (an inverse correlation between education level and preference for *Shariʿa* as opposed to the positive correlation between religiosity and preference for *Shariʿa*). However, both education and religiosity appear to play a role and are included in the model. Women as a group also have a lower preference for *Shariʿa*, although those who identify as a "housewife" in the employment question tend to prefer *Shariʿa* more often than the general population.

Bivariate analysis

Using the weighted data from the telephone poll, standard Spearman correlations for ordinal variables indicated a significant ($p < .01$) relationship between both independent variables (religiosity and education) and the dependent variable (the preference for *Shari'a*), with rho's (hereinafter "r") of .158 and –.148, respectively.[55] While significant, neither of these results indicate a strong correlation with either of the independent variables. In the course of reviewing the data, it appeared that this analysis might not adequately describe the interaction between variables. For purposes of determining the independence of the tested variables the Spearman's r for education and religiosity was calculated. The results indicated an r of –.112 with a significance at $p < .01$. It is not surprising that there is some inverse correlation between the two, but it is notable that the correlation is relatively low, though significant.

Pearson's correlation is only reliable in evaluating continuous variables, which would not typically include Likert scale questions, though in the case of an education scale in which each value represents approximately three years, it might be justifiable. Even so, the calculations were made and helped to inform later regression analysis. There is an inverse correlation between education and the preference for enforcing *Shari'a* in Turkey, with a Pearson's r of –.174.[56] Religiosity has a positive and lower correlation – a Pearson's r of only .026. Although education is more highly correlated (though inversely), it is still only a low correlation. However, the analysis of significance (standard two-tailed) is more notable.[57] Education has a significance measure of ($p < .01$), which indicates that the relationship is significant even though the correlation is relatively low. Using Pearson, religiosity has a lower significance of ($p > .1$), which does not indicate a significant relationship between it and views of *Shari'a*. If Pearson analysis were reliable for these variables, it would create a basis for the hypothesis that education is a better predictor of preference for *Shari'a* than religiosity, a claim that tends to be supported by qualitative data reviewed in Chapter Six.[58] However, it did prompt exploring regression models. For the purposes of determining the independence of the tested variables, the Pearson's r for education and religiosity was calculated. The results indicated an r of –.043 with a significance at $p > .05$. This is lower correlation and significance than Spearman analysis indicated, but it may be attributed to the unreliability of Pearson's in this case.

There are a number of variables from the telephone poll with a significant Spearman correlation. In addition to education, a number of other questions significantly correlated with *Shari'a* preferences with a significance at $p < .01$. Six variables had a Spearman's r of greater than .2: *Shari'a* provides for religious freedom (.348), requires women to cover (.346), provides that sons inherit twice that of daughters (.204), testimony of women is generally equal to half that of a man (.244), allows men to marry up to four wives (.201), and drinking wine is a *hadd* crime (.235). Several other variables indicated strong significance with correlations less than .20. These included the following: *Shari'a* requires that the basic health and educational needs of all be met (Spearman's r of .119); *Shari'a* prohibits Muslims from eating pork (.141); *Shari'a* forbids Muslims from drinking alcohol (.136); *Shari'a* prohibits a Muslim from changing religion (.099); *Shari'a* forbids the taking of interest (.135); *Shari'a* forbids homosexuality (.094); highway robbery is a *hadd* crime (.140); treason is a *hadd* crime (.166); theft is a *hadd* crime (.092); murder is a *hadd* crime (.102); fornication is a *hadd* crime (.103); kidnapping is a *hadd* crime (.156); false accusation of adultery or fornication is a *hadd* crime (.106); arson is a *hadd* crime (.126); homosexuality is a *hadd* crime (.191); and a Muslim may live a moral life in a non-Muslim country (Spearman's r of –.167, indicating that those who prefer *Shari'a* are less likely to believe that this is possible). The correlation between preferences for *Shari'a* and most of these views is not entirely surprising. Another interesting relationship is that those who desire the enforcement of *Shari'a* appear more likely to view homosexuality as a *hadd* crime than any of the actual *hadd* crimes, except winedrinking, a view which is at odds with traditional jurisprudence. This may indicate that understandings of *Shari'a*, or at least *hadd* jurisprudence, may reflect cultural values rather than the details of *fiqh* literature.

Education had a number of significant correlations with other variables. It inversely correlates with the belief that *Shari'a* provides religious freedom (r of –.205) and the view that *Shari'a* prohibits a Muslim from changing religion (–.134), both with significance at $p < .01$. Higher education positively correlates with gender (.255), indicating that men tend to have more education than women in the population, the view that *Shari'a* prohibits Muslims from changing religion (.134), the view that adultery is a *hadd* crime (.085), and the view that theft is a *hadd* crime (.116).

Religiosity had a significant minor correlation with a number of the positive or inclusive statements regarding Islam, such as *Shari'a* requires that the basic health and educational needs of all be met ($r = .096$) and provides religious freedom (.18). It also correlates with descriptive statements associated with traditional understandings of Islam, such as *Shari'a* requires that Muslim women cover their hair (.086), prohibits them from eating pork (.103), forbids them to drink alcohol (.105), prohibits Muslims from changing religion (.114), and forbids homosexuality (.108). The only significant correlations between religiosity and the possible *hadd* crimes list was with the belief that homosexuality is a *hadd* crime (.103) and that winedrinking is a *hadd* crime (.170). It is notable here that religiosity correlates with the view that homosexuality is a *hadd* crime, while it is not within the context of classical jurisprudence.

Although the implications are quite limited, there are a number of variables from the telephone poll with a significant Pearson correlation. The results are provided for reference and comparison. In this paragraph, and then in the following three, correlations refer to Pearson calculations. In addition to education, four other questions significantly correlated with *Shari'a* preferences: whether *Shari'a* provides for religious freedom, requires women to cover, provides that sons inherit twice that of daughters, and whether testimony of women is generally equal to half that of a man. The correlation between preferences for *Shari'a* and these beliefs are not entirely surprising. For religious freedom, the Pearson's r is .362, with strong significance ($p < .01$). For covering, the Pearson's r is .34, with a strong significance ($p < .01$) – very similar. The correlation with inheritance is slightly lower; the Pearson's r is .227, with a high significance ($p < .01$), and with regard to the gender of a witness, it is .248 with high significance ($p < .01$). Another interesting relationship is that those who desire the enforcement of *Shariʿa* appear more likely to view homosexuality as a *hadd* crime than any of the actual *hadd* crimes, a view which is at odds with traditional jurisprudence.

Education also inversely correlates with the belief that *Shariʿa* provides religious freedom (r of –.201, with significance at $p < .01$). Among those who believe that *Shariʿa* could be appropriately enforced by the state, there was a negative correlation between education and both the view that *Shariʿa* rules must conform to the dominant *madhab* in the jurisdiction and that *Shariʿa* rules ought to be codified. The first is a more important relationship and might be explained by higher education, which tends to discourage a preference for traditional *fiqh* rules, even among those who believe that *Shariʿa* rules may be appropriately enforced by states.

Religiosity had some notable correlation with views on alcohol and the acceptability of interest within Islam. The correlation between religiosity and the view that *Shariʿa* forbids drinking alcohol is measured at .092, with a strong significance ($p < .01$). It is even more highly correlated with the belief that winedrinking is a *hadd* crime (.122 with high significance). Between religiosity and the belief that interest is prohibited by *Shariʿa*, the correlation was 0.073 and also had a moderate significance approaching $p < .05$. So, at least in these cases, religiosity correlates to some degree with traditional understandings of *fiqh* rules.

The findings that use Pearson's are not hugely different from those that use the Spearman analysis. However, most of the relationships are relatively minor, and none of the correlations adequately explains views related to *Shariʿa*. Ultimately, bivariate analysis is not sufficient to make predictive statements about the survey data.

Linear regression and crosstab analysis

Linear regression modeling requires three assumptions.[59] First, it relies on the independence of responses, a factor related to the sampling. Second, it must have a normally distributed error. Third, it must have constant covariance. Although the size and the randomness of the sample using standard political polling methodology and RDD software is likely sufficient to meet the requirements of the first assumption, checking residuals and a q–q plot did not indicate a normal distribution, thus making a standard linear regression model unreliable.[60] The model included gender, education, employment, and religiosity as independent variables, and the preference for *Shariʿa* was the dependent variable. Running a linear regression gave results similar to those indicated in a Pearson's r bivariate analysis. That is, the inverse relationship between education and the preference for *Shariʿa* was significant. It also indicated that gender was significant, with women being less likely to prefer *Shariʿa*. Religiosity itself was not significant in this analysis.[61] Because this mode of analysis was not statistically reliable, crosstab and binary regression analysis were used.

The crosstab comparing the three values of education and preference for *Shari'a* used in the qualitative analysis of interviews clearly indicates that those with a university education tend not to prefer *Shari'a* at a rate higher than the sample population. Those with a high school education align with the population as a whole, and those with an elementary education or less tend to prefer *Shari'a* at a rate higher than the sample population. It is also notable that a lower percentage of participants with some university education were undecided than in the other two groups.

This indicates that religiosity is also connected to the preference for *Shari'a*, but neither of these creates a predictive model that includes other significant variables. Since the linear regression model was not reliable, the earlier analysis justified developing a binary logistic regression model, considering simple preference or nonpreference for *Shari'a*, along with university education, gender, identification as a housewife, and identification as not/not very religious. Although not completely predictive, this model indicates that university education likely plays

Table 5.3 Crosstab evaluation of education and *Shari'a* preference

	Agree or Strongly agree that Shari'a *ought to be the law of the state*	*Neither agree nor disagree*	*Disagree or strongly disagree*
2-yr or 4-yr College, Masters, or PhD	31 (13.5%)	12 (5.3%)	185 (81.2%)
High school or secondary school	67 (19.8%)	43 (12.5%)	232 (77.7%)
Elementary education or less	85 (26.5%)	41 (12.8%)	195 (60.7%)

Similarly, the very religious tend to prefer *Shari'a* more than the general population do, the religious tend to reflect the sample population, and the non/not religious tend not to prefer *Shari'a*.

Table 5.4 Crosstab evaluation of religiosity and *Shari'a* preference

	Agree or Strongly agree that Shari'a *ought to be the law of the state*	*Neither agree nor disagree*	*Disagree or strongly disagree*
Very Religious	13 (30.9%)	5 (11.9%)	24 (57.2%)
Religious	159 (21.7%)	81 (11.1%)	492 (67.2%)
Not very or not at all religious	8 (7.8%)	8 (7.8%)	87 (84.4%)

a significant role in the preference for *Shariʿa*. This relationship is even stronger for women. Although women identifying as housewives are more likely to prefer *Shariʿa* than the sample population, they also tend to be less likely to have a university education and are more likely to be very religious.

Binary logistic regression model

The Likert scale for *Shariʿa* preference was converted to binary by making those who neither agree nor disagree, disagree, and strongly disagree zero. Those who agree or strongly agree were made one. The goal was to isolate those who positively responded that they want a religious state.

Model

A binary logistic regression model was created in order to show the connection or lack of connection between the variables. In order to run a binary model, several models were run using dummy variables for the values of education, gender, employment, and age. For the purposes of this analysis, variables that were not found to have a statistically significant impact on the dependent variable (preference for a *Shariʿa*-based state) were removed.

Variables

In order to change the reporting data from the survey to binary coded answers, the Likert scale answers were changed so that instead of being answered one through five, they were answered zero or one. For instance, The five-point Likert scale for the question indicating a participant's preference for a *Shariʿa*-based state was converted to a binary variable by making those who neither agree nor disagree, disagree, and strongly disagree zero and by making those who agree or strongly agree one, the goal being to isolate those who responded positively to a religious state. Two of the chosen independent variables, college education and employment status as a "housewife," both went through similar changes (i.e., someone reporting employment as "housewife" is reported as a one, all else as a zero).[62] The tested value for religiosity considered "not at all religious" and "not very religious" one and the other three answers zero.[63] The independent variable "gender" was already binary with zero representing "male" and one "female."

Reliability

The Nagelkerke R squared was .083, suggesting the independent variables represent 8.3% of the variability in the dependent variable. According to the Hosmer and Lemeshow test and classification table, the predicted values of the model are accurate 80.6% of the time in predicting those who want a *Shariʿa*-based state in Turkey.

Table 5.5 Binary logistic regression table – Preference for *Shari'a*

	B (*SE*)	*B* (*SE*)	*B* (*SE*)	*B* (*SE*)
University Education (at least four-year degree):	–.855** (.234)	–.865** (.235)	–.679** (.244)	–.635** (.246)
Gender (Female):		–.097 (.167)	–.666* (.272)	–.673* (.273)
Identification as a Housewife for Employment:			.815** (.287)	.790** (.288)
Not Religious or Not Very Religious:				–.961* (.478)

The dependent variable is the preference for a state based on *Shari'a*. Standard errors are in parentheses. ** indicates $p < 0.01$, and * indicates $p < 0.05$.

Results

The binary logistic models were split into four. The first tested only the variable for university educated against a preference for a *Shari'a* state. The second tested both university education and gender. The third tested university education, gender, and status as a housewife. The fourth added not/not very religious.

The first model reveals evidence that those who are university educated (those with a four-year degree or above) are less likely to be in favor of a *Shari'a*-based state. The beta for university education in the first model is –.855 (standard error .234). Thus, the odds of someone without a university education having a preference for a *Shari'a* are 2.35 (1/.425) times greater than those with a university education. These results were found to be significant at the ($p < .01$) level.

The second model, besides undergirding the point about education above while holding gender constant, reveals there is no statistically significant connection between gender and a preference for a *Shari'a*-based state. The results for education did not change materially from the first to the second model and are similarly statistically significant ($p < .01$). Holding education constant, gender, despite having a slightly negative *B* value (–.097), had an extremely high *p*-value (not significant at the .05 level) and an extremely low standard error (.167). This suggests that there was unexplained variability in the independent variable "Gender" when holding educational status constant.

The third model attempted to explain some of the variability in gender by adding the employment status "Housewife" as an independent variable. All three variables were now significant at the $p < .05$ level. When holding gender and status as a housewife as constants, the odds of someone without a university education having a preference for *Shari'a* are 1.97 (1/.507) times greater than those with a university education ($p < .01$). Women, when holding university education and status as a housewife constant, are 1.95 (1/.514) times less likely than men to prefer a *Shari'a*-based state ($p < .05$). Finally, those who self-identified their employment status as "Housewife," while holding university education and gender as constant, were 2.26 times more likely to prefer a *Shari'a*-based state than those who chose other forms of employment ($p < .01$).

The fourth model kept all three of the previous independent variables and added religiosity as measured by those who self-reported as either not very religious or not at all religious (choices four and five on the survey) versus those who are very religious, religious, or not sure (choices one, two, and three). When holding university education, gender, and status as a housewife as constants, those with a religiosity score of not/not very religious were 2.61 (1/.383) times less likely to prefer a *Shari'a* state than those who were very religious, religious, or not sure. These findings were significant at $p < .05$. Gender remained significant at $p < .05$, and the values university educated and housewife were both significant at $p < .01$. When holding the other independent variables constant, all remained very similar to their values from the third model.

Conclusion

The inferences that may reasonably be drawn from the data are modest. There are clearly some factors – such as gender, education, identification as a housewife, and religious identity – that interact in shaping preferences for *Shari'a*. The model seems to indicate that university education and identification as a housewife may be the most significant observed factors related to *Shari'a* preference when controlling for the other observed factors. It is not surprising that those who favor *Shari'a* are inclined to view it positively and in ways that comport with Turkish norms, or that those who oppose it tend to view it negatively and at odds with Turkish norms. Comparing the results to similar studies in other societies, it appears that the role of Islam and perceptions of *Shari'a* in Turkey are distinctive. Perhaps the most interesting data from the large-*n* studies is found in the open-ended questions asking respondents to define *Shari'a* and then to indicate who ought to enforce it. The qualitative interviews analyzed in Chapters Six and Seven open up the possibility for answering causal questions with greater confidence and context.

Notes

1 Note that the expected correlation between level of education and desire for *Shari'a* would be inverse, that is, that those with higher levels of education would be expected to be less likely to desire *Shari'a*. The relationship between religiosity and desire for *Shari'a* would be expected to be a direct correlation, but of lower magnitude.

2 As of 2013, 46% of Turks regularly used the Internet; however, there is little reliable data on the demographic characteristics of those users. There is a general assumption that they tend to be younger and wealthier than the general population. Facebook usage at the time of the study included 40% of the Turkish population, presumably with a similar bias. The Internet survey did not reflect the population of Facebook users in terms of gender (more male), age (younger), or education (higher). Responses also appeared to reflect a polarization that might be the result of response bias, that is, those without strong preferences may have been less likely to participate. *See e.g.*, "Internet Stats and Facebook Usage in Europe Year-End 2013," available at http://www.internetworldstats.com/stats4.htm.

3 Margins of error for means of responses were calculated at the 0.05 significance level. That is, there is a 5% probability that the margins of error for the mean response for a question of the survey do not contain the mean response for the entire population of Turkey. In other words, there is a 95% probability that the mean response for the entire population of Turkey is the same as the mean response of the survey, within the margin of error stated for a response. Margins of error are reported as percentages of the mean response. Calculated margins of error are noted for each survey question. *See* Jay L. Devore, *Probability and Statistics for Scientists and Engineers.* 7th ed. Boston: Brooks/Cole Cengage Learning, 2009.

4 *See Nokta*, October 17, 1986.

5 Necat Erder, *Türkiye'de Siyasi Partilerin Seçmeleri ve Toplum Düzeni*. Istanbul: TÜSES Foundation, 1999 at 68–69.

6 *Id.*

7 *See* Ali Çarkoğlu, "Religiosity, Support for Şeriat and Evaluations of Secularist Public Policies in Turkey." *Middle Eastern Studies* 40.2 (2004).

8 *See* Çarkoğlu and Kalaycıoğlu.

9 *See* Ali Çarkoğlu and Binnaz Toprak, *Religion, Society and Politics in a Changing Turkey*, Istanbul: TESEV, 2007 at 81.

10 Pew Research Religion & Public Life Project, "The World's Muslims: Religion, Politics and Society." April 30, 2013 at 201.

11 The unweighted percentages are 4.6% very religious, 81.5% religious, 5.6% not very religious, 1.4% not at all religious, and 7% were not sure or did not answer.

12 *See* Çarkoğlu and Toprak at 41. Note that this study divided religiosity into six categories rather than five. If the two middle categories (religious and very religious are combined, they approximate the "religious" category in this study (low 80s).

13 Data in this and the following paragraph come from the Internet survey, which is admittedly nonrepresentative. This data is presented because these questions were not asked in the shorter telephone survey. Obviously, it only represents the views of the participants. Weighting to Turkish demographic norms is noted where it might be helpful.

14 The raw percentage was about 67 in the Internet survey. The weighted response was 66%, which is fairly close to the 63.8% rate found in the 1999 TESEV survey. *See* Çarkoğlu at 128.

15 This is an increase from the TESEV study in 2006. *See* Çarkoğlu and Toprak at 97.

16 In a similar question, the 2006 TESEV study indicates 22.1%.

17 References to religion or religious law rather than Islam tended to inversely correlate with the desire to enforce *Shari'a* as law.

18 There appears to be some basis for this in the interview questions related to influential religious leaders discussed later.

19 Notably, those who identify *Shari'a* as primarily "moral" generally did not support its enforcement as law.

20 The importance of freedom as a part of authentic religious experience is further developed in the interviews discussed later.

21 These three statements were used in the telephone poll, the Internet survey, and interviews.

22 These two statements were used only in the Internet survey and interviews.

23 *See* e.g., Clark B. Lombardi, "State Law as Islamic Law in Modern Egypt: The Incorporation of the *Shari'a* into Egyptian Constitutional Law." *Studies in Islamic Law and Society* 19 (2006) at 103–105.

24 Çarkoğlu and Toprak at 87.

25 *Id.*

26 Pew Research Religion & Public Life Project at 202.

27 *Id.*

28 *Id.*

29 *See* Abdullahi Ahmed An-Naim, *Toward an Islamic Reformation: Civil Liberties, Human Rights, and International Law*. Syracuse, NY: Syracuse University Press, 1990 at 90–91.
30 *See, e.g.*, Nilüfer Göle, *The Forbidden Modern: Civilization and Veiling.* Ann Arbor: University of Michigan, 1996; Leila Ahmed, *A Quiet Revolution: The Veil's Resurgence, from the Middle East to America.* New Haven & London: Yale University Press, 2012; Madhavi Sunder, "Piercing the Veil." *Yale Law Journal* 112 (2003): 1399.
31 A similar question in a 1999 TESEV survey found that 76% agreed at that time. *See* Çarkoğlu at 125.
32 Çarkoğlu and Toprak at 29.
33 The 1999 TESEV survey asked a similar question, but in terms of enforcing the traditional rule in contemporary Turkey. Not surprisingly, only 13.9% accepted that proposal. *See* Çarkoğlu at 122.
34 *Id.* at 120.
35 As a matter of Hanafi *fiqh*, this is a much more complicated issue. *See* Rudolph Peter, *Crime and Punishment in Islamic Law: Theory and Practice from the Sixteenth to the Twenty-first Century*. Cambridge: Cambridge University Press, 2005, p. 65, "According to most schools, apostasy is a hadd crime, to be punished with death . . . Unlike the other schools, the Hanafites and the Shiites do not regard apostasy as a hadd offence. Further, they hold that only male apostates are to be executed, whereas female apostates must be imprisoned until they repent . . . "
36 *See, e.g.*, Frank Vogel and Samuel Hayes, *Islamic Law and Finance: Religion, Risk and Return*. Leiden: Brill, 1998; Haider Ala Hamoudi, "The Muezzin's Call and the Dow Jones Bell: On the Necessity of Realism in the Study of Islamic Law." *American Journal of Comparative Law* 56 (2008): 442.
37 *See* Peters at 148–173, discussing the enforcement of Islamic criminal law in Saudi Arabia, Libya, Pakistan, Iran, Pakistan, Sudan, and Northern Nigeria.
38 With regard to *hadd* crimes, "The distinguishing feature is that claims of God, unlike claims of men, cannot be waived by men." *Id.* at 53.
39 *Id.* at 64–65.
40 Pew Research Religion & Public Life Project at 221.
41 *Id.* at 220.
42 *Id.* at 219.
43 *See generally id.* at 218–221.
44 *See id.* at 52–55.
45 One modernist approach to this issue.
46 *See* Tariq Ramadan, "We Must Not Accept This Repression: The Muslim Conscience Demands a Halt to Stonings and Executions." *The Guardian*, March 30, 2005.
47 Pew Research Religion & Public Life Project at 207.
48 *Id.* at 212.
49 *See* Pew Research Religion & Public Life Project at 218–221.
50 Brinkley Messick, *The Calligraphic State: Textual Domination and History in a Muslim Society.* Berkeley: University of California Press, 1993 at 54–57. *See also* Powers at 383.
51 *E.g.*, the lesser share in inheritance and the lesser weight in testimony.
52 Public reason proposed by Rawls is intended to regulate political discourse and decision-making in the liberal state. He distinguishes between "public reasons" and "nonpublic reasons." Public reasons are truths that are widely accepted, premises rooted in a society's conception of political justice and "guidelines of inquiry" that establish standards for evaluating competing arguments. Nonpublic reasons comprise those that do not fit into these categories – most notably religious reasons – which are often the basis for moral and policy preferences. On its face, Rawls' conception of public reason does not seem open to theological argument. *See* John Rawls, *Political Liberalism.* New York & Chichester: Columbia University Press, 1993 at 220–254.

53 The American Association for Public Opinion Research (AAPOR) documents the studies here: http://www.aapor.org/Response_Rates_An_Overview1.htm#.UztIRoUa2ko

54 A study by Visser, Krosnick, Marquette, and Curtin indicated that surveys with lower response rates (near 20%) yielded more accurate measurements than did surveys with higher response rates (near 60 or 70%). Penny S. Visser, Jon A. Krosnick, Jesse Marquette and Michael Curtin, "Mail Surveys for Election Forecasting? An Evaluation of the Colombia Dispatch Poll." *Public Opinion Quarterly* 60 (1996): 181–227. Keeter et al. compared results of a 5-day survey employing the Pew Research Center's usual methodology (with a 25% response rate) with results from a more rigorous survey conducted over a much longer field period and achieving a higher response rate of 50%. In 77 out of 84 comparisons, the two surveys yielded results that were statistically indistinguishable. Among the items that manifested significant differences across the two surveys, the differences in proportions of people giving a particular answer ranged from 4 percentage points to 8 percentage points. Scott Keeter, Courtney Kennedy, Michael Dimock, Jonathan Best, and Peyton Craighill, "Gauging the Impact of Growing Nonresponse on Estimates from a National RDD Telephone Survey." *Public Opinion Quarterly* 70.5 (2006): 759–779. Curtin et al. tested the effect of lower response rates on estimates of the Index of Consumer Sentiment (ICS). They assessed the impact of excluding respondents who initially refused to cooperate (which reduces the response rate 5–10 percentage points), respondents who required more than five calls to complete the interview (reducing the response rate about 25 percentage points), and those who required more than two calls (a reduction of about 50 percentage points). They found that excluding these respondent groups had no effect on estimates of the ICS using monthly samples of hundreds of respondents. Richard Curtin, Stanley Presser and Eleanor Singer, "The Effects of Response Rate Changes on the Index of Consumer Sentiment." *Public Opinion Quarterly* 64.4 (2000): 413–428. Holbrook et al. assessed whether lower response rates are associated with less unweighted demographic representativeness of a sample. By examining the results of 81 national surveys with response rates varying from 5% percent to 54%, they found that surveys with much lower response rates were only minimally less accurate. Allyson Holbrook, Jon Krosnick and Alison Pfent, "The Causes and Consequences of Response Rates in Surveys by the News Media and Government Contractor Survey Research Firms," in *Advances in Telephone Survey Methodology*. Ed. James M. Lepkowski, N. Clyde Tucker, J. Michael Brick, Edith D. De Leeuw, Lilli Japec, Paul J. Lavrakas, Michael W. Link and Roberta L. Sangster. New York: Wiley, 2007, pp. 499–528.

55 Note that correlation between education and *Shari'a* preference was inverse in the study; that is, higher education tended to correlate with a preference not to enforce *Shari'a*.

56 Correlations between the responses were measured by calculation of the Pearson r correlation coefficient. The value of Pearson r, ranging from –1 to 1, indicates a negative or positive correlation and the extent to which a correlation is present. Positive numbers indicate a direct correlation (as one variable increases, so will the other), while negative numbers indicate an inverse correlation (as one variable increases, the other will decrease). Additionally, larger numbers (either positive or negative) indicate greater correlation, while a value of 0 indicates no correlation and a value of 1 or –1 indicates perfect correlation. *See* Devore at 470.

57 Two-tailed significance represents the probability that the correlation has occurred by chance. Generally, a 0.05 significance level is considered significant, while any significance level lower than this is considered to have stronger significance. A significance level of 0.025, for example, indicates a probability of 2.5% that a correlation was due to chance, while a significance level of 0.005 indicates a 0.5% probability that a correlation was due to chance, and so on. *Id.*

58 Note that the unweighted correlations support the same conclusions. The unweighted correlation between education and preference for *Shari'a* in the study is 0.197 with

a significance of < 0.01 (high). The unweighted correlation between religiosity and preference for *Shariʿa* is 0.027, with a low significance of > 0.1 (low).

59 *See e.g.*, Sanford Weisberg, *Applied Linear Regression*. Hoboken, NJ: John Wiley & Sons, 2013 at 133–146.

60 In an OLS linear regression, it is assumed that the residuals are normally distributed. The typical way of testing this is a Kolmogorov–Smirnov test on the model. The results of both it and a Shapiro Wilk test were both statistically significant, suggesting the residuals in this model are not normal.

61 The independent variables were found to be significant in explaining the dependent variable according to an F test. The R^2 was 0.073, suggesting that that the model explains 7.3% of the variability in the dependent variable. Gender, identification as a housewife, having high school education, and having a four-year university education were all statistically significant to a $p < .05$ level. All significant data (except for identification as a housewife) suggest a tendency to choose a government not based on *Shariʿa*.

62 Independent variables were tested as categorical. Ultimately, the values not shown were found to be insignificant.

63 Religiosity was a very complex variable to analyze. In the linear regression, it did not test as significant. I tested each individual value in the five-point scale individually in a binary regression, but the only significant result was for "not at all" religious, which showed perfect collinearity with the preference not to have *Shariʿa*. Of the 13 people who identified as "Not at all religious," 5 disagreed and 8 strongly disagreed that they would like to have a *Shariʿa*-based state in Turkey. As such, a model using that value did not provide useful information regarding the other variables. It was not surprising that "religious," "unsure," and "not very religious" did not produce significant results given the earlier analyses; however, it was somewhat surprising that "very religious" was not more significant. None of the combinations other than the one presented in the model above indicated significance at $p < .05$.

6 Analysis of qualitative interviews

This chapter will review my qualitative research, which asked Turkish citizens to explain why they hold particular views related to *Shari'a*. The interviews identify some surprising overlaps that transcend economics, education, political preferences, and religious ideology. Turks generally, including both "secularists" and the very religious, seem to share a strong preference for traditional moral values while at the same time embrace a libertarian approach to law and religion.

Hundreds of people went through the initial screening interviews in order for me to obtain sets of candidates who represented the nine independent variable combinations (three levels of education by three levels of religiosity). These screening interviews varied between 1 and 20 minutes in length. Candidates who appeared to fit a particular combination of variables, and agreed to extensive interviews, were then asked to complete a hard copy version of the online survey. After the results were scanned, candidates were interviewed for an additional 40 to 120 minutes. The initial portion of those interviews asked explanatory questions related to the survey and considered the causes for the candidates' particular views. The later portion explored significant religious influences and the sources for their views related to *Shari'a* and religion more generally. Two full sets of interviews representing each of the nine independent variable combinations were completed. Four interviewees fell into categories different from those anticipated in the screening interviews, and six random university students went through complete interviews in order to explore the possible trends among younger, educated Turks, for a total of 28 in-depth interviews using the survey. An additional six people active in institutions with connections to Fethullah Gülen or the Hizmet Movement were interviewed more generally, without the use of the survey instrument. All names were changed in order to protect the privacy of participants in the study.

The sample for the case studies was Turkish citizens thought to represent the nine combinations of scores for independent variables in the project. Interviews were conducted primarily in the Beyoğlu district of Istanbul, so there is a possibility that the causal mechanisms of preferences differ from residents in other parts of Turkey. However, Beyoğlu is one of the most diverse neighborhoods in Turkey and includes migrants from throughout the country.[1]

Each of the interviewees began by completing the survey on their own time. I reviewed and scored the surveys, applying the same methodology used in analyzing the large-*n* results, to confirm that my assumed values for the independent variables were accurate. This raised questions regarding the causal mechanisms resulting in particular preferences for secularism and the enforcement of *Shari'a* rules. The interviews focused on confirming variable scores and process tracing, working backward from a preference for *Shari'a*, to confirm possible causes indicated by the survey or to uncover alternative causal factors. Interviews were conducted in the spring of 2013, prior to the *Gezi* protests. Level of education, the main independent variable, was assigned a value of lower, middle, or higher. The dependent variable had three possible values, each corresponding with a preference for enforcing *Shari'a*. As a potentially competing factor, religiosity was tested for correlation as well.

This chapter addresses results from the initial portion of the interviews that related directly to the survey questions, while the following chapter deals with the results from the more narrative portions of the interviews. Consistent with the underlying thesis of the project, interviews are considered first according to education level, beginning with those with a university education, then moves to those between a primary school education and a high school diploma, and then concludes with those who have a primary school education or less. This chapter will focus on the survey questions and pattern tracing to elaborate understandings of *Shari'a*. More-detailed narratives will be reserved for the following chapter, which will examine the influences that shaped those understandings.

University educated

Fifteen university-educated Turks participated in in-depth interviews. Two identified themselves as very religious, three as religious, and ten as non/not very religious. One clear result among this group (as with the large-*n* surveys) is that these people tend to disapprove of state enforcement of *Shari'a* – in fact, not a single person in this category desires that *Shari'a* be enforced in Turkey. However, the conception of *Shari'a* within this group is more polarized to the extent that religious persons construed it as consistent with Turkish constitutional secularism, whereas non/not very religious persons tended to view it in strict and perhaps more traditional terms.

The two very religious, university-educated interviewees provide an interesting contrast. Fatma is a university assistant professor, raised in a wealthy, conservative family. She maintains a deep faith commitment, but she works in a community that she considers antagonistic toward her faith. Ahmet recently graduated from a public university in Istanbul with a degree in business administration. He also believed he was marginalized in the university setting. Both oppose the enforcement of *Shari'a* by the state, but they have somewhat different views regarding the content of *Shari'a*.

Fatma asserted that traditional Islamic jurisprudence cannot be enforced because of the changed context of contemporary Turkey, and her survey responses to questions regarding the content of *Shari'a* indicate a rejection of many traditional *fiqh* rules – such as those related to head covering for women, apostasy, homosexuality, inheritance by women, and testimony by women. However, she did agree that the consumption of alcohol and pork was prohibited – views consistent with the traditional rules. Her list of *hadd* crimes also comported with traditional jurisprudence, although she did not include apostasy because she does not believe that the issue is settled (a defensible position). She did explain, though, that she does not believe the traditional punishments can be enforced by the state in a way that comports with Islamic justice. As such, she believes that *hadd* crimes constitute civil crimes only to the extent that they harm others but are private religious offenses in all cases.

Although she occasionally covers her head as a matter of respect at funerals and other solemn gatherings, she does not generally wear a head covering in public, even though nearly all female members of her family do. This viewpoint is representative of a significant group of religious people in Turkey, who object to particular popular or traditional requirements associated with Islam as a result of considerable personal exploration and religious commitment. In choosing attributes that define Islam for her, she listed all options that would likely be considered virtues (mercy, love, justice, etc.), along with family, education, prayer, participation at the mosque, and human rights.

As with many respondents, Fatma distinguishes between Turkish secularism, which she characterized as attempting to exercise control over religion, and her ideal, which she indicated would be limited to ensuring the free exercise of religion and the separation of religion and the state. She insisted that the state should not play a role in protecting citizens from religious social pressure, a view she considers paternalistic and outdated. However, she also expressed deep concern that the Turkish government was promoting a particular view of Islam, making it inherently political, and thus potentially corrupting authentic religious sentiment.

In clarifying why she does not want *Shari'a* enforced in Turkey, Fatma explained that divine law is not the product of medieval *fiqh*. She believes that enforcing rules that are not certain or that cannot be enforced justly is contrary to the requirements of Islam. The approach she described sounded a bit like Sanhouri's to the extent that it emphasized enforcing rules known with certainty; however, she explicitly rejected the *ijma* of the classical jurists as a basis for that certainty. Fatma emphasized that the content of any *Shari'a* rule to be enforced must be subject to analysis using the best tools of science and interpretation available. With regard to process, her assertion that *Shari'a* rules ought to be enforced only when done with guarantees of procedural justice may be consistent with similar views expressed by Tariq Ramadan regarding the problems inherent in using *hadd* punishments in nation-states.

With regard to her personal religious practice, Fatma tries to pray five times a day but is often unable to fulfill this obligation because of work. She goes to a mosque for Friday prayers when she is able, but she does not attend at the university where she teaches for fear that she would be judged by her coworkers. She fasts during Ramadan and gives *zakat* (as do most Turks). She occasionally participates in a book group for women hosted by a friend of hers. She recounted several stories related to keeping her religious life separate from her professional life, in part for fear that she will not be promoted or that she will be otherwise ostracized by her peers. The picture of the academic community she described is extremely tolerant of most differences in ways that she appreciates deeply. However, it is also profoundly intolerant of religious commitment and expression, at least from her perspective. She explained that she has always been careful to ensure that no one sees her pray. As a junior professor, she explained that she is vulnerable if her colleagues perceive her as being overly religious.

Ahmet described similar feelings of fear. As a person who identifies as very religious, he worries that he will be dismissed or discounted by his peers. He explained that he felt very alone on campus and was one of the few students who prayed in the mosque on campus or attended Friday prayers there. Although he tends to understand the content of *Shari'a* in more traditional terms than Fatma, he similarly considers the requirements of Islam as consistent with Turkish law. He indicated that he believes that *Shari'a* provides for equality regardless of gender, race, religion, or other difference. Unlike Fatma, he does believe that Islam requires women to cover, and that it forbids apostasy and homosexuality. At the same time, Ahmet believes that charging interest in financial transactions is allowable under Islamic jurisprudence. Although he agrees with traditional inheritance rules and polygamy, he objects to distinctions between testimony based on gender. Like Fatma, he does not consider apostasy a *hadd* crime, but he also left highway robbery off his list (which is considered a *hadd* crime in traditional jurisprudence). The list of traits identified with Islam by Ahmet is nearly identical to Fatma's, including all of the positive virtues along with pious obligations, but he adds *jihad* and working hard to the list. The only distinction he made between Turkish secularism and his ideal was that he believes that Turkish secularism removes religious symbols from public life.

There did seem to be a degree of conflict between a commitment to traditional understandings of Islamic rules and the contemporary legal and economic system in Turkey. For example, at one point, Ahmet indicated that *Shari'a* is both a personal moral obligation and an obligation of the state. He also insisted that morality must be the standard for law. Later in the interview, he indicated that he does not want *Shari'a* to be enforced in Turkey. He explained that he was not confident that the government could enforce the rules in a way that would both uphold constitutional protections and comport with the requirements of Islam (perhaps another reference to Tariq Ramadan). However, he was more optimistic than Fatma regarding the reliability of classical *fiqh* as a basis for many, though perhaps not all, legal rules. Similarly, although he supports the ideal of government noninterference with religion, he also indicated that government has an obligation to protect citizens from coercive religious pressures. Consistent with someone who feels marginalized on the basis of faith, Ahmet expressed that religion and religious people are under attack in Turkey, while secularism and nonreligious people are not. With regard to religious practice, Ahmet prays five times a day, goes to Friday prayers, keeps the Ramadan fast, and gives *zakat*.

The two most striking commonalities between these two interviews are the level of personal energy both people exert to reconcile their deeply held religious convictions with their professional and intellectual lives and the common sense of oppression by peers that they feel because of their religion. Fatma clearly had deeper concerns about sharing her religious convictions and practices at the university. With regard to their views of *Shariʿa* and its enforceability in Turkey, both expressed the conviction that classical *fiqh* rules do not adequately reflect God's ideal, and that the modern nation-state cannot guarantee just enforcement even for those rules that are known with certainty (itself a disputed notion). This was particularly true for any rule requiring capital punishment.

Three university-educated interviewees identified as religious: Hakan, Sevgi, and Dilek. All three were in their early to mid-20s and agreed that *Shariʿa* ought not to be enforced in Turkey. Beyond this, their answers varied significantly. This might be explained in part by the breadth and diversity of the group that identifies as religious in Turkey. It is the largest single category, and in some polls it constitutes a majority. However, it is possible that identifying as religious has become an important social signifier that has a wide variety of meaning in terms of both belief and practice.

At the time of the interviews, Hakan was 21 and approaching the completion of his business degree in university. He identified as very religious in high school but became less so. He still plays the *nei*, and his connection to Sufi music still has spiritual significance for him. He acknowledges that some people want to enforce *Shariʿa* in Turkey, but he indicated that he does not "support or actively oppose" this perspective. However, he noted that enforcing traditional *fiqh* rules would have far less impact on men, which concerns him deeply.

Hakan seems to have responded to the survey with the assumption that the traditional *fiqh* understanding of law constitutes *Shariʿa*. For example, he indicated that it does not provide for substantive equality based on difference, nor does it guarantee economic rights like health and education. For him, it absolutely denies freedom of religion. The only questions in which he was not certain of the traditional *fiqh* rule, or perhaps its applicability, were the cases of apostasy, gender-based inheritance, gender-based testimonial weight, and its applicability to non-Muslims. Interestingly, when asked to identify traits he associates with Islam, Haryettin chose primarily practice-related traits such as prayer, mosque attendance, and community. The only positive virtues he identified were charity and friendship, but he also identified political activity and wealth, which he indicated was a criticism of the politicization of religion that concerns him in Turkey.

With regard to secularism, his view reflects a suspicion of the current government and a desire for greater separation, with the notable exception of controlling religious education. However, he indicated that religious education ought to be presented in a more historical and comparative context than the current curriculum allows. He believes that secularism and nonreligious citizens are threatened in Turkey and not religion and religious people.

With regard to his personal religious practice, Hakan described himself as unconventional. He rarely prays or attends mosque except on religious holidays, but he does feel that his music constitutes a meaningful spiritual practice. He said that he identifies with Sufism much more than with traditional jurisprudence, a phenomenon that he believes is common and growing in Turkey.

Sevgi came to the interview in a hip designer t-shirt and a haircut she described as "radical." Based on initial impressions, I expected her to be antagonistic toward religion. However, she expressed a deep commitment to her faith and to personal reflection. She identified herself as part of a growing community of young people who self-identify as religious but choose not to abide by traditional external norms of dress and head covering because those externals do not necessarily reflect an "authentic" experience of Islam.

Sevgi's responses related to the content of *Shari'a* were similar to Hakan's in that they tended to reflect traditional *fiqh* rules or uncertainty where she believed there was dispute. Notably, she disagreed with him in insisting that *fiqh* rules that make differences based on gender or religion are actually *Shari'a* rules. However, in the interview she did distinguish between the *fiqh* rules that are presumed to be *Shari'a* and the rules that are ultimately divine (which she identified as the "true *Shari'a*"). This created some degree of cognitive dissonance for her. For example, she is certain that God requires Muslims to pray five times a day, a requirement she does not abide by. This causes her some guilt, but she is also motivated to try to pray more. Sevgi also believes that Muslim women ought to cover their hair as a requirement of *hijab*, but she does not cover her hair. This causes her some degree of conflict, but less than does praying because, from her perspective, the requirements of *hijab* are inherently more subjective and personal than are the standards for prayer.

When asked about *hadd* crimes, another traditional category, she identified all of the crimes on the list (including distractors) except homosexuality, apostasy, and winedrinking. Interestingly, she identified all of the crimes that involve harm to others. In the interview, she indicated that law enforced by the state should really only punish activity that harms others. Although she accepts the possibility that *Shari'a* might be enforceable by the state, she does not want that for Turkey because she does not believe it could be applied justly and consistently. She expressed concern that state involvement with religion tends to be corrupting, so it was no surprise that the main distinction between Turkish secularism and her ideal was that the latter would not be subject to government control.

Dilek presented a case for the integration of an authentic religious commitment with the principles of Turkish constitutional secularism. The following is a translation from a portion of her interview:

> We are not a religious state. That was the point of the Republic. Secularism protects freedom. People don't even know what *Shari'a* means. We don't want to be like Iran or Saudi Arabia. We have freedom and a good economy. My family is Muslim and I believe in God, but I don't support the beliefs of Islamists. Rumi had the right view of Islam for Turks. I want freedom for everyone, including for girls to cover, but I don't believe that I need to cover to be a good Muslim. Iranians were free, and now they are not. Turkey should not go in that direction.

The view that religion can be privatized to some degree to conform with Kemalist principles of secularism is a view that appeared frequently in both the telephone poll and the Internet survey. Like Hakan and Sevgi, Dilek generally understands *Shari'a* to mean the rules found in classical *fiqh* manuals. Like Sevgi, she made a distinction between those rules and what God actually requires. For example, she does not consider drinking alcohol, apostasy, interest, or homosexuality problematic. She also objects to gender-based distinctions in inheritance or testimony, along with polygamy.

With regard to secularism, Dilek considers it more important than religious freedom per se because it ultimately ensures greater freedom from coercion. She would prefer that Turkey have greater separation between the state and religion. She expressed concern that the AKP government is threatening the tradition of constitutional secularism. Although her commitment to Republican principles is not unusual, it is notable that Dilek was raised in eastern Turkey in the city of Urfa and identifies as both Turkish and Kurdish. Dilek was less comfortable talking about personal religious practice than either Hakan or Sevgi. She explained that such things are very private to her.

All three of the religious university-educated interviewees expressed discomfort with political Islam and attempts to enforce classical *fiqh* rules – especially in cases where they do not apply equally to men and women. As a group, they all expressed a need to reimagine Islamic jurisprudence in a contemporary context or to interpret it through the lens of Turkish constitutional secularism. They do not agree as to the rules of classical *fiqh* or what is ultimately required by God, but they all expressed some degree of internal conflict in reconciling their faith with their conceptions of justice.

Ten university-educated people who self-identified as non/not very religious participated in in-depth interviews, representing a wide variety of backgrounds, including Kurdish, Laz, Armenian, and Alevi. The entire group opposed the imposition of *Shari'a* in Turkey and generally had one of two basic approaches to *Shari'a*. In interviews, eight people described *Shari'a* in terms of the classical rules they understood. Two people admitted that they picked options that would seem to indicate a modernist, or at least a nontraditional, approach to Islamic legal rules, not because they believed that approach was authentic, but because their understanding of the traditional rule was so offensive that they would not choose it in the survey. Some from this group were extremely uncomfortable discussing religion at all, and one person (Altan, who will be discussed more in the next chapter) became agitated and hostile discussing *Shari'a* because he considers it a justification for oppression that he had personally experienced. Although everyone in this group had or was in the process of receiving a university education, several admitted that religion was unimportant to them and that they knew relatively little about Islam. Two interviews stand out, those with Seda and Emir.

Seda is a very articulate academic who was 31 at the time of the interview. She identified as "not very religious," the category in the survey between "religious" and "not at all religious." In her own words:

> Most people accept religion on faith without investigation. *Shari'a* as law is a problem because the sources are not sufficient to form a legal system. Any approach to *fiqh* is the reasoning of men and out of context. God uses

> stories, not rules. *Human* reason is the key. Law should be practical. Even attempts to know *Shari'a* should be rooted in knowledge/logic. "*Shari'a*" in Turkey would be another law of men – not God's law. The social structure remains largely feudal and such a change could be used to consolidate power . . . Power expressed in law can change behavior – not will. No one covers in my family. My grandmother still prays (and covers for funerals). I believe in God and the idea that life is a test, but I believe that religion is social; it gives parents a way to answer the ultimate questions of children.

Seda's answers sometimes indicated her understanding of the traditional rules, as in the immorality of homosexuality or taking interest, but she identified many *fiqh* rules as inauthentic and violative of the spirit of Islam (e.g., covering for women and polygamy). She recognized some rules as traditional but was uncertain whether they really constituted *Shari'a* rules (apostasy and gender-based rules for inheritance and testimony). She identified *zina*, murder, and homosexuality as *hadd* offenses, but she did not identify highway robbery, theft, apostasy, or winedrinking as such. When asked, she identified *hadd* crimes with those things she believes to be most inimical to Islam. She complained that the entire field of traditional *hadd* jurisprudence emphasizes certain minor offenses (e.g., theft) while ignoring murder, thereby providing disproportionate punishments, which is contrary to Islamic principles of justice. This approach is consistent with the view she expressed in the survey of Islam being a source of virtues as opposed to devotional practices. In terms of personal religious practice, Seda indicated almost none. She makes a significant distinction between faith, which she admits to, and practice, which she actively avoids.

With regard to secularism, Seda noted that Turkish secularism lacks a sufficient emphasis on freedom of expression. As a legal principle, she believes that secularism is threatened in Turkey and that it is more important than freedom of religion. Even so, she indicated that Turkish law ought to require restaurants to close during the day in Ramadan and that boys and girls ought to be in different classes in secondary school. She explained that she desires these policies not because they are associated with Islam, but because they are cultural and provide a basis for national consensus.

Emir was 27 at the time of his interview and working as a writer. His family is Kurdish and his mother is Alevi. Although he does not want Turkey to enforce *Shari'a* rules, he did indicate concern that it might be foreseeable in the current political climate:

> I suppose *Shari'a* might be able to be enforced in a fair and democratic context. If not, it should not be treated as civil law. I have no idea what the specifics would look like or what purpose it would serve other than meeting a sense of religious obligation for some. It would be better for the *ulema* [traditional scholars of Islamic jurisprudence] to take responsibility for *Shari'a* rather than the government. Otherwise, it is more likely to be used as a tool for the privileged to consolidate their control over the legal and political system.

In questions related to content, Emir generally identified *Shari'a* with traditional rules, except in circumstances where he did not know the traditional rule (in his case, inheritance and *hadd* punishments). Like most respondents, he does not believe that *Shari'a* rules apply to non-Muslims. He used the following terms to describe Islam: community, mercy, *jihad*, prayer, forgiveness, and avoiding sin. He indicated that he tried to emphasize essentials rather than check everything that might have some role in Islamic religious practice and ethics. In a similar fashion, he chose only one attribute for Turkish secularism (control of religion) and his ideal (removing religious symbols and content from public life). Unlike the other members of the less- or nonreligious group, he indicated that religious freedom is more important than secularism. Although Emir does not actively practice Islam, it appeared he reflected deeply on questions of faith. He was thoughtful, engaging, and interesting.

While the interviewees with university educations were quite diverse, they all opposed the establishment of a legal system in Turkey that would enforce *Shari'a* rules. Among the nonreligious, some vehemently rejected the idea that religious law could be enforced after the establishment of the Turkish Republic. The more religious members of the group had similar concerns regarding any compromise of constitutional secularism and democracy, but they tended to reimagine traditional *Shari'a* rules in ways that might be consistent with existing Turkish law, or they relegated those rules to the sphere of private moral commitment in which law would play no role.

High school educated

There were six high school–educated participants in the in-depth interviews. Two each identified as very religious, religious, and non/not very religious, respectively. None of the six agreed that Turkey should enforce *Shari'a*. Unlike the university-educated group, they tended to have a more conventional understanding of *Shari'a*. They also tended to be more supportive of the AKP government.

Both of the very religious high school graduates had similar responses to the survey questions. They agreed that *Shari'a* conformed to traditional *fiqh* rules, albeit with some notable exceptions. Both interviewees questioned whether apostasy was a breach of Islamic law, and one had similar questions regarding homosexuality. Both interviewees objected to disparate inheritance rules based on gender and to polygamy. One expressed similar disagreement with the principle that legal testimony by women carries less weight than that of men. With regard to *hadd* crimes, both interviewees agreed that Islamic jurisprudence requires punishment for *zina*, theft, and winedrinking. Neither person listed highway robbery or apostasy as a *hadd* crime. Both expressed the conviction that Islamic jurisprudence conforms to Turkish norms of civil law. According to one interviewee:

> We are a secular republic with a Muslim government. The state may enforce parts of *Shari'a*, but it would be difficult. Real freedom began in the 80s. Prime Minister Erdoğan is a great leader and has made us great again – the

> best since Atatürk. There is no problem being a Muslim and living in a secular republic . . . I am very proud of development of the past ten years. I am much better off than my parents. We love America. Prime Minister Erdoğan and President Obama are good friends because Obama is a Muslim. People should be free to choose how to live. Turkey is a Muslim nation, and we should be free to live as Muslims.

Both interviewees identified Islam with traditional virtues, but one emphasized devotional practice and the other political involvement. They share similar views regarding Turkish secularism, but one expressed dissatisfaction with the level of control the government exercises over religious practice. In particular, he expressed anger that, in the past, Friday sermons had been distributed to local imams by *Diyanet*. Both people have a regular devotional life and are active in a local mosque.

The two self-identified religious interviewees indicated a similar commitment to Turkish secularism, but both expressed less interest in politics generally. One was a 25-year-old personal trainer, and the other was 19 and studying for the university entrance exam. Both identified *Shari'a* rules as the rules from traditional *fiqh* except where they conflict with Turkish law, such as apostasy, drinking alcohol, and the disparate treatment of women (inheritance, testimony, and hair covering). The one issue upon which they disagreed was polygamy. The personal trainer identified Islam with family, love, and friendship, while the student identified it with a long list of virtues, family, and human rights. Both expressed the view that Turkish secularism has changed over the last ten years and that there should be greater protection from religious coercion. According to the personal trainer:

> I believe in God, but I hate politics. I just want to have a good life. Everything is best if everyone is free. Don't bother me and I won't bother you – and I'm a big guy. I work with lots of wealthy people and some foreigners. I do okay, but rich people have gotten the most in the last 20 years. I believe, but it's not a big part of my life. It might be when I have a family. *Shari'a* has nothing to do with my life. It's mostly rules from 1,000 years ago. It doesn't even have much to do with Islam the way we live it in Turkey.

The student expressed similar sentiments:

> I am preparing for the university entrance exam. I don't have time for religion and believe it is social. My family is not too religious. Religion is fine as a social matter. I attend Mosque with my extended family at holidays and it is meaningful. Religious ceremony is meaningful, but it shouldn't be used to exclude or oppress.

The perspectives indicating Muslim identity as well as deep commitments to Kemalist principles were fairly consistent with the responses of religious high school graduates in the telephone poll and the Internet survey. However, it is possible that the degree of frustration with the current government is not representative. This might be explained by the fact that both interviewees are young. It is also possible that the student might attend university and ultimately be more appropriately compared with religious university graduates.

The two non/not very religious high school graduate participants in the study are, aside from a shared commitment to Turkish nationalist principles and an objection to the imposition of *Shariʿa* as law, very different people. Kadir is a businessperson who was 38 at the time of the interview. He identified himself as politically conservative and a supporter of the AKP government. In general, his answers were very similar to those given by the religious high school graduates described above. That is, although he identifies as a Muslim, he identifies more closely with his Turkish national identity. Nergis works in the tourist industry and was 30 at the time of the interview. Nergis comes from an Alevi family, but she considers that identity to be primarily social and cultural:

> *Shariʿa* is pointless. I don't believe in Islam. My family is Alevi, but it is cultural and social for us – mostly at deaths and births. I wasn't raised with any religious instruction. My parents believe in God, that he is good and merciful. It is personal to them. I feel no pressure to conform because they don't know their own faith. It makes me angry that people want to impose their religious rules on me – especially these days.

Like some of the nonreligious university-educated interviewees and many of the nonreligious participants in the telephone poll and the Internet survey, Nergis identified *Shariʿa* with traditional rules and made no effort to reconcile them with Turkish secularism. She did not know what crimes require *hadd* punishments but had the general sense that traditional punishments are harsh and inconsistent with Turkish law. The only trait she identified with Islam is being involved in political activities.

Nergis expressed anger at the AKP government and at the followers of Gülen, who she blames for the increasing role of religion in public life. She believes that both secularism and authentic religion are threatened in Turkey, and her ideal of secularism emphasizes the separation of religion and the state. Notably, she was one of the few respondents in any of the phases of the study to indicate that students in universities should not be allowed to wear head coverings. Nergis noted that discussing religion makes her angry and resentful.

More than the other two educational groups, the high school graduates expressed a deep commitment to Turkish nationalism and Kemalist principles, regardless of their religiosity or party affiliation. It might be that this group shares these characteristics in part as a result of the national program of socialization in public schools. Nationalist and Republican principles are a regular part of the public education system, along with a standardized curriculum of religious education, and university education contains fewer of these elements.

Primary school education or less

Seven people with a primary school education or less were interviewed as part of the study. Two each identified as very religious or non/not very religious, and three identified as religious. The group represents a variety of perspectives, but they tend to share a common commitment to a more traditional understanding of Islam and Islamic jurisprudence.

Both of the very religious interviewees with a primary school education or less gave similar responses to the survey questions. They agreed that *Shari'a* conforms to traditional *fiqh* rules with the exception of apostasy, which they considered allowable at least in part because it was not a violation of Turkish civil law. With regard to *hadd* crimes, one person chose all of the options, including the distractors, and the other person chose every option except apostasy. Both people expressed the conviction that Islamic jurisprudence ought to be kept separate from Turkish norms of civil law. According to one interviewee: "Turkey is moving in the right direction. I am very proud of our republic, our economy, and our laws. Islam is helping the country. *Shari'a* is good, but the law is different. It is how I live my life."

Both interviewees identified Islam with traditional virtues, but one emphasized prayer as well. They had nearly identical views regarding the relationship between law and religion, considering Turkish secularism their ideal for civil law. This group did not believe that government ought to protect citizens from social pressure to conform to religious norms. Both expressed satisfaction that the government was no longer enforcing head covering bans in universities. This group may have been the most optimistic about the legal and political trajectory of Turkey, and both people enthusiastically supported the AKP government and Prime Minister Erdoğan in particular.

Three interviewees with a primary school education or less self-identified as religious. Halil was 45 at the time of the interview and works as a maintenance person for an apartment building. Melek was 66 and works as a cook. Zeynep was 52 and works as a cleaning person.

Halil was born in the southeastern city of Diyarbakir into a Kurdish family and migrated to Istanbul in the early 1990s in order to find work to support his family. He prays regularly and is active in a local mosque. He indicated that the traditional rules of *fiqh* constitute *Shari'a*, but he was not sure whether non-Muslims were subject to it. He identified all of the options in the survey as *hadd* crimes, which he clarified as meaning that all were considered sins in Islam and could be criminalized. He described Islam in terms of the virtues listed in the survey, as well as prayer, mosque attendance, and *jihad*. Halil was the only person in the full-length interviews to indicate that Turkey ought to enforce *Shari'a*. He explained that living according to *Shari'a* was a personal and moral obligation that could be, but was not required to be, enforced by the state (his own personal preference). For purposes of consistency, he believes that the state ought to choose a *madhab* for particular rules, even though his family was raised honoring the *Shafi'i* school rather than the historically more influential *Hanafi* school. He would expect the parliament to draft legislation implementing *Hanafi* rules as law, particularly in the areas of family law and public morality. However, he would want judges to be able to interpret those laws without having to rely only on *Hanafi* jurisprudence:

> We need Islam. Under the AKP, things are much better, but we should do what is required by the Quran. This would be a good thing. Then we will have more freedom . . . I don't know how it would work exactly. I guess we would pass laws approved by the *ulema*. The Ottomans did that.

As with the very religious interviewees in this group, Halil considered Turkey's secularism to be ideal. He said that he feels free to practice his religion and is confident that the country will continue to allow religion to play a greater role in public life. He conveyed a deep distrust of government in general, but he expressed confidence in the AKP government. He cited the complete payment of IMF loans owed by Turkey as evidence of AKP success and the efficacy of Islam. The distinction between the state and the AKP could become increasingly complicated for people like Halil, because the ruling party has been in power long enough to deeply influence nearly all realms within the state bureaucracy.

One of the most fascinating people interviewed in the study is Melek. She came across as confident, self-possessed, and profoundly practical. Although she would like to be retired, she continues to work in order to help support her family. She described her view of *Shariʿa* in traditional terms except in the area of gender. She explained that, regardless of religious tradition, men and women must be treated equally under the law. In identifying crimes that require *hadd* punishments, she only chose adultery and murder. She explained that, while the rest might be included in "the books," they do not require anything more than civil law. Not only did she object to the idea of *Shariʿa* enforced as law ("that's what Iran does"), she stated that "ancient rules" should not even apply to Muslims as a moral standard:

> I don't want "*Shariʿa*" because it is too severe. That isn't Islam, but the empty idea of children. I'm a believer. I try to be a good person and help people. These are the greatest obligations of a Muslim. The Republic was a good idea and has done many good things. Being more publicly religious hasn't helped anyone but politicians. The *Cemaat* [here referring to those who follow Fethullah Gülen] is more about money than faith. If we enforce *Shariʿa*, freedom will go, and that is not Islam. My husband sees things the same way. You need real freedom in order to have real religion.

Melek described Islam in terms of family, love, human rights, prayer, friendship, and hard work. She identified secularism as an important Turkish ideal, but she would prefer that it emphasize freedom of expression rather than protection from social pressure. For that reason, she disapproves of the current state of Turkish secularism, which she considers compromised and under threat. As evidence, she proffered the effective end of the ban on head covering in universities. Although Melek considers herself a faithful Muslim, she does not cover her hair. The view she presented in the interview was that in Turkey external expressions of piety, including women covering their hair, were largely political acts.

Zeynep shared a number of traits in common with Melek – including gender, ethnicity, educational background, and family structure – but she presented herself as somewhat more conservative. Even so, she was not optimistic that *Shari'a* rules would be good for herself, her family, or the nation. Like many of the participants in the interviews, she accepted a traditional understanding of those rules, with the exception of the rules treating women differently than men. In any event, she does not believe that those rules apply to non-Muslims. Like Halil, she identified all of the crimes in the survey list as *hadd* crimes because she understood them all to constitute sins within Islam. That being said, she made it clear that she considers these personal moral obligations, and that they should only be enforced by the state when they cause harm to others. Her faith seemed to be a very important part of her life, informing every aspect of her daily existence. She identified Islam with all of the virtues and pious practices listed in the survey, notably excluding anything political:

> Turkey now has many religious schools abroad and this makes me happy. Foreigners enjoy Turkish culture, food, recreation, etc. What is the *Shari'a*? I don't know. People can say all kinds of things. It's mostly terrorists or extremists who say they want *Shari'a* – but their interpretation . . . I go to the Mosque and pray. It is an important part of Turkish culture.

In discussing secularism, she expressed satisfaction with the status quo but would prefer it if there was less social pressure to conform to someone else's view of Islam, while at the same time including more commonly acceptable Islamic symbols and values in the public sphere. Although she believes that individual freedom is more important than secularism, she would like to end coeducation in public high schools.

Yusuf and Elif were the two individuals in the interviews with primary school educations or less and who self-identified as not very religious. Yusuf was 41 at the time of the interview and runs his own business. Elif was 36 at the time of the interview and works as a cleaning person. They hold very different political views, but they reached similar conclusions in their assessment of *Shari'a* and its appropriateness in Turkish law.

Despite having little education, Yusuf became a successful entrepreneur, moving from the central Anatolian city of Yozgat to Istanbul after completing his military service. He expressed great pride in Turkey and for his time in the military. He identified that experience as the foundation for his commitment to secularism. Though he considers himself Muslim, noting that "all Turks are Muslims," he considers it a cultural identification that has very little impact on his life. He accepts that traditional *fiqh* rules equate with *Shari'a* except with regard to apostasy and issues resulting in different rules based on gender. "Those are not modern, and

Turkey is a modern Muslim country." He guessed that *zina*, highway robbery, theft, murder, homosexuality, and apostasy were probably in the tradition *hadd* crimes, but he admitted that he really was not sure. He associates the ideal of Islam with a commitment to family, charity, mercy, prayer, the mosque, friendship, and avoiding sin, but in the interview he insisted that religion is a private matter:

> Government should not be mixed with religion. The AKP is religious, but they don't force it on us. They have improved the economy. My business is good, and I just want a good future for my children. I'm not very religious, but religious people are fine if they respect my freedom. We have fought hard to make Turkey a modern country, and we will not become like Iran.

Yusuf insists that Turkish secularism protects freedom of religion and expression, but he is concerned by the extent to which the government involves itself in religious affairs. His preference would be to emphasize the separation of religion and the state but to still deter the more coercive elements of religion (groups he identified as "extremists").

Like Yusuf, Elif indicated that she supports the AKP despite not being very religious, but she also admitted that she is concerned that their economic policies do not help the poor. She was more supportive of the Refah government in the 1990s because "they helped the poor as Islam teaches." Elif identified several traditional rules with *Shari'a*, such as the prohibition on drinking alcohol and the *hijab* for women, but she objected to the rules on apostasy, inheritance, and testimony. She also said that the question of homosexuality is very confusing for her. She identified all of the crimes on the survey list as *hadd* crimes except homosexuality, apostasy, and winedrinking because "those do not involve other people." She identified Islam with the virtues of family, charity, mercy, justice, love, and friendship, but she expressed suspicion toward those who bring religion into politics:

> I don't know if *Shari'a* should be law. We don't have it now and the economy is good. It might not matter, but I don't know. I'm not very religious, but the government has helped many people live a better life. We are all Muslim, so our government ought to include our values without compulsion.

Elif identified the main difference between Turkish secularism and her ideal as the difference between the control of religion and stricter separation between religion and the state. Although she did not identify religion as primarily cultural to the extent that Yusuf did, it was very clear that for Elif Islam is an integral part of being Turkish (even for those, like her, who do not identify as religious).

The group of study participants with a primary school education or less was quite diverse, but there were some common themes in both the surveys and the interviews. More than the other two groups, they seemed to consider Islam an inherent component of Turkish identity. This may have existed in the other groups, but this was not as common or as clearly communicated. Even the less religious people in this group were somewhat sympathetic to the idea of enforcing "*Shari'a*" if all that meant was codifying existing cultural values.

Reflections on the survey group of interviews

The people interviewed represent the tremendous diversity within Turkey. There were some clear similarities that correlated with religiosity, but attitudes toward law and the state tended to follow education level more closely, supporting the thesis that provided the impetus for this study. I will begin with reflections related to the role of religiosity and then move to education.

The most consistent trait among people identifying as very religious was their commitment to devotional practice. Most pray five times a day and visit their local mosque with some regularity. All of them expressed a commitment to the five pillars of Islam – confession, prayer, fasting, almsgiving, and pilgrimage – even if they were not perfectly consistent in living those principles. The other common factor, which was also shared by those identifying as religious, was their understanding of *Shariʿa*. In this group, nearly everyone had a basic understanding of Islamic ethics and the traditional requirements of *Shariʿa* according to *fiqh* (usually *Hanafi fiqh*, though in one case, *Shafiʿi*). However, all of them objected to rules that they could not reconcile with their basic conceptions of justice. This most often included punishment for apostasy or the application of rules that treat women differently than men. The university-educated members of this group argued for an explicit reevaluation of traditional methodology, perhaps consistent with Islamic modernism. Others in the group tended to argue that certain rules could not appropriately be enforced by the state, even if they do in fact constitute *Shariʿa*.

The group identifying as religious tended to be somewhat less consistent in understanding religiosity. A few people had a consistent devotional practice, while others did very little except on religious holidays. As a group, they were less deferential to traditional rules. To the extent that *Shariʿa* had any place within government for these interviewees, it was somewhat narrower than for the very religious group.

The non/not very religious group was perhaps the most polarized. University-educated people tended to dismiss the relevance of *Shariʿa* completely, while those with a primary school education or less viewed it as something the government might appropriately consider, even though they viewed religion in primarily cultural terms. This group also had demonstrably higher variance in their answers than did the other two groups.

Education appears to have played a greater role in forming views related to the appropriate relationship between religion and the state. It also plays a role in how *Shariʿa* is understood. This is obviously a more complicated dynamic.

The university-educated interviewees all mentioned the importance of privacy in religion and wrestled with the implications. In each case, they concluded that many (if not all) of the traditional *fiqh* rules would be inappropriate as law in Turkey. Unlike the other groups, these people were less comfortable with a religious legal framework that appeared to be incompatible with the Turkish system of law and government.

The more religious participants tended to argue for the need to reinterpret the sources of Islamic jurisprudence in a contemporary context that they believed would reconcile them with modern notions of justice in Turkey. The nonreligious participants took the traditional rules at face value and rejected the entire system from which the rules emerged because they conflicted with contemporary legal norms in Turkey.

Although the high school–educated group represented a variety of perspectives, they had some interesting commonalities. First, they tended to object less frequently to the idea that religion might play a role in law. Second, they tended to understand religion in a cultural context more than either of the other groups. Finally, they mentioned Turkish nationalism and the values of Atatürk more than the other two groups. I would postulate that this group is likely socialized in a common manner more than the other two groups. All but one of the participants graduated from public high schools (the one attended a religious *imam-hatip* school). Public high schools in Turkey share many elements of a common curriculum, particularly with regard to religion and civics as described in Chapter Three. Although such programs of education and socialization cannot guarantee particular outcomes, this group shared a reverence for the ideals of the Turkish Republic that seemed to exceed that of the other groups. At the very least, they mentioned them with much greater frequency. Since university education is less controlled and is intended to encourage independent inquiry, it might be that the impact of national socialization in public primary and secondary schools is diluted for those who attend university. Similarly, those who do not attend high school are likely to be shaped by factors other than the national secondary school curriculum. Because military service is compulsory for men – though wealthy and university-educated Turks might be able to avoid it – it is possible that military service provides a similar basis for revering foundational principles of the Turkish Republic because it too has been imagined as a vehicle for socialization. The interviews do indicate that men tended to mention Atatürk, the Republic, and the nation more often than did women.

The group of participants who had completed primary school or less all spoke of religion and religious tradition with a degree of reverence not found in the other groups when taken as a whole. They all considered religion a source of values that would likely inform the creation of law. However, they all had an appreciation for the constitution and the legal system in Turkey. None of them desired for Turkey to be like Iran or Saudi Arabia (the only countries consistently identified with enforcing *Shariʿa* in the study). Even the self-identified religious person who did desire to codify *Shariʿa* did not imagine enforcing the entire body of classical Islamic jurisprudence. He seemed to want something more symbolic, which acknowledged the central role of Islam in Turkish values and morality.

This qualitative review of the interviews supports the notion that education tends to impact the *preference* for *Shariʿa* more than religiosity. However, religiosity does affect *conceptions* of *Shariʿa*. The interviews appear to indicate a spectrum, ranging from less educated people who tend to give greater deference to religious tradition to more educated people who feel freer to openly criticize, reject, or argue for a reimagining of that system.

Hizmet/Gülen-affiliated participants

Six people who actively participate in institutions identified as part of the Gülen Community or the Hizmet Movement were interviewed as part of the study. In screening interviews, people who actively identified with these groups tended to be uncomfortable with some of the survey questions (although they arguably represent a disproportionately large part of the Internet survey sample). Given the growing importance of these institutions within Turkey, I felt that it was critical to interview people from these movements. These interviews did not use the survey, were more casual than the other interviews, and were open-ended. Note that this small sample itself represents tremendous diversity of backgrounds and particular religious views. Although there is a great degree of economic support and coordination among institutions affiliated with or inspired by Gülen, they are by no means monolithic.

The first interview subject was a 20-year-old university student named Akif. Akif attended a Gülen-inspired high school in Istanbul and is a second-year student at Fatih University (also Hizmet-affiliated). He has been inspired by the writings and teachings of Fethullah Gülen, but Akif wanted to make it clear that he has explored them outside of the context of his formal education in discussion groups and in student organizations. He expressed a reverence for *Shari'a* and the *fiqh* tradition and insisted that they are not inconsistent with modern constitutional and legal principles. Even so, he does not want *Shari'a* to be enforced by the Turkish state – not because it is not binding, but because he does not believe that a modern constitutional state could do so justly. Consistent with the preaching of Gülen, Akif believes that democracy and the rule of law are perfectly compatible with Islam.

Mehmet was 42 at the time of the interview and works as a university professor. He was extremely sincere and sophisticated in discussing his faith. He first became interested in the writing of Fethullah Gülen in college. He is actively involved in a community of likeminded people at his university, and he participates in volunteer opportunities regularly. He acknowledges that *Shari'a* is God's law and that the classical tradition of *fiqh* attempted to understand those rules. He honors the tradition, but he indicated that he does not believe that tradition ought to be given the weight of civil law in Turkey. He explained that where such rules have been enforced by governments – such as in Iran, Saudi Arabia, or Sudan – they have not resulted in justice and prosperity. He attributes this perceived failure to three things: corruption, fragmentation of the Muslim community, and the application of rules developed for medieval societies in a modern context. Mehmet asserted that "Muslims in places like Turkey and the United States have freedom to obey God according to their consciences. Justice in a secular or non-Muslim system is still justice, but injustice justified by religion is not authentic Islam."

Mehmet would prefer that wise and pious leaders elected by the people establish a just society that reflects the core principles of Islam and honors human freedom. Although he has been very supportive of the AKP government, he expressed concern that money and power have attracted some to government service and to Hizmet for the wrong reasons.

Arzu was the only woman associated with Hizmet I was able to interview. At the time, she was 32 and working as a school administrator. She was very articulate, thoughtful, and impressive. She became interested in Gülen while at university, and she married a young man she met in the religious community. She is deeply religious, but she is also a practical and free thinker. Although there are times when she wears a headscarf for solemn occasions, such as funerals, she does not believe that it is a requirement incumbent upon her as a Muslim woman. She admitted that bucking common norms within her religious community could be frustrating, but she was grateful that her community has honored her decisions of conscience. Given her disagreement with members of her religious community on moral questions, Arzu would be very uncomfortable if the Turkish government were to enforce rules as if they bore the authority of *Shari'a*. She indicated that she is more comfortable with a "secular" state that allows her to practice her faith as she deems appropriate. She indicated some degree of frustration with Turkish secularism to the extent that it entails control of religion, but she would prefer it to a religious state.

Hikmet was a 46-year-old high school teacher. He has two children, and more than once he mentioned his financial struggles to support his family. He came across as somewhat dour and unhappy. He was suspicious of this project and was critical of research in Turkey conducted by non-Muslims, stating that it was inappropriate for me to study Islamic law or societies. According to Hikmet, *Hanafi* jurisprudence ought to be the basis for civil law in Turkey. He insisted that this would be consistent with democracy, constitutionalism, and rule of law. He was not concerned that classical *fiqh* rules might be inconsistent with existing laws. With regard to the questions of gender inequality, he explained that people could more authentically live their lives under *Shari'a* rules. This interview was shorter than the rest because Hikmet believed that the answers to my questions related to *Shari'a* were quite clear. I was very thankful that he consented to the interview because Hikmet was well read and intentional in his convictions, which are likely representative of a significant number of Turkish Muslims.

Levent was 39 and worked at a nonprofit organization affiliated with Hizmet at the time of the interview. He has a degree in business administration and is very proud of the work his organization does because he helps to provide opportunities for people that would otherwise not exist. He has clearly thought deeply about his faith and has committed himself to work that is consistent with his convictions. Although he expressed satisfaction at AKP successes over the previous 11 years, he has far more confidence in the role of the private sector to effect change. Thus, it is unsurprising that he does not trust the state to enforce Islamic legal norms. He noted that those who have been inspired by Gülen have experienced persecution in the past, and it is possible that a so-called *Shari'a* state could be equally if not more oppressive, even in Turkey:

> I put my trust in Allah, not in politicians. As long as we have freedom to practice our religion and to conduct our business, we will build an Islamic society,

> one that is authentic and freely chosen. One that government will not be able to manipulate. We have our own media [*Zaman* and Samanyolu]. We have our own schools. We have our own universities. We have many charitable organizations and foundations. We work in every province and throughout the world. We are changing Turkey, not politicians.

Levent expressed concern that government, even one perceived as being sympathetic, could become corrupt.[2]

Kudret was 44 at the time of the interview and a very successful businessperson. His family is politically conservative and owns a number of businesses. The family is connected to a number of Hizmet-related charities as well as to the AKP. Kudret is very astute, but he admitted that he does not know much about the tradition of Islamic jurisprudence. The view he presented in the interview is that government ought to be concerned with public safety and with facilitating commerce. Beyond that, government ought to be minimized so that people can make their own choices. Kudret has spent a significant amount of time in Europe and in the United States. He would prefer that Turkey adopt the U.S. approach to law and religion, but he expects that it will take time. With regard to *Shari'a*, he does not know how the tradition ought to be understood today. He is far more concerned with his own personal moral obligation to abide by it, and he relies on the work of Gülen to better understand his faith.

The interviewees with connections to Hizmet were very diverse, which is encouraging because it indicates that members of these organizations can cooperate to support common causes and yet allow for difference and some degree of dissent. The network of civil society organizations inspired by Gülen is clearly extensive. Some of these participants credited Hizmet organizations for much of the educational and economic development in Turkey over the previous ten years – although that might be going a bit too far. As a group, they seemed to believe that they are contributing to something meaningful and constructive, and in most cases they were suspicious of government, even one led by people nominally affiliated with their causes. Their understandings of *Shari'a* mostly deferred to the teaching of Gülen, which is not surprising. It is, however, a bit problematic because Gülen himself is not very explicit in his public teaching about the content of *Shari'a* and about the role of the state in enforcing Islamic norms.

Notes

1 *See About Beyoğlu Municipality*. Beyoğlu Municipality, 2011, available at http://en.beyoglu.bel.tr/beyoglu_municipality/default.aspx?SectionId=1652.

2 New of fraud investigations related to the AKP in late 2013 and the subsequent criticism of Hizmet and the targeting of Hizmet members by the government make these observations all the more relevant.

7 Influences in the formation of views toward *Shari'a*

Both the quantitative and the qualitative data indicate that the meanings attributed to *Shari'a* vary widely within Turkey, and that Turkey's overall profile differs from most predominantly Muslim countries. It is also clear that there has been a shift in preferences and views within Turkey over the last 20 years. Religion now plays a more open and central role in public discourse, but great value is placed on the opportunity for public discourse, personal choice, and dissent. One of the most surprising and interesting results of the interviews was the collection of narratives describing how people developed their personal religious beliefs, particularly beliefs related to the role and content of *Shari'a*. Details from some of the more interesting and representative conversations follow.

Ekrem

Ekrem, a 27-year-old male barber, moved to Istanbul from Tokat with his family when he was in primary school. He strongly supports Prime Minister Erdoğan and the AKP government for two main reasons: (1) their success in developing the economy and (2) the increased prominence given to religion. He repeatedly referred to Turkey as a "Muslim nation." Like most of the participants in the study, Ekrem indicated that his family had been the primary source of religious education in his life. He also noted the role of religious education in public schools but dismissed it as "a waste of time." He claimed that he learned more about Islam from the television channel Samanyolu[1] than he did from the national school curriculum. One question asked of all participants was, "Is there any public figure (writer, religious leader, scholar, musician, actor, television commentator, etc.) whose views on religion you find interesting or persuasive?" Ekrem's response to this question was, "I don't like the religious people on TV; they do it for the money mostly. It's also confusing because they disagree with one another." Skepticism of public figures was fairly common in the interviews. It also raised the fascinating issue of pluralism within Turkish religious views. Turkish media and publications contain a wide variety of religious perspectives – including traditional, modernist, syncretist, shamanist, and new age – and a host of other approaches to religion are readily available on bookstore shelves. For Ekrem, as well for other participants in the study, this cacophony has created confusion and a widely felt desire for authoritative religious voices. Ekrem found that authority in the prime minister. Others found it in Fethullah Gülen or some other religious figure. Ekrem explained this dynamic as a sort of heuristic. He does not have the training to determine what approaches to faith are authentic, so when he finds a leader with religious convictions whom he respects and trusts, he defers to them on matters of faith and policy. This or similar approaches seem to have been adopted by many of the people interviewed, although there was great variety among those acknowledged as reliable teachers of Islam.

Dilek

Dilek is the 25-year-old female graduate student, originally from Urfa, who was discussed in Chapter Six. She expressed strong opposition to "Islamists" and described her fascination with Rumi and the Sufi traditions native to Anatolia. Like several of the women interviewed, she does not wear any sort of head covering, even though she adamantly supports the right to do so regardless of location or context. Dilek spoke very sweetly about the role her mother played in teaching her to pray and learning about Islam generally. She also indicated that she has read extensively on the subject of Islamic spirituality. Given her interest in esoteric religion and mystical traditions, I was somewhat surprised that she noted her fondness for the television show *The Fifth Dimension* (*Beşinci Boyut*), which aired on Samanyolu between 2005 and 2011. The series is strikingly similar to the 1990s CBS show *Touched by an Angel*. The formula for most episodes was a family going through crisis, gently aided by a duo of angels. Several interviewees mentioned this show, identifying it as meaningful to people across age groups and educational backgrounds. Although family dramas hold value for Dilek, she has no fondness for "television *hocas*" (preachers). She did say that she enjoys the relatively new genre of programming, which mixes practical information on health, food, and exercise with Islamic spirituality.

Yusuf

Yusuf, the 41-year-old male business owner described in Chapter Six, was satisfied with the AKP government so long as no particular religious view was imposed on him. He indicated that his family and school were the main sources of his religious education. He was thankful that his parents never forced him to practice or believe anything in particular. They wanted him to decide for himself what he believed and how he would live. His mother covers, but he does not believe that it is necessary. Yusuf insisted that religious leaders ought to be rational, and he complained that woefully few are. He did mention that Yaşar Nuri Öztürk was reasonable in most of his writing and public speaking. Yusuf added that some religious journalists are also fairly reasonable, but he could not remember any particular names.

Elif

Born in the Black Sea region in 1976, Elif worked as a cleaning person at the time of her interview. She did not identify as religious, but she has supported the AKP. She learned most of what she knows about religion from her grandmother. She described public religious figures as confusing and self-interested. Elif described religious-oriented television dramas as more beneficial, saying, "they are about real life." She added that she enjoys dramas based on the Ottoman period but that she is glad she did not have to live back then. Other interviewees shared a number of similar views.

Halil

Halil worked in a residential building as a doorperson in Istanbul. He was 45 at the time of the interview and has lived in the Beyoğlu neighborhood since 1991, when he moved there from the southeastern city of Diyarbakir. Halil learned about religion at home from his family and from television. He showed particular interest in his community at his local mosque, where he prays regularly: "Our *hoca* is a very good man." He also indicated that he respects Fethullah Gülen and the many ministries inspired by him. Halil described religion as a key touchstone that brings people together and provides the opportunity to start over: "My father died last year, but our family came together for the first time in many years to pray. God gave us another chance."

Altan

Altan, 29 at the time of the interview, works as a sales representative for a large Turkish company based in Istanbul. He has a university degree in business and is fluent in English. Although he identifies culturally as Muslim, he expressed discomfort with questions related to religion in general and with *Shari'a* in particular: "We all know what it is, but most of us don't want to live that way." For Altan, *Shari'a* requires women to cover, which is antithetical to his view of free expression. More than any other participant in the study, Altan expressed antipathy toward public religious figures and religious media. His parting comment made this particularly clear: "I'd rather read Bertrand Russell."

Fatma

Fatma, the 33-year-old academic described in Chapter Six, identifies as a very religious person who chooses not to cover. She originally learned about religion from her family, but she had classes in school that were also influential. As an adult, she has read extensively on religious topics (though it is not her field of study). Like many of the people who were interviewed after completing the survey, Fatma was exposed to the "*Gülen Cemaati*" in school. Her attitude toward Gülen and Hizmet matched those of many others surveyed. She expressed respect for "*Hoca Efendi*'s" teaching (using the honorific for an esteemed teacher), but she was never really comfortable in the groups who were affiliated with him. She was very uncomfortable with the level of conformity and the relative marginalization of women that she observed in those groups. More recently, she has developed an interest in some contemporary figures identifying with the Sufi tradition. She mentioned Ömer Tuğrul İnançer as one such figure.[2]

Hakan

Hakan is the 20-year-old religious university student described in Chapter Six. He learned about Islam from family and friends, but his family was not very religious. He tried to be faithful and observant in high school. He attended a religious discussion group (not affiliated with Gülen) in high school. He attended a regular (*Anadolu*) high school and his teachers led the group. He went with his brother at first and then went alone. At about the same time, Hakan learned to play the *nei*, and as an important instrument in *Mevlevi* devotion, it has had religious significance for him. Hakan said that being religious gives him a sense of purpose and well-being. It makes him feel "special." He, too, was influenced by television, particularly *The Fifth Dimension*; they were "real" stories of faith, he said. Hakan eventually found organized religion somewhat empty: "I believe it is used to control people." When he first showed interest in Islam, his grandparents mocked him, afraid that he would become a "*Cemaat* guy." Hakan believes Muslims want a good life like everyone else, but strict religious groups make that harder. He likes some contemporary Sufi thinkers, such as Inançer, but he believes many use too much Persian and Arabic, making them inaccessible. Another aspect that concerns Hakan about many popular understandings of Islam is what he described as "the inequitable treatment of women."

Ahmet

Ahmet is the very religious 22-year-old university student described in Chapter Six. He was one of the most social and engaging participants in the study. For him, religion is deeply connected to family. He began learning to read the Quran before beginning school at the age of six. He went to a religious primary school and started at an *imam-hatip* (religious) high school, but then he switched for university entrance purposes. He studied in a private Quran course for six years while he was in school. In fact, he said that it was harder for him to learn to read Turkish. Ahmet observed that most people in his public university are less religious than he is. However, he emphasized that he is exploring and appropriating his faith and not taking the word of an imam or public figure. In high school, he participated in a discussion group sponsored by a "[Gülen] *Cemaati*"[3] organization. Ahmet said that he enjoys Gülen's books, but that they are very difficult to understand. His experience with the "*Cemaat*" group in school was more negative. He opined that the leaders exercised too many inappropriate forms of control. He described one instance when he participated in a discussion group (in Turkish, a *sohbet*) after prayers. The group was held in a small room, and Ahmet sat on a couch because his knee was injured and hurting. "The *abiler* [a word used in Hizmet to indicate leaders, literally meaning "older brothers"] chastised me and insisted that I sit on the floor as a matter of tradition and deference." Ahmet objected, explaining that he believes that attitudes of the heart to be more important than legalism. He also described the experience of marginalization as a person of faith. When he was in high school and would visit his brother at university, his brother asked him not to mention that he prayed or attended the mosque. Ahmet was more than a bit surprised, and he felt ashamed about his faith for the first time. As he described it, "being a Muslim is becoming more shameful in Turkey. My grandmother doesn't even know that I pray." According to Ahmet, his conservative relatives and friends accept a certain level of religious devotion or practice, but they do not attempt to deepen or challenge their faith, and the result is that they do not grow or change. Ahmet indicated that he wants to be different. He said that he wants his faith to be authentic and a basis for positive change in his life and in the life of his community.

Sevgi

Sevgi is the religious woman described in Chapter Six who was finishing university at the time of her interview. Her outward appearance resembled some former students of mine who were involved in the underground music scene. She had spiky hair, shaved on one side, wore a few large pieces of metal jewelry, and sported a ripped t-shirt. Although she indicated that she believes that she should cover as a matter of faith, she does not. Her family is religious, but her mother does not cover either. Sevgi described her faith as the product of personal exploration even more than as the result of the influence of her family. She especially enjoys the religious-themed novel *Selim ve Hande* by Halit Ertuğrul.[4] Like many Turks, she ascribes to the intelligent design theory of creation.[5] Although she was exposed to the teaching of Gülen in her university exam prep course, Sevgi was not very impressed with the approach or the way the movement was structured (it was "too hierarchical"). She added that it can be very strict and does not reach people in an authentic way; instead, it emphasizes conformity and a narrow brand of politics. She was also wary of it because of its perceived closeness to the United States and its government. Sevgi explained that she is a pacifist and that the United States had become the primary driver of large-scale military actions in the world, something she believes to be antithetical to Islam and to Christianity. She did indicate that she respects Nihat Hatipoğlu, a formally trained theologian who would appear regularly on the Star TV channel in Turkey, particularly during Ramadan.[6]

Sevgi has reached out for guidance in the past as she wrestled with the issue of homosexuality (though she made no indication that she herself identified as anything other than straight). She found it difficult to reconcile the experience of her gay friends, who said that they did not choose to be gay, with the popular view that homosexuality itself is a sin. After calling the *Diyanet fatwa* line a number of times unsuccessfully, she sent a lengthy email inquiry to the Directorate. She received a reply affirming that homosexual acts are forbidden by Islam but that being attracted to the same sex did not itself constitute sin. Instead, homosexuality was described as a struggle or temptation, such as the physical propensity for alcohol addiction, that gives people the opportunity to honor Allah by turning away from temptation. With some degree of ambivalence, Sevgi accepted this view as authoritative. Although she admitted that this might not ultimately conform to what she chooses to believe, it is the wrestling with texts, traditions, and logical arguments that she claims make her religious experience authentic:

> This is important for true religion. Turks become atheists as a response to perceived hypocrisy or because they are too legalistic. Religious life appears or becomes oppressive to them. Those who were legalistic and dogmatic in religion take that with them and tend to become dogmatic atheists.

Seda

Seda, a woman who studied philosophy in university, identified herself as not very religious. She was extremely articulate in expressing her views and explaining why she held particular opinions. She complained that most people accept religion on faith without adequate investigation and reflection. Although she finds value in Islamic tradition, she explained her belief that God uses stories, rather than rules, to communicate with human beings: "Revelation consists more of parables and narratives than rules, and God expects us to use the reason he gave us." Seda explained that family was important in the formation of her views. She explained that no women in her family cover, but that her grandmother does pray regularly.

She admitted to believing in God and in the idea that life is a test, but she asserted that religion is primarily social, giving parents a way to answer the ultimate questions asked by children. Seda complained that religion classes in school provided her no history or context for understanding her tradition – only the content of certain prayers and rituals. She mentioned hearing in middle school that followers of Gülen intended to spread their influence within Turkish politics and beyond.[7] Neither she nor her family took these ideas seriously, but in retrospect she said that she believes that they have done exactly that. Seda lamented that what was once about belief is now about power: "Political hegemony of any type is bad, but it is made worse combined with religion because of its ability to control." When asked whether there were any religious figures she respected, she noted that Dücane Cündioğlu thinks about religion and reason.[8] She also mentioned that she occasionally likes to watch Öztürk on television because he explains how religion is used to control people – a view she has sympathy for.

Seda told an interesting story to indicate the role that religion plays in her life, even though she does not practice or consider herself religious:

> At the end of high school I was staying with my religious grandmother. The earthquake of '99 took place at 3:15 a.m. I woke up to the shaking. The sky

> looked red and I heard strange rumblings and horns. I really thought it was the Judgment and was comforted. My grandmother awoke and rushed under a doorframe. I asked her what she was doing. She said that it was what we do in an earthquake. So the secular granddaughter thought it was the judgment and the religious grandmother realized it was an earthquake and responded practically. Then I became frightened.

Seda admitted there are elements of religion that are deeply embedded in her psyche, but she also indicated that this creates some degree of internal conflict. She indicated a concern that she believes many of her peers also hold – that traditional approaches to Islam tend to marginalize and subordinate women in practice, even if that is not the intent of the textual tradition. She noted that women have a similar problem in some Christian cultures as well. She actually mentioned a number of similarities between the United States and Turkey, so I asked her why that might be. She shared the following insight:

> Turks are immigrants who had a multiethnic empire, and the United States is a nation of immigrants. It is no wonder that Turkey and the U.S. are similar in some ways. Politics, and particularly religious politics in Turkey, has changed us, homogenized us. It was better when there was more diversity of views and expressions.

Melek

Melek is the 66-year-old cook and housewife who identified as religious and had a primary school education described in Chapter Six. She emphasized the role of her faith in inspiring her to help others and to provide a good example for her children and grandchildren. She carried herself with great dignity and confidence in the interview. She does not wear a head covering, and she does not believe that it is required by the Islamic injunction to dress modestly. Like most of the people completing the full survey and participating in the interview portion of the study, Melek mentioned the "*Cemaat*," and she did so in mostly negative terms. She asserted that, "they are more about money than faith." She indicated that the only public religious figure she respects is Öztürk because he is rational and focuses on the primary text of the faith, the Quran. She graciously offered to give me her copy of his book *The Meaning of the Holy Quran*. She appeared disappointed when I declined, telling her that I owned a copy, but she was encouraged that I had translated one of his books into English. After more discussion, Melek did say that she also believes that Zekariya Beyaz, a prominent professor of religion and sociology, was worth listening to.[9] Like most of the people interviewed, she mentioned the role of family in forming her views of Islam and *Shari'a*. As one of the older people with children to be interviewed, I was also interested in the ways she approached teaching her children. Melek explained that she was intentional in providing spiritual and moral life lessons by example to her children and grandchildren. "Love, helping others, and doing no harm – this is what we try to live and teach." She also emphasized the importance of hope and focusing on the positive. She offered to share a personal faith story as an example:

> My daughter has had chronic myelogenous leukemia for seven years. Nothing is worse for a parent than facing the death of a child. Her treatment is awful, and we could have lost hope. Instead, we all made a decision to face this struggle with faith.[10] She has now fallen in love and feels much better. We are hopeful that she is entering remission. But even if she leaves us, we know that Allah has brought good things to our family in the midst of tragedy and struggle. She found love, we found hope, and all of us found some peace.

Zeynep

Zeynep also completed primary school and identified as religious. She was 52 and working as a housekeeper at the time of the interview. Like most people, she identified her family as the main source of her education regarding Islam and *Shari'a*. Although she prays and attends mosque regularly, she noted that religious devotion is an important part of Turkish culture: "Our whole family practices; we are Turkish." When considering religious leaders she finds influential, Zeynep included Öztürk and Nihat Hatipoğlu "because they explain Islam clearly and sensibly." She also mentioned the importance of religious programming, mostly on Samanyolu, and especially *The Fifth Dimension* and *The Mirror*.[11] For Zeynep and her family, fasting is an important devotional practice. From an early age, she began fasting not only during Ramadan but also during other religious observances throughout the year. She has taught her son to do the same. Toward the end of the interview, Zeynep told the story of her introduction to prayer and fasting. When she was ten, her mother would give her money for each day she fasted during Ramadan. Since it was a positive experience, Zeynep wanted to participate in the prayers as well. Her mother brought her to the mosque and told her to bow and rise up along with everyone else. "Because I didn't know the prayers yet, my mother told me to say 'Allah' both when I bowed down and when I stood up." By the time she was 12, Zeynep had memorized the formal prayers and recited them regularly. Although she emphasized the importance of religious education and cultural identification, she made it very clear that "my religion is ultimately between me and Allah."

Emir

Emir is the ethnically Kurdish, 27-year-old writer with both Alevi and *Shafi'i* influences described in Chapter Six. His maternal grandfather was an Alevi elder from Syria, and his paternal grandfather was from the predominantly Armenian city of Yerevan. He expressed pride that his paternal grandfather had met Said Nursi, generally regarded as the most influential Islamic scholar in the early decades of the Turkish Republic.[12] All four of Emir's grandparents were very religious, but his parents were less so. He identified as not very religious, but he had a deep understanding of Islamic thought based on his own study. His parents wanted him to make his religious commitments freely, so he read widely on Islam. He also read the Gospels and the *Torah* in order to compare them to the Quran as texts and as sources of spiritual inspiration. Emir was not particularly impressed by popular religious scholars, but he did say that he enjoys Nursi's *Risale-i Nur* and Ismet Özel's[13] well-known poem *Yearning* (*Münacaat*).

He shared two interesting stories, one from his youth and one more recent. He explained that he used to hang out with his friends at the neighborhood mosque in the city of Kars when he was in junior high. His buddy was the son of the imam at the mosque, which allowed them to get away with mischief other kids could not. One day Emir and his friends cut the power to the mosque, including to the sound system, during the Friday sermon (a time when the mosque would be very full). When the imam discovered what they had done, Emir and his friends were banned from the mosque for a year. This struck the boys as a severe punishment because they enjoyed the community of the mosque. It was a place where older people were patient and encouraging, and where there was always water.

Emir also told a more recent story to illustrate the relationship between religion and funerals for many of Emir's peers and to explain a bit of his family's iconoclasm. His paternal grandmother had died recently, unexpectedly, and without prolonged suffering. His father was so relieved she did not suffer that he laughed at a joke at the funeral. The officiating imam was not amused and became very angry, publicly chastising and cursing Emir's father for laughing at such a somber occasion, which only made him laugh more.

Nergis

Nergis is the nonreligious woman from an Alevi family described in Chapter Six. She works in the tourism sector, and, although she did not attend university, she speaks several foreign languages and has had exposure to many foreign cultures. She described her Alevi identity as entirely cultural and social, something that becomes important for her at deaths and births. Unlike most of the others in the study, Nergis did not receive religious instruction from her family. Her parents believe in a good and merciful God. For them religion is personal and private because they are marginalized for their Alevi identity. Nergis said that her family placed no pressure on her to conform, and that most members of her family had little understanding of their own religious tradition.

She recalled a family story from her childhood. When she was about ten, her family visited her father's cousin. He wasn't religious, but he had a Quran on his shelf. At one point, Nergis reached for the Quran to look at it, but her father's cousin reached over to take it before she could touch it. He insisted that she could not even touch it because she was not ritually clean. He could, though, even though he was not practicing his faith. At her request, he read to her some passages about miracles, and they discussed the readings. Neither Nergis nor her relative believed that the stories were real. They agreed regarding the substance of their nonbelief, but it still seemed to bother Nergis that she was not even allowed to touch the Quran because of her age, her lack of belief, or her gender (she was not sure which). Although she had the standard course in religious education in high school, she hated it and this frustrated her teacher. She could not think of a single religious figure she found interesting or worthwhile. When pressed, she said, "Give me an atheist like Dawkins." She finished the interview by sharing a story highlighting the tension or disconnect between belief and nonbelief in her family. Her mother has epilepsy, and when Nergis was 14 she remembered witnessing her mother having a seizure. At the end of the seizure, her mother began to recite the *shahada*, the basic confession of faith in Islam, as she regained her faculties – an act that made no sense to Nergis then or now. Not surprisingly, Nergis expressed anger at the prospect of having religious rules imposed upon her by anyone – by her family, by her community, or by her government.

Hizmet/Gülen-affiliated participants

The six participants in the study from Hizmet/Gülen-affiliated organizations were asked similar questions in a more abbreviated fashion and gave relatively homogeneous responses. All but one person indicated that their family was deeply influential in the formation of their views of Islam and *Shari'a*. All six credited Fethullah Gülen as the primary source of religious knowledge in their lives. Four people indicated that the work of Rumi was important to them, and two mentioned Said Nursi. Most of the people in this group mentioned the importance of media outlets, such as *Samanyolu* and *Zaman*, but they were more divided with regard to political leaders like Prime Minister Erdoğan and President Gül. This seemed to indicate trust of Hizmet-affiliated civil society organizations and distrust of political parties.

With regard to *Shari'a* itself, this group of interviewees displayed an interesting guardedness and ambivalence. As a group, they tended to be uncomfortable talking about *Shari'a* explicitly. When pressed, one person offered that it is of course a requirement of Allah, but its enforcement as law is not considered appropriate by most Turks. "We are not extremists who call for *Shari'a*, but we live in a Muslim country. Our law ought to protect our religious freedom." This and similar statements seemed to imply that civil law ought to reflect Islamic values without importing the classical *fiqh* tradition. This appears to be consistent with Gülen's public positions on *Shari'a* and *fiqh*. He does not deny the authority of the classical tradition, but he does seem to allow for a modernist application of the values underlying those rules within the limits of democratic and constitutional frameworks.

Observations

The interviews present a fascinating patchwork of perspectives that indicate some areas of commonality and a few clear divisions. First, it is clear that a number of Kemalist and Republican principles are deeply embedded in and impact religious views. Rule of law, constitutionalism, democracy, gender equality, and some form of secularism were valued to some degree by nearly every participant. As a result, the understandings of *Shari'a* tended to have modernist implications, except in the case of those who rejected it completely. Except for those actively participating in Hizmet/Gülen-affiliated organizations, more than 75% of interviewees mentioned the "*Cemaat*" in some form and almost always in a critical light. As many participants put it, even most of those who identified as religious or very religious, organizations tied to or inspired by Fethullah Gülen had become influential. It had become a pathway to greater wealth and political power for many, particularly within the AKP. With the rapid increase in power came increased opportunity for abuse. A number of people clarified that they did not mean to criticize Islam, religious people, or Gülen. Instead, they criticized any human organization in which power was being abused. The six participants from Gülen organizations tended to be somewhat defensive when asked about these perceptions. Most made a clear distinction between Hizmet and nonreligious organizations, particularly the AKP. As a group, they seemed deeply concerned by abuses of power and problems created by excessive nationalism.

Although a wide variety of factors influenced the religious perceptions of the interviewees, a number of notable individuals and organizations stood out. Obviously, Fethullah Gülen was the single most mentioned influence (positive or negative) other than family. Yaşar Nuri Öztürk was mentioned by a surprising number of participants as well. Other influential figures mentioned included religious scholars Nihat Hatipoğlu and Zekariya Beyaz, the poet Ismet Özel, and the writers Halit Ertuğrul and Dücane Cündioğlu. Ömer Tuğrul İnançer was mentioned by three people and falls into an interesting category of popular figures providing religious and spiritual advice without a formal education in the field. Similarly, political leaders, such as now-President Erdoğan and former President Gül, provide some degree of religious inspiration for a number of those interviewed. Traditional sources of spiritual guidance in Anatolia, such as Mevlana Jelaluddin Rumi and Said Nursi, remain important figures today. Media companies including the *Zaman* newspaper and the Samanyolu television network are playing an increasingly important role. It was especially surprising that so many participants in the study mentioned a single Samanyolu television series, *The Fifth Dimension*, as an important source of religious knowledge.

Notes

1 One surprising result of the interviews was the important role of Samanyolu and its religious-themed dramatic programming in forming religious mores and identity among diverse groups of people. *See* Chapter Three for a more detailed discussion of the role of the media in shaping religious values.

2 İnançer was mentioned by a few participants. He was trained as an attorney and as a musician. Music led him to a deeper exploration of Sufism and has become the main subject of his writing and speaking. He is described in greater detail in Chapter Three.

3 The term *Cemaat* (literally community) is usually used in a pejorative manner to refer to organizations inspired by or affiliated with the teaching of Fethullah Gülen. It is not the word used by people involved in those organizations, and they would likely take

offense at its negative connotations. I only use the term to the extent that it was used by subjects in my research.

4 Halit Ertuğrul was one of a number of novelists who provided a religious counter-narrative to the socialist and modernist voices of the 1970s. His novel, *Selim ve Hande*, is his most notable work. Çimen Günay-Erkol, "Issues of Ideology and Identity in Turkish Literature during the Cold War," in *Turkey in the Cold War: Ideology and Culture*. Ed. Cangül Örnek and Çagdas Üngör. New York: Palgrave Macmillan, 2013, pp. 123–124.

5 Marc Kaufman, "In Turkey, Fertile Ground for Creationism." *Washington Post*, November 8, 2009, available at http://www.washingtonpost.com/wp-dyn/content/article/2009/11/07/AR2009110702233.html.

6 Nihat Hatipoğlu (a writer and theologian) is a popular religious figure who appears on Turkish religious television channels such as Samanyolu and Kanal 7. *See* Jeanette Jouili, "Re-fashioning the Self through Religious Knowledge: How Muslim Women Become Pious in the German Diaspora," in *Islam and Muslims in Germany*. Ed. Ala Al-Hamarneh and Jörn Thielmann. Leiden: Brill, 2008, p. 473.

7 She referred to the so-called "*Büyük Orta Doğu Projesi*" (The Great Middle East Project), which is usually used to refer to Gülen and Hizmet in negative and conspiratorial terms. However, it is patently evident that Gülen's influence and the influence of institutions inspired by him have increased dramatically since 2000.

8 *See* Chapter Three for background on Cündioğlu.

9 *See* Chapter Three for background on Zekariya Beyaz.

10 Here she described her family struggle to face disease, disability, and perhaps death as a form of *jihad* (*cihat*).

11 *Ayna* (The Mirror), is another religious oriented popular drama produced and aired on Samanyolu.

12 Nursi was also ethnically Kurdish and a scholar in the Shafi'i school of jurisprudence. In addition to giving voice to objections against state limitations on freedom of expression rooted in religion, particularly related to forms of dress, he was also profoundly influential in the development of Gülen's thought. *See* Chapter Three for a more detailed discussion.

13 Ismet Özel is one of the most prominent poets in Turkey today and is particularly notable for his conversion from being a widely known Marxist intellectual to one of the country's most noted Islamic thinkers. He is an extremely sophisticated writer, whose articles freely mix ideas from European literature and philosophy with Islamic theology and spirituality. Although he addresses a wide variety of political and philosophical issues, the central question he considers is the meaning of being a Muslim in the Republic of Turkey. *See, e.g.*, Scott Morrison, "To Be a Believer in Republican Turkey: Three Allegories of Ismet Özel." *The Muslim World*, 96 (2006): 507–521; Laurent Mignon, "Kays Mutlu: Ismet Özel: Individualität und Selbstdarstellung eines Türkischen Dichters." *Bulletin of the School of Oriental and African Studies University of London* 68.3 (October 2005): 465.

Conclusion

Words in both law and religion can shape power relationships and are often highly disputed. "*Shari'a*" lies within the overlap of these two spheres and provides a unique subject for the study of meaning in that liminal space. Islamic jurisprudence in the 19th-century Ottoman Empire continued to develop, but still operated within the context of the *madhabi* tradition of *taqlid*, with a formal preference for the *Hanafi* school. Madrasas trained scholars in Sunni schools of thought, the state enforced *Shari'a* rules, a Caliph led the community, and a *Sheikh al-Islam* answered complex legal questions. The attempt to integrate European code traditions into the Islamic legal system of the Ottomans with the enactment of the *Mecelle* in 1877 was consistent with other early modernist attempts at legal reform and even had some roots in classical jurisprudence.[1] This led to a more formal disconnect from tradition upon the founding of the Turkish Republic with the dismantling of *madhabi* institutions, the abolition of the Caliphate, the adoption of a secular constitution, and the enactment of civil codes.

Within the contemporary secular milieu, *Diyanet*, Öztürk, Gülen, and others developed new approaches to Islamic jurisprudence in Turkey. Generally, these approaches incorporate elements of modernism. Of course, there are other important groups – including the Alevis, various Sufi *tariqats*, *Salafis*, and others – but they did not come up as frequently in the study. Although Öztürk remains an interesting and important voice, *Diyanet* and Gülen are more influential because they have extensive networks of institutions (including mosques, schools, and civil society networks). *Diyanet* and Gülen both acknowledge the importance of traditional *fiqh*, even though they diverge from its rules (unlike Öztürk, who rejects the tradition). The ultimate success of these approaches to jurisprudence depends largely on popular support. However, the landscape of understandings among Turkish citizens is varied and evolving. This uncertainty invites more empirical studies on the meanings attributed to *Shari'a* and Islamic jurisprudence by Turkish citizens, as well as the broader question of the role of religion within the Turkish Republic.

The analysis in Chapters Five through Seven supports a number of important findings. First, there is a trend of increasing support for *Shari'a* within Turkey. Additionally, university education appears to correlate (inversely) with this preference with greater significance than religiosity. Still, the study indicates that Turks under 30 are more likely to be religious than those between 30 and 50 and that those under 30 who identify as religious are more likely to have a university education. It is clear that interpretations of *Shari'a* in Turkey differ from those in other predominantly Muslim countries, but that does not mean that greater convergence could not emerge. The influence of the AKP in combining commitments to Islamic ethics, center-right politics, neoliberal economics, and Kemalist Republican values has likely accentuated this distinction by validating the consistency of secular constitutionalism and Islam. It will be interesting to observe whether these patterns shift with the current Hizmet–AKP rift and the Erdoğan presidency.

Turks who desire the enforcement of *Shari'a* are more likely to have a modernist understanding of how rules are derived and to conceive of a sphere of *Shari'a* within a constitutional legal system that applies mainly to issues of personal status. Those who oppose the establishment of *Shari'a* are more likely to conceive of it in negative terms. Thus, "*Shari'a*" seems to have taken on new meanings as groups have either appropriated or criticized it. It is a quintessential example of fractured and contextual meaning at the center of both religious and legal tradition. The open-ended questions in the surveys and the interviews reveal a wide variety of meanings attributed to *Shari'a*, and this fracturing of meaning may be consistent with post-structural semiotic critiques based on metalanguage (as in Barthes)[2] or power structures (as in Foucault).[3] Further, they give credence to the postmodern turn in the work of some scholars of Islamic jurisprudence (such as Hallaq), warranting further linguistic and sociological research.

The study also indicates that Turks increasingly want a legal system that reflects their values. To the extent that Kemalist secularism is in tension with broadly held Islamic values in Turkey, it is likely to be unsustainable – as in the case of the prohibition against head coverings in universities. This may be especially true for the case of limits on individual liberties. Enforcing new limits on liberty in the name of values (or Islam) is likely to evoke strong opposition as it did in the *Gezi* protests that referenced limits on public displays of affection and on the sale or use of alcohol.

Fethullah Gülen was the single most mentioned influence in the empirical studies; however, outside of communities inspired by his work, most of those interviewed had deep reservations regarding his followers, if not the man himself. It is possible that this dynamic has changed since the *Gezi* protests and the rising tensions between the AKP and Hizmet. Yaşar Nuri Öztürk was also mentioned by a significant number of those interviewed and is worth considering in depth, even though his influence is admittedly narrower. Other religious scholars mentioned were Nihat Hatipoğlu, Zekariya Beyaz, Said Nursi, and Mevlana Jelaluddin Rumi. Several writers were mentioned in the interviews, including the poet Ismet Özel and the writers Ömer Tuğrul İnançer, Halit Ertuğrul, and Dücane Cündioğlu. Most of these religious writers and thinkers are considered in greater detail in Chapter Three. Political leaders also seem to provide some degree of religious inspiration or guidance, particularly Recep Tayyip Erdoğan and Abdullah Gül. The *Zaman* newspaper and the Samanyolu Television, along with the plethora of religious media publishers and broadcasters, have perhaps the greatest influence in shaping views related to religion and law. It appears that religious discourse at a variety of levels plays a more open role in Turkish civil society than it did prior to the election of the first AKP-led government in 2002.

However, one surprising result from the interviews is the apparent similarity between the experience of religious conservatives in Turkey and religious conservatives in the United States. Both groups are employing similar strategies and tactics to advance an agenda. Both groups have intentionally invested in specialized education, have generated their own press infrastructure and supply of entertainment, and have created multiple layers of civil society organizations, all serving as a basis for political mobilization (or at least contributing to such mobilization).

The rise of private evangelical schools and homeschooling in the United States parallels the establishment of *imam-hatip* schools and religiously inspired high schools in Turkey. The rise of Fox News is analogous to the growth of *Zaman*. In the 1990s, religious conservatives in the U.S. supported cable networks including TBN, PTL, The Family Channel, and programs like *The 700 Club* and *Touched by an Angel*. Only a decade later, Turkish religious conservatives supported Samanyolu, Kanal 7, and Dost with programs ranging from Quran classes to *The Fifth Dimension*. The similarities are striking. It is probable that politicians and business leaders were aware of the success of American religious conservatives and actively adopted their strategies. The profound influence of organizations inspired by Fethullah Gülen in Turkey may have made the deployment of these strategies more consistent and effective. To their credit, religious conservatives have presided over important democratizing reforms and laudable economic growth in Turkey. There is some degree of irony that Hizmet leaders and Gülen himself now complain of the kind of control and marginalization that many interviewees in the study levied against the "*Cemaat*" at a time when Hizmet was benefitting from government access.

Although there is increasing support for *Shari'a* in Turkey, it is unlikely that religious leaders would risk losing political or economic influence by proposing constitutional reforms that require conformity with *Shari'a*. Prohibitions on interest or limiting rights to divorce – *Shari'a* rules enforced by a number of predominantly Muslim states – could compromise economic stability and political support for religious politicians in Turkey. It is more likely that *Shari'a* in Turkey will mean expanding religious freedom along with symbolic nods to some traditionally Islamic moral norms. Periodic attempts to enforce religious norms may occur; however, if the *Gezi* protests provide any example, this type of legal reform is likely to be met with significant resistance.

Notes

1 *See* "Report of the Commission Appointed to Draft the Mejelle." *Arab Law Quarterly* 1.4 (1986): 367–372; *See also* Findley 2010 at 94.

2 *See generally*, Roland Barthes, *Elements of Semiology*. New York: Hill and Wang, 1968.

3 *See generally*, Michel Foucault, *The Order of Things: An Archaeology of the Human Sciences*. London: Tavistock, 1970.

Bibliography

Acar, Ismail, "A Classical Scholar With a Modern Outlook: Fethullah Gulen and His Legal Thought." In *Mastering Knowledge in Modern Times: Fethullah Gulen as an Islamic Scholar*, Ed. Ismail Albayrak. New York: Blue Dome, 2011, pp. 65–84.

Agrama, Hussein A., *Questioning Secularism: Islam, Sovereignty, and the Rule of Law in Modern Egypt*. Chicago: University of Chicago Press, 2012.

Ahmad, Feroz, *The Making of Modern Turkey*. London: Routledge, 1993.

Ahmad, Feroz, *The Young Turks: The Committee of Union and Progress in Turkish Politics, 1908–1914*. Oxford: Clarendon Press, 1969.

Ahmed, Leila, *A Quiet Revolution: The Veil's Resurgence, from the Middle East to America*. New Haven & London: Yale University Press, 2012.

Akarli, Engin Deniz, "Law in the Marketplace: Istanbul, 1730–1840." In *Dispensing Justice in Islam*, Ed. M. K. Masud, R. Peters, and D. S. Powers. Leiden: Brill, 2006.

Akgündüz, Ahmed, "Shariʿah Courts and Shariʿah Records: The Application of Islamic Law in the Ottoman State." *Islamic Law and Society* 16.2 (2009): 202–230.

Aksakal, Mustafa, *Ottoman Road to War in 1914*. Cambridge: Cambridge University Press, 2008.

Albayrak, İsmail (Ed.), *Mastering Knowledge in Modern Times: Fethullah Gülen as an Islamic Scholar*. New York: Blue Dome Press, 2011.

Ames, Edward S., "Non-Religious Persons." *American Journal of Theology* 13 (1909):541.

Anderson, Pamela Sue, "Gender and the Infinite: On the Aspiration to Be All There Is." *International Journal for Philosophy of Religion* 50.1–3 (2001): 191–212.

An-Naim, Abdullahi Ahmed, *Islam and the Secular State*. Cambridge, MA: Harvard University Press, 2008.

An-Naim, Abdullahi Ahmed, *Toward an Islamic Reformation: Civil Liberties, Human Rights, and International Law*. Syracuse and New York: Syracuse University Press, 1990.

Arat, Yeşim, *Rethinking Islam and Liberal Democracy*. Albany, NY: SUNY Press, 2005.

Asad, Talal, *Formations of the Secular: Christianity, Islam, Modernity*. Stanford, CA: Stanford University Press, 2003.

Asad, Talal, *Genealogies of Religion: Discipline and Reasons of Power in Christianity and Islam*. Baltimore, MD: Johns Hopkins University Press, 1993.

Atatürk, Mustafa Kemal, *A Speech Delivered by Mustapha Kemal, President of the Turkish Republic, October 1927*. Leipzig: K.F. Koehler, 1929.

Baer, Marc David, *The Dönme: Jewish Converts, Muslim Revolutionaries, and Secular Turks*. Stanford, CA: Stanford University Press, 2009.

Balistreri, Alex E., *Translating the Republic: Muslim Discourse on Modernity and the Rise of the Turkish Newspaper Zaman*. Doctoral dissertation, Princeton University, 2008.

Baran, Zeyno, *Torn Country: Turkey between Secularism and Islamism.* Stanford, CA: Hoover Institution Press, Stanford University, 2010.

Barkey, Karen, *Empire of Difference*. Cambridge, MA: Cambridge University Press, 2008.

Barton, G., P. Weller and I. Yilmaz (Eds.), *The Muslim Work and Politics in Transition: Creative Contributions of the Gülen Movement.* London and New York: Bloomsbury, 2013.

Barthes, Roland, *Elements of Semiology*. New York: Hill and Wang, 1968.

Bein, Amit, *Ottoman Ulema, Turkish Republic: Agents of Change and Guardians of Tradition.* Stanford, CA: Stanford University Press, 2014.

Bein, Amit, "Politics, Military Conscription, and Religious Education in the Late Ottoman Empire." *International Journal of Middle East Studies* 38.2 (2006): 283–301.

Bellah, Robert N., "Civil Religion in America." *Daedalus* 117.3 (1988): 97–118.

Berger, Peter, *The Sacred Canopy: Elements of a Sociological Theory of Religion.* New York: Anchor Books, 1990.

Berkes, Niyazi, *The Development of Secularism in Turkey*. Montreal: McGill University Press, 1964.

Berkes, Niyazi (Ed.), *Turkish Nationalism and Western Civilization: Selected Essays of Ziya Gökalp*. New York: Columbia University Press, 1959.

Bourdieu, Pierre, *The Field of Cultural Production: Essays on Art and Literature*. New York: Columbia University Press, 1993.

Bozdoğan, Sibel and Reşat Kasaba (Eds.), *Rethinking Modernity and National Identity in Turkey*. Seattle: University of Washington Press, 1997.

Brown, Daniel W., *Rethinking Tradition in Modern Islamic Thought*. Cambridge, UK and New York: Cambridge University Press, 1996.

Brown, Jonathan A. C., *Hadith: Muhammad's Legacy in the Medieval and Modern World.* Oxford: OneWorld, 2009.

Burak, Guy, "The Second Formation of Islamic Law: The Post-Mongol Context of the Ottoman Adoption of a School of Law." *Comparative Studies in Society and History* 55.3 (2013): 579–602.

Çağaptay, Soner, *Islam, Secularism, and Nationalism in Modern Turkey: Who Is a Turk?* London and New York: Routledge, 2006.

Çakmak, Diren, "Pro-Islamic Public Education in Turkey: The *Imam-hatip* School." *Middle Eastern Studies* 45.5 (2009): 825–846.

Çarkoğlu, Ali, "Religiosity, Support for Şeriat and Evaluations of Secularist Public Policies in Turkey." *Middle Eastern Studies* 40.2 (2004): 111–136.

Çarkoğlu, Ali and Binnaz Toprak, *Religion, Society and Politics in a Changing Turkey.* Istanbul: TESEV, 2007.

Çarkoğlu, Ali and Ersin Kalaycıoğlu, *Turkish Democracy Today: Elections, Protest, and Stability in an Islamic Society*. London: I. B. Tauris, 2007.

Çınar, Alev, *Modernity, Islam, and Secularism in Turkey: Bodies, Places, and Time*. Minneapolis: University of Minnesota Press, 2005.

Çınar, Alev, "The Justice and Development Party: Turkey's Experience with Islam, Democracy, Liberalism and Secularism." *International Journal of Middle East Studies* 43.3 (2011): 529–541.

Çınar, Menderes, "Turkey's Transformation under the AKP Rule." *Muslim World* 96 (2006): 469–486.

Coulson, Noel J., *A History of Islamic Law*. Lahore: Lahore Law Times Publications, 1979.

Council on Foreign Relations, "U.S.-Turkey Relations: A New Partnership." *Independent Task Force Report No. 69*, 2 May 2012.

Daly, Mary, *Beyond God the Father: Toward a Philosophy of Women's Liberation*. London: Women's Press, 1986.

Davison, Andrew, *Secularism and Revivalism in Turkey: A Hermeneutic Reconsideration*. New Haven: Yale University Press, 1998.

Davison, Roderic, *Reform in the Ottoman Empire*. Princeton, NJ: Princeton University Press, 1963.

Demiralp, Seda, "The Odd Tango of the Islamic Right and Kurdish Left in Turkey: A Peripheral Alliance to Redesign the Centre?" *Middle Eastern Studies* 48.2 (2012): 287–302.

Deringil, Selim, "There Is No Compulsion in Religion: On Conversion and Apostasy in the Late Ottoman Empire: 1839–1856." *Comparative Studies in Society and History* 42.3 (2000): 547–575.

Deringil, Selim, *The Well-protected Domains: Ideology and the Legitimation of Power in the Ottoman Empire, 1876–1909*. London: I. B. Tauris, 1998.

Devji, Faisal, *Landscapes of Jihad*. Ithaca: Cornell University Press, 2005.

Dressler, Markus, "Religio-Secular Metamorphoses: The Re-Making of Turkish Alevism." *Journal of the American Academy of Religion* 76.2 (2008): 280–311.

Durkheim, Émile, *The Elementary Forms of the Religious Life*. Mineola, NY: Dover Publications, Inc., 2008.

Earl, Edward Mead. "The New Constitution of Turkey." *Political Science Quarterly* 4.1 (1925): 73–100.

Ebaugh, Helen R., *The Gulen Movement: A Sociological Analysis of a Civic Movement Rooted in Modern Islam*. London: Springer, 2010.

Eliade, Mircea, *The Myth of the Eternal Return: Cosmos and History*. Princeton, NJ: Princeton University Press, 2005.

Eligür, Banu, *The Mobilization of Political Islam in Turkey*. Cambridge: Cambridge University Press, 2010.

Erder, Necat, *Türkiye'de Siyasi Partilerin Seçmeleri ve Toplum Düzeni*. Istanbul: TÜSES Foundation, 1999.

Ergene, Boğaç, "Evidence in Ottoman Courts: Oral and Written Documentation in Early-Modern Courts of Islamic Law." *Journal of the American Oriental Society* 124.3 (2004): 471–491.

Ergül, F. Aslı, "The Ottoman Identity: Turkish, Muslim or Rum?" *Middle Eastern Studies* 48.4 (July 2012): 629–645.

Fadel, Mohammad, "The Social Logic of Taqlīd and the Rise of the Mukhataṣar." *Islamic Law and Society* 3.2 (1996): 193–233.

Feener, R. Michael, "Muslim Legal Thought in Contemporary Indonesia." In *Islamic Law in Contemporary Indonesia: Ideas and Institutions*, Eds. Mark E. Camack and R. Michael Feener. Cambridge: Harvard University Press, 2007, pp. 14–25.

Feuerbach, Ludwig, *The Essence of Christianity*. Mineola, NY: Dover Publications, 2008.

Findley, Carter V., *Bureaucratic Reform in the Ottoman Empire: The Sublime Porte, 1789–1922*. Princeton, NJ: Princeton University Press, 1980.

Findley, Carter V., *Turkey, Islam, Nationalism, and Modernity: A History, 1789–2007*. New Haven and London: Yale University Press, 2010.

Fortna, Benjamin C., *Imperial Classroom: Islam, the State and Education in the Late Ottoman Empire*. Oxford: Oxford University Press, 2002.

Foucault, Michel, *The Order of Things: An Archaeology of the Human Sciences*. London: Tavistock, 1970.

Foucault, Michel, *Religion and Culture*. New York: Routledge, 1999.

Freud, Sigmund, *The Future of an Illusion*. Mansfield Centre, CT: Martino Pub., 2010.

Fukuyama, Francis, *The End of History and the Last Man*. New York: Free Press, 2006.

Gabriel A. Almond, Emmanuel Sivan, and R. Scott Appleby, *Fundamentalism: Genus and Species*. Chicago: University of Chicago Press, 1995.

Gaer, Joseph, *How the Great Religions Began*. New York: Dodd Mead, 1981.

Geertz, Clifford, *Islam Observed: Religious Development in Morocco and Indonesia*. Chicago: University of Chicago Press, 1968.

Geertz, Clifford, "Religion as a Cultural System," in *The Interpretation of Culture: Selected Essays*. London: Fontana Press, 1993.

Gerber, Haim, "Rigidity versus Openness in Late Classical Islamic Law: The Case of the Seventeenth-Century Palestinian Muftī Khayr al-Dīn al-Ramlī." *Islamic Law and Society* 5.2 (1998): 165–195.

Gerber, Haim, *State, Society and Law in Islam: Ottoman Law in Comparative Perspective*. New York: SUNY Press, 1994.

Göle, Nilufer, *The Forbidden Modern: Civilization and Veiling*. Ann Arbor: University of Michigan Press, 1996.

Gül, Ayşen, "Turkish Prime Time Television: Mass Culture and Tabloidization." *Communication Faculty Magazine* 23 (2005): 57.

Gülen, Muhammed Fethullah, *The Essentials of the Islamic Faith.* Clifton, NJ: Tughra Books, 2006.

Gülen, Muhammed Fethullah, *M. F. Gülen: Essays, Perspectives, Opinions.* Clifton, NJ: Tughra Books, 2002.

Gülen, Muhammed Fethullah, *Toward a Global Civilization of Love & Tolerance.* Clifton, NJ: Tughra Books, 2004.

Günay-Erkol, Çimen, "Issues of Ideology and Identity in Turkish Literature During the Cold War." In *Turkey in the Cold War: Ideology and Culture*, Ed. Cangül Örnek and Çagdas Üngör. London: Palgrave Macmillan, 2013, pp. 109–129.

Hale, William, *Turkish Politics and the Military.* London: Routledge, 1994.

Hallaq, Wael, *Authority, Continuity, and Change in Islamic Law.* Cambridge, UK and New York: Cambridge University Press, 2005.

Hallaq, Wael, *The Formation of Islamic Law.* Aldershot, Hants, Great Britain; Burlington, VT: Ashgate/Variorum, 2004.

Hallaq, Wael, *A History of Islamic Legal Theories: An Introduction to Sunni Usul al-fiqh.* Cambridge: Cambridge University Press, 1997.

Hallaq, Wael, *The Impossible State: Islam, Politics, and Modernity's Moral Predicament.* New York: Columbia University Press, 2013.

Hallaq, Wael, *An Introduction to Islamic Law*. Cambridge and New York: Cambridge University Press, 2009.

Hallaq, Wael, *The Origins and Evolution of Islamic Law*. Cambridge, UK and New York: Cambridge University Press, 2005.

Hallaq, Wael, *Shari'a: Theory, Practice, Transformations.* Cambridge, UK and New York: Cambridge University Press, 2009.

Hamoudi, Haider Ala, "The Muezzin's Call and the Dow Jones Bell: On the Necessity of Realism in the Study of Islamic Law." *American Journal of Comparative Law* 56.2 (2008): 423–499.

Hanioğlu, M. Şükrü, *A Brief History of the Late Ottoman Empire*. Princeton, NJ: Princeton University Press, 2008.

Hanioğlu, M. Şükrü, *Preparation for a Revolution: The Young Turks, 1902–1908*. New York: Oxford University Press, 2001.

Hart, Kimberly, *And Then We Work for God: Rural Sunni Islam in Western Turkey*. Stanford, CA: Stanford University Press, 2013.

Hart, Kimberly, "Performing Piety and Islamic Modernity in a Turkish Village." *Ethnology* 46.4 (2007): 289–304.

Hefner, Robert W. (Ed.), *Shari'a Politics: Islamic Law and Society in the Modern World.* Bloomington: Indiana University Press, 2011.

Hegel, Georg W. F., *The Philosophy of History.* New York: The Colonial Press, 1899.

Hendrick, Joshua D., *Gülen: The Ambiguous Politics of Market Islam in Turkey and the World.* New York: New York University Press, 2013.

Hill, Enid, "Al-Sanhuri and Islamic Law: The Place and Significance of Islamic Law in the Life and Work of 'Abd al-Razzaq Ahmad al-Sanhuri, Egyptian Jurist and Scholar 1895–1971" *Arab Law Quarterly* 3.1, 33–64, 3.2, 182–218 (1988).

Hodgson, Marshall, *The Venture of Islam, Volume 2*. Chicago: University of Chicago Press, 1974.

Holyoake, George Jacob, *Origin and Nature of Secularism*. London: Watts & Co., 1896.

Huntington, S. P., "The Clash of Civilizations?" *Foreign Affairs* 72.3 (1993): 22–49.

Ibn Rushd, *The Distinguished Jurist's Primer Volume I.* London: Garnet Publishing, 1994.

İnalcık, Halil, *The Ottoman Empire: The Classical Age 1300–1600*. New York: Praeger, 1973.

Jackson, Sherman A., *Islamic Law and the State: The Constitutional Jurisprudence of Shihab al-Din al-Qarafi*. Leiden: Brill, 1996.

James, William, *The Varieties of Religious Experience: A Study in Human Nature*. New York, NY: Penguin Books, 1982.

Johansen, Baber, "A Perfect Law in an Imperfect Society: Ibn Taymiyya's Concept of 'Governance in the Name of Sacred Law.'" In *The Law Applied: Contextualizing the Islamic Shari'a*, Ed. Bernard G. Weiss, Peri Bearman, and Wolfhart Heinrichs. London & New York: I. B. Tauris, 2008, pp. 259, 261.

Jouli, Jeanette, "Re-fashioning the Self through Religious Knowledge: How Muslim Women Become Pious in the German Diaspora," in *Islam and Muslims in Germany*. Ed. Ala Al-Hamarneh and Jörn Thielmann. Leiden: Brill, 2008.

Kalaycioğlu, Ersin, *Party Identification, Islam and Secularism in Turkey*. Sabanci University Research Database 18, 2008.

Kalaycioğlu, Ersin, "The Mystery of the Turban: Participation or Revolt?" *Turkish Studies* 6.2 (2005): 233–251.

Kamali, Mohammad H., *Freedom of Expression in Islam.* Cambridge: Islamic Texts Society, 1997.

Kamali, Mohammad H., *Shari'ah Law: An Introduction.* Oxford: Oneworld, 2008.

Kandiyoti, Deniz (Ed.), *Women, Islam and the State.* Philadelphia: Temple University Press, 1991.

Kandiyoti, Deniz and A. Saktanber (Eds.), *Fragments of Culture: The Everyday of Modern Turkey*. New Brunswick, NJ: Rutgers University Press, 2002.

Kaplan, Sam, "Din-u Devlet All over Again? The Politics of Military Secularism and Religious Militarism in Turkey Following the 1980 Coup." *International Journal of Middle East Studies* 34.1 (2002): 113–127.

Karpat, Kemal, *Studies on Ottoman Social and Political History*. Leiden: E.J. Brill, 2002.

Karpat, Kemal, *The Politicization of Islam: Reconstructing Identity, State, Faith, and Community in the Late Ottoman State*. New York: Oxford University Press, 2001.

Kasaba, Reşat, *A Moveable Empire: Ottoman Nomads, Migrants, and Refugees*. Seattle: University of Washington Press, 2009.

Kasaba, Reşat (Ed.), *Cambridge History of Turkey, Vol. IV: Turkey in the Modern World.* Cambridge: Cambridge University Press, 2008.

Kayaoğlu, Turan, *Legal Imperialism: Sovereignty and Extraterritoriality in Japan, the Ottoman Empire, and China*. Cambridge: Cambridge University Press, 2010.
Kazanciğil, Ali and E. Özbudun (Eds.), *Atatürk, Founder of a Modern State*. London: C. Hurst, 1981.
Kinzer, Stephen, *Crescent & Star: Turkey Between Two Worlds*. New York: Farrar, Straus and Giroux, 2001.
Koyuncu-Lorasdağı, "The Prospects and Pitfalls of the Religious Nationalist Movement in Turkey: The Case of the Gülen Movement." *Middle Eastern Studies* 46.2 (2010): 221–234.
Kreiser, Klaus, "Turban and Türban: 'Divider between Belief and Unbelief': A Political History of Modern Turkish Costume." *European Review* 13.3 (2005): 447–458.
Kuru, Ahmet T., *Secularism and State Policies Toward Religion: the United States, France, and Turkey*. Cambridge and New York: Cambridge University Press, 2009.
Lewis, Bernard, *Emergence of Modern Turkey*. London: Oxford University Press, 1968, 2002.
Lewis, Franklin, *Rumi – Past and Present, East and West: The Life, Teachings, and Poetry of Jalâl al-Din Rumi*. London: Oneworld, 2007.
Libson, Gideon, "On the Development of Custom as a Source of Law in Islamic Law: Al-rujūʿu ilā al-ʿurfi aḥadu al-qawāʿidi al-khamsi allatī yatabannā ʿalayhā al-fiqhu." *Islamic Law and Society* 4.2 (1997): 131–155.
Lombardi, Clark B., *State Law as Islamic Law in Modern Egypt: The Incorporation of the Shariʿa into Egyptian Constitutional Law*. Leiden and Boston: Brill, 2006.
Mango, Andrew, *Atatürk: The Biography of the Founder of Modern Turkey*. Woodstock, NY: The Overlook Press, 1999, 2000.
Mardin, Şerif, *Religion and Social Change in Modern Turkey*. Albany, NY: State University of New York Press, 1989.
Masud, M. K., R. Peters, and D. S. Powers. *Dispensing Justice in Islam: Qadis and Their Judgments*. Leiden and Boston: Brill, 2006.
McCarthy, Justin, *Muslims and Minorities: The Population of Ottoman Anatolia and the End of Empire*. New York: New York University Press, 1983.
Meeker, Michael E., *A Nation of Empire: The Ottoman Legacy of Turkish Modernity*. Berkeley: University of California Press, 2002.
Mermer, Ali, *Aspects of Religious Identity: The Nurcu Movement in Turkey Today*. Unpublished thesis, Durham University, 1985, available at http://etheses.dur.ac.uk/1614/
Messick, Brinkley M., *The Calligraphic State: Textual Domination and History in a Muslim Society*. Berkeley: University of California Press, 1993.
Metcalf, Barbara, "Remaking Ourselves: Islamic Self-Fashioning in a Global Movement of Spiritual Renewal." In *Accounting for Fundamentalisms: The Dynamic Character of Movements*, Ed. R. Scott Appleby and Martin E. Marty. Chicago: University of Chicago Press, 1994, pp. 706–725.
Morrison, Scott, "To Be a Believer in Republican Turkey: Three Allegories of Ismet Özel." *The Muslim World* 96.3 (2006): 507–521.
Nafi, Basheer M., "The Rise of Islamic Reformist Thought and Its Challenge to Traditional Islam." In *Islamic Thought in the Twentieth Century*, Ed. Suha Taji-Farouki and Basheer M. Nafi. London: Institute for Ismaili Studies, 2004, pp. 28–60.
Navaro-Yashin, Yael, *Faces of the State: Secularism and Public Life in Turkey*. Princeton, NJ: Princeton University Press, 2002.
Newman, William, *The Social Meanings of Religion: an Integrated Anthology*. Chicago: Rand McNally, 1974.
Nurbaksh, Javad, *The Psychology of Sufism*. New York: KNP, 1993.

Nursi, Said, "Savunma." In *Modern Türkiye'de Siyasî Düşünce*, Ed. Tanıl Bora and Murat Gültekingel. Istanbul: İletişim, 2005, pp. 1093–1094.

Opwiss, Felicitas, *Maslaha and the Purpose of the Law.* Leiden: Brill, 2011.

Otto, Jan M., *Sharia Incorporated: a Comparative Overview of the Legal Systems of Twelve Muslim Countries in Past and Present.* Leiden: Leiden University Press, 2010.

Özdikmenli-Demir, Gözde and Birsen Şahin-Kütük, "The Role of Parents, Siblings, Peers, Relatives and Other Agents in Turkish-Muslim Emerging Adults Religious Socializations." *Archive for the Psychology of Religion* 3 (2012): 363.

Ozgur, Iren, "Social and Political Reform through Religious Education in Turkey: The Ongoing Cause of Hayrettin Karaman." *Middle Eastern Studies* 47.4 (2011): 569–585.

Öztürk, Yaşar Nuri, *Kur'an'daki Islam.* Istanbul: Yeni Boyut, 1997.

Öztürk, Yaşar Nuri, *Kur'an Verileri Açisindan Laiklik.* Istanbul: Yeni Boyut, 2003.

Öztürk, Yaşar Nuri, *Reconstruction of Religious Life in Islam: Returning to the Quran*, Trans. Ali Hayrani Öz. Istanbul: Yeni Boyut, 1999.

Özyürek, Esra, "Convert Alert: German Muslims and Turkish Christians as Threats to Security in the New Europe." *Comparative Studies in Society and History* 51.1 (2009): 91–116.

Özyürek, Esra, *Nostalgia for the Modern: State Secularism and Everyday Politics in Turkey.* Durham, NC: Duke University Press, 2006.

Pak, Soon-Yong, "Articulating the Boundary between Secularism and Islamism: The *Imam-hatip* Schools of Turkey." *Anthropology & Education Quarterly* 35.3 (2004): 324–344.

Pandya, Sofiya and N. Gallagher (Eds.), *The Gülen Hizmet Movement and its Transnational Activities: Case Studies of Altruistic Activism in Contemporary Islam.* Boca Raton: Brown Walker Press, 2012.

Parla, Taha, *The Social and Political Thought of Ziya Gökalp.* Leiden: E.J. Brill 1989.

Peirce, Leslie, "A New Judge for Aintab: Shifting Legal Environment of a Sixteenth-Century Ottoman Court." In *Dispensing Justice in Islam*, Ed. M.K. Masud, R. Peters and D.S. Powers. Leiden: Brill, 2006, pp. 71–93.

Peirce, Leslie, "State, Society, and Law in Islam: Ottoman Law in Comparative Perspective." *Islamic Law and Society* 2.3 (1995): 365–371.

Peletz, Michael G., *Islamic Modern Religious Courts and Cultural Politics in Malaysia.* Princeton, NJ: Princeton University Press, 2002.

Perry, Michael J., *Under God?: Religious Faith and Liberal Democracy.* Cambridge, UK and New York: Cambridge University Press, 2003.

Peters, Rudolph, *Crime and Punishment in Islamic Law: Theory and Practice from the Sixteenth to the Twenty-first Century*. Cambridge: Cambridge University Press, 2005.

Pew Research Religion & Public Life Project, "The World's Muslims: Religion, Politics and Society." 30 April 2013.

Poulton, Hugh, *Top Hat, Gray Wolf, and the Crescent: Turkish Nationalism and the Turkish Republic*. New York: NYU Press, 2001.

Powell, Russell, "Evolving Views of Islamic Law in Turkey." *Journal of Law and Religion* 28 (2013): 474–481.

Powers, David, "Four Cases Relating to Women and Divorce in Al-Andalus and the Maghrib, 1100–1500." In *Dispensing Justice in Islam: Qadis and Their Judgments*, Ed. M.K. Masud, R. Peters, and D.S. Powers. Leiden: Brill, 2006: 383–409.

Qutb, Sayyid, *Social Justice in Islam.* Oneonta, NY: Islamic Publications Intl., 2000.

Rahman, Fazlur, *Islam & Modernity: Transformation of an Intellectual Tradition.* Chicago: University of Chicago Press, 1982.

Rahman, Fazlur and E. Moosa, *Revival and Reform in Islam: A Study of Islamic Fundamentalism.* Oxford: Oneworld, 2000.

Rawls, John, *Justice as Fairness*. Cambridge, MA: Harvard University Press, 2001.
Rawls, John, *Political Liberalism*. New York & Chichester: Columbia University Press, 1993.
Rawls, John, *A Theory of Justice*. Cambridge: Belknap Press, 1999.
Rida, Rashid, *Usr al-Islam wa Usul al Tashri al Amm*. Cairo: al-Manar Press, 1956.
Riley-Smith, Jonathan S. C., *The Crusades, Christianity, and Islam*. New York: Columbia University Press, 2008.
Rippin, Andrew, *Muslims: Their Religious Beliefs and Practices*, Ed. John Hinnel and Ninian Smart. New York: Routledge, 2005.
Roy, Olivier, *The Failure of Political Islam*. Cambridge, MA: Harvard University Press, 1994.
Schacht, Joseph, *An Introduction to Islamic Law*. Oxford, Oxfordshire and New York: Clarendon Press, 1982.
Schacht, Joseph, *The Origins of Muhammadan Jurisprudence*. Oxford: Clarendon Press, 1953.
Schick, Irvin and Ertuğrul Tonak (Eds), *Turkey in Transition*. Oxford: Oxford University Press, 1987.
Schimmel, Annemarie, *Mystical Dimensions of Islam*. Chapel Hill: University of North Carolina Press, 1975.
Schimmel, Annemarie, *Rumi's World: The Life and Work of the Great Sufi Poet*. Berkeley, CA: Shambhala, 2001.
Shah, Idries and Doris Lessing, *Learning How to Learn: Psychology and Spirituality in the Sufi Way*. New York: Penguin, 1996.
Shaw, Stanford and Ezel Kural Shaw, *History of the Ottoman Empire and Modern Turkey, Volume II: Reform, Revolution, and Republic: The Rise of Modern Turkey, 1808–1975*. Cambridge: Cambridge University Press, 1977.
Shively, Kim, "Taming Islam: Studying Religion in Secular Turkey." *Anthropological Quarterly* 81.3 (2008): 683–711.
Silverstein, Brian, *Islam and Modernity in Turkey*. New York, NY: Palgrave Macmillan, 2011.
Silverstein, Brian, "Islamist Critique in Modern Turkey: Hermeneutics, Tradition, Genealogy." *Comparative Studies in Society and History* 47.1 (2005): 134–160.
Sunder, Madhavi, "Piercing the Veil." *Yale Law Journal* 112 (2003): 1399.
Sunier, Thijl, Nico Landman, Heleen van der Linden, Nazli Bilgili, and Alper Bilgili, *Diyanet: The Turkish Directorate for Religious Affairs in a Changing Environment*. Amsterdam and Utrecht: VU University of Amsterdam and University of Utrecht, 2011.
Tapper, Richard (Ed.), *Islam in Modern Turkey: Religion, Politics and Literature in a Secular State*. London: I. B. Tauris, 1991.
Taşkın, Yüksel, "Upsurge of the Extreme Right in Turkey: The Intra-Right Struggle to Redefine 'True Nationalism and Islam." *Middle Eastern Studies* 44.1 (2008): 131.
Taylor, Charles, *A Secular Age*. Cambridge, MA: Belknap Press of Harvard University Press, 2007.
Tillich, Paul, *The Dynamics of Faith*. New York: Harper One, 2009.
Toprak, Binnaz, *Islam and Political Development in Turkey*. Leiden: E.J. Brill, 1981.
Trimingham, J. Spencer, *The Sufi Orders in Islam*. Oxford: Oxford University Press, 1998.
Tuğal, Cihan, *Passive Revolution: Absorbing the Islamic Challenge to Capitalism*. Stanford, CA: Stanford University Press, 2009.

Tunç, Aslı, “Mediated Justice: Turkish Newspapers’ Coverage of Controversial Criminal Cases.” *Turkish Studies* 11.44 (2010): 643.

Turam, Berna, *Between Islam and the State: The Politics of Engagement.* Stanford, CA: Stanford University Press, 2007.

Turner, Victor W., *The Ritual Process: Structure and Anti-structure.* Chicago: Aldine Pub. Co., 1969.

Tylor, Edward B., *Primitive Culture: Researches into the Development of Mythology, Philosophy, Religion, Language, Art, and Custom.* New York: Gordon Press, 1976.

Ulutaş, Ufuk, “Religion and Secularism in Turkey: The Dilemma of the Directorate of Religious Affairs.” *Middle Eastern Studies* 46.3 (2010): 389–399.

Vahide, Şukran, *Islam in Modern Turkey: An Intellectual Biography of Bediuzzaman Said Nursi.* New York: State University of New York Press, 2005.

Vahide, Şukran, “Toward an Intellectual Biography of Said Nursi.” In *Islam at the Crossroads: On the Life and Thought of Bediuzzaman Said Nursi*, Ed. Ibrahim M. Abu-Rabi. New York: SUNY Press, 2003, pp. 1–20.

Vogel, Frank and Samuel Hayes, *Islamic Law and Finance: Religion, Risk and Return.* Leiden: Brill, 1998.

Walton, Jeremy, “Confessional Pluralism and the Civil Society Effect: Liberal Mediations of Islam and Secularism in Contemporary Turkey.” *American Ethnologist* 40.1 (2013): 182–200.

Weber, Max, *Essays in Sociology*. Oxford: Oxford University Press, 1958.

Weber, Max, “Objectivity in Social Science and Social Policy.” In *The Methodology of the Social Sciences*, Ed. and Trans. E. A. Shils and H. A. Finch, New York: Free Press, 1949, pp. 50–112.

Weber, Max, *The Protestant Ethic and the Spirit of Capitalism*. New York: Oxford University Press, 2011.

Wellman, James K. Jr. (Ed.), *Belief and Bloodshed: Religion and Violence across Time and Tradition*. Plymouth: Rowman & Littlefield Publishers, 2007.

Wellman, James, *Evangelical vs. Liberal: The Clash of Christian Cultures in the Pacific Northwest*. Oxford: Oxford University Press, 2008.

White, Jenny B., *Islamist Mobilization in Turkey: A Study in Vernacular Politics*. Seattle: University of Washington Press, 2002.

Yavuz, Hakan, “Political Islam and the Welfare (Refah) Party in Turkey.” *Comparative Politics*, 30.1 (October 1997): 63–82.

Yavuz, Hakan, *Islamic Political Identity in Turkey*. New York: Oxford University Press, 2003.

Yavuz, Hakan, *Secularism and Muslim Democracy in Turkey*. Cambridge, UK and New York: Cambridge University Press, 2009.

Yavuz, Hakan and John Esposito, *Turkish Islam and the Secular State: The Gülen Movement*. Syracuse: Syracuse University Press, 2003.

Yazıcı, Serap, *Başkanlık ve Yarı-Başanlık Sistemleri: Türkiye icin Bir Değerlendirme.* Istanbul: Istanbul Technical University Press, 2010.

Yılmaz, Hakan, *In Search of a Turkish Middle Class: Economic Occupations, Political Orientations, Social Life-Styles, Moral Values: Summary of the Basic Findings.* Istanbul: Bogazici University, 2008.

Yılmaz, İhsan, *Muslim Laws, Politics and Society in Modern Nation States: Dynamic Legal Pluralisms in England, Turkey and Pakistan.* Aldershot & Burlington: Ashgate, 2005.

Yılmaz, İhsan, "Secular Law and the Emergence of Unofficial Turkish Islamic Law." *Middle East Journal* 56.1 (2002): 113–131.

Yükleyen, Ahmet, "Production of Mystical Islam in Europe: Religious Authorization in the Süleymanlı Sufi Community" *Contemporary Islam* 4 (2010): 269–288.

Yükleyen, Ahmet, "Sufism and Islamic Groups in Contemporary Turkey." In *Turkey in the Modern World*, Ed. R. Kasaba. Cambridge, UK and New York: Cambridge University Press, 2008, pp. 381–387.

Zizek, Slavoj, "The Clash of Civilizations at the End of History." *Cultural Inquiry* (2007), available at https://www.scribd.com/doc/19133296/Zizek-The-Clash-of-Civilizations-at-the-End-of-History.

Zürcher, Erik J., *Turkey: A Modern History*. London and New York: I. B. Tauris, 1997, 2004.

Index